The Alger Hiss Espionage Case

T. Michael Ruddy
Saint Louis University

THOMSON

WADSWORTH

Australia • Canada • Mexico • Singapore • Spain • United Kingdom • United States

Publisher: Clark Baxter
Assistant Editor: Paul Massicotte
Editorial Assistant: Richard Yoder
Marketing Manager: Caroline Croley
Marketing Assistant: Mary Ho
Advertising Project Manager: Tami Strang
Project Manager, Editorial Production:
Jennifer Klos
Print Buyer: Kristine Waller

Permissions Editor: Sarah Harkrader
Production Service: Shepherd, Inc.
Photo Researcher: Suzie Wright
Copy Editor: Francine Banwarth
Cover Designer: Preston Thomas
Cover Image: Bettmann/CORBIS
Cover Printer: Webcom
Compositor: Shepherd, Inc.
Printer: Webcom

For more information about our products, contact us at:
Thomson Learning Academic Resource Center
1-800-423-0563
For permission to use material from this text or product,
submit a request online at http://www.thomsonrights.com

Any additional questions about permission can be
submitted by email to thomsonrights@thomson.com

Library of Congress Control Number:
2003115531

ISBN: 0-15-508560-3

Wadsworth/Thomson Learning
10 Davis Drive
Belmont, CA 94002-3098
USA

Asia
Thomson Learning
5 Shenton Way #01-01
UIC Building
Singapore 068808

Australia/New Zealand
Thomson Learning
102 Dodds Street
Southbank, Victoria 3006
Australia

Canada
Nelson
1120 Birchmount Road
Toronto, Ontario M1K 5G4
Canada

Europe/Middle East/Africa
Thomson Learning
High Holborn House
50/51 Bedford Row
London WC1R 4LR
United Kingdom

Latin America
Thomson Learning
Seneca, 53
Colonia Polanco
11560 Mexico D.F.
Mexico

Contents

Preface

Consistent with the purpose of the American Stories series, the Alger Hiss affair serves as a vehicle for considering a number of historical themes that run through early Cold War America. First, and probably most obvious, it provides a perspective on the emerging Cold War tensions dividing the two former allies, the United States and the Soviet Union, tensions strongly affected by the ideological differences between communism and the democratic-capitalist system. This ideological divide influenced international events as well as events on the domestic scene. Secondly, the Hiss affair offers a case study of the growing anti-Communist movement that by 1950 would be identified with the notorious Senator Joseph McCarthy of Wisconsin, an important topic that historians are still debating today as new archival evidence confirms that there indeed was Soviet espionage activity in the United States during the 1930s and 1940s. On one level, in light of this new evidence, the actions of Senator McCarthy and other political figures identified with the anti-Communist crusade might be interpreted as a rational response to this Communist activity that potentially threatened American national security. Nevertheless, in pursuit of their cause, their words and actions fostered an often-exaggerated fear of domestic Communist subversion in government and in other areas of American life, from Hollywood to universities, that deeply affected the lives of many Americans. Third, related to the second theme, the Hiss case helps illuminate the social and cultural milieu of the time. Finally, Hiss's travails provide a fascinating insight into American politics. Since Alger Hiss had been an official in two Democratic administrations—Franklin D. Roosevelt's and Harry S. Truman's—his struggle encapsulates the political rivalry between the Democratic and Republican parties. On the more personal level, Congressman Richard M. Nixon's exploitation of the case for his own political ends serves as a means to consider the role of political opportunism in the exercise of public policy. Furthermore, Alger Hiss, with his Ivy League pedigree—Johns Hopkins University and Harvard Law—personified the elite who had so dominated American politics and government from the early days of the republic. This elite was one of Nixon's targets then and throughout his political career.

The Alger Hiss case represents in microcosm many of the forces and influences that comprised the anti-Communist phenomenon of the immediate post-World War II period that came to be known as McCarthyism. An examination of Hiss's story has something to offer to those interested in American international and political, as well as social and cultural, history.

Prologue

In the Pumpkin Patch

On August 3, 1948, Whittaker Chambers, a confessed former Communist and at that time senior editor at *Time* magazine, appeared before the House Committee on Un-American Activities (HUAC) and accused Alger Hiss, the president of the Carnegie Endowment for International Peace, of belonging to the Communist Party during the 1930s while Hiss was a member of the administration of President Franklin D. Roosevelt. From that day in August, an interested American public followed the emerging dispute between these two individuals with keen interest as Hiss denied the charges and endeavored to clear his name, ultimately filing a libel suit against Chambers.

But then on December 2, the affair took a surprising turn. Served a subpoena by HUAC, Chambers led congressional investigators into a pumpkin patch on his Maryland farm and pulled microfilm containing classified State Department documents from a hollowed-out pumpkin. Chambers claimed he had received these materials from Hiss.

These "pumpkin papers" were the first indication the American public had that the Hiss-Chambers dispute involved much more than alleged membership in the Communist Party. It involved espionage, accusations that Hiss had served as a clandestine agent of the Soviet Union, providing sensitive classified materials to the Kremlin. More, it involved espionage by a prominent member of the Roosevelt-Truman administrations, a man who had been in a position to influence policy. To many Americans, these charges were tantamount to treason. Alger Hiss had betrayed his country. If proven true, these charges would validate the accusations made by Republican members of Congress that Americans up to this time had been inclined to discount as merely part of the political in-fighting that characterized the Washington scene. The anti-Communist crusade, which in the 1950s would adversely affect the lives of so many individuals both inside and outside government, had been festering since the end of

World War II. Hiss's ultimate conviction and the consequent vindication of the charges made by administration critics propelled this crusade to a new level.

Time magazine, the publication Chambers worked for, in its December 13, 1948, issue, published the following description of that momentous discovery in the pumpkin patch.

"INVESTIGATIONS: THE DUSTY BOMB"

He looked as unprepossessing as a baker—a calm, pudgy little man who kept an old pipe in the pocket of his untidy blue serge suit. But his looks were deceiving. Whittaker Chambers, a senior editor of TIME, a Quaker, was a brilliant intellectual. Before 1938, he had been a Communist courier for the Soviet "apparatus" in Washington, D.C.

Sitting in the jammed, floodlighted congressional committee room last summer, he made his enormous, softly worded accusation—that Alger Hiss, a former high State Department official, had also been a Communist. The nation was shocked. Hiss shocked it again. He vehemently denied every accusation and filed a $75,000 libel action against his detractor. Chambers, who thought that his own word as an ex-Communist was enough, produced no more evidence to back his charge.

But there was more evidence—a plump, heavy package which had been lying in a Brooklyn attic like a dusty bomb during all the ten years in which Chambers had been trying to live down his past.

SIXTY-FIVE DOCUMENTS

Last month Chambers was called for deposition hearings by Hiss's attorney, William Marbury of Baltimore. He was subjected to questioning in connection with the slander suit which made him believe "that Hiss was determined to destroy me—and my wife, if possible." He went to his farm at Westminster, Md., waited two days for his anger to cool.

Then he went back to Marbury's quiet book-lined law office. There, from the package which he had brought back from Brooklyn, he handed over 65 copies of confidential State Department documents. Some were typewritten; three were memoranda in handwriting (later identified by California's Congressman Richard Nixon as that of Alger Hiss).

Lawyer Marbury and Federal Judge W. Calvin Chesnut took an appalled look, secretly turned the documents over to the Department of Justice. Suddenly, Chambers was engulfed in something far bigger and infinitely uglier than his original controversy with Alger Hiss.

MOMENT OF SILENCE

At first no hint of the new disclosure leaked out. But early last week, Robert E. Stripling, chief investigator for the House Committee on Un-American Activities, got an inkling of what had happened.

He rounded up Congressman Nixon, drove to Maryland, found Chambers in the cowbarn at his farm, finishing the evening milking. They bluntly accused him of withholding evidence from the congressional committee. After a long moment of silence Chambers admitted that they were right. Did he have more information? He would not say.

The next day Stripling telephoned Chambers to come to the committee's Washington office; on arrival he was served with a subpoena which directed him to turn over all forms of documents and evidence in his possession. Chambers looked at the legal form; then, matter-of-factly, he admitted that he had more evidence, and promised to turn it over.

He was asked why he had not produced the documents before; why had he kept them hidden for so many years? He was a Quaker; he recoiled at the idea of hurting anyone or of ruining anyone's life.

That night two committee investigators tramped up to the door of the farmhouse. Chambers examined their credentials, switched on a string of yard lights, and led them to his garden. He pointed to a rude circle of squash, each of which had been arranged to point at a yellow pumpkin, and said: "Here's what you're looking for."

After a moment of hesitation, one agent leaned over curiously and examined the pumpkin. Its stem had not been severed and it appeared to be growing on the vine. But close examination revealed that its top had been sliced off and then carefully replaced. Its hollow interior held three aluminum capsules of microfilm.

AMAZING HAUL

Chambers explained that he had picked the pumpkin as a hiding place that morning before leaving for Washington, said that he had been afraid Communists might search his house and barn while he was away.

Next day, with the aid of the FBI, the committee began sorting through its amazing haul. The microfilm yielded a three-ft. pile of photostatic copies of highly confidential military and State Department dispatches. One came from Ambassador William Bullitt in Paris. One bore a heading which explained that it had been handed to the German Ambassador by Under Secretary of State Sumner Welles. They were dated during the years 1937 and 1938.

The uses to which Soviet Russia could have put such material in the years before World War II were obvious. By following key words in the documents, experts might have been able to crack the code from which they had been translated. They would also have formed a guide to U.S. thinking about Soviet Russia, Italy, Germany and Japan, would have furnished valuable clues to future U.S. diplomatic maneuvers.

The Alger Hiss Case and Cold War America

Front pages of newspapers throughout the country on December 4, 1948, headlined the discovery of classified State Department documents in a hollowed-out pumpkin on the farm of Whittaker Chambers, a senior editor at *Time* magazine.[1] Americans were already familiar with Chambers and his accusations against Alger Hiss, former State Department official and current president of the Carnegie Endowment for International Peace. In August, Chambers had appeared before the House Committee on Un-American Activities (HUAC) and accused Hiss of being a member of the Communist Party during the 1930s. Since then, news accounts had followed the story from congressional committee hearings to the federal court, where Hiss filed a slander suit. But the classified State Department documents pulled from the pumpkin on that December day took the dispute to a new, more serious, level. Conflicting, seemingly unverifiable, statements by two individuals and accusations of Communist Party membership, that in itself enough to ruin a person's reputation, were replaced by concrete evidence of espionage. From this time until Alger Hiss's conviction for perjury in January 1950, the case consumed the attention of Cold War America.

The principal antagonists in the case were studies in contrasts. The accuser, Whittaker Chambers, was a Columbia University dropout, an itinerant writer and translator, who by his own admission had been an active member of the Communist Party until he became disillusioned in the late 1930s. While a member of the party, he had worked on the staffs of two Communist periodicals, *The Daily Worker* and *The New Masses*. He had also been recruited for the

Soviet underground, which ultimately led to his encounter with Alger Hiss.

The accused, Alger Hiss, was a respected member of the Washington establishment. Hiss graduated from Johns Hopkins University and Harvard Law School, where he was elected to the *Law Review* staff and became a protégé of Professor Felix Frankfurter, a future Supreme Court justice. When Hiss completed his studies, Frankfurter secured a clerkship for him with Supreme Court Justice Oliver Wendell Holmes. Later, choosing government service over a lucrative private law practice, Hiss came to Washington as one of the many idealistic young men eager to participate in Franklin Roosevelt's New Deal effort to lift the country from the depths of the depression. He worked in the Agricultural Adjustment Administration, did legal work for the Nye Committee, a Senate committee investigating the munitions industry during World War I, and ultimately ended up in the State Department, where he rose to positions of significant responsibility. During World War II, he played a leading role in the creation of the United Nations. In that capacity, he attended the much maligned 1945 Yalta Conference as a lesser advisor to President Roosevelt. In 1946, Hiss resigned his State Department post and accepted the prestigious position of president of the Carnegie Endowment for International Peace.

Hiss's New Deal credentials, his ties to the Democratic Party, and particularly his links to the Roosevelt-Truman foreign policy were critically important in the tension-charged political atmosphere at the beginning of the Cold War. Conservative Republicans accused the Roosevelt and Truman administrations of pursuing policies that impotently responded to Kremlin pressures. To these critics, nowhere was this more evident than in the fate suffered by Poland and the other countries of Eastern Europe, doomed to endure Soviet domination. Thus the charges Chambers leveled were as much an indictment of these two Democratic administrations as they were a personal attack on Hiss's reputation. The affair, therefore, encapsulated many of the forces and concerns that enveloped American society and politics in postwar America.

In the late 1940s, the euphoria of the World War II victory succumbed to the insecurities of the Cold War as international events exposed the threatening intentions of Soviet communism. Relations between the United States and Soviet Union, former wartime allies, steadily deteriorated. By 1948, when Chambers came forward with his accusations, Soviet forces were already tightening their control over Eastern Europe, and Truman in 1947 had issued his Truman Doctrine, committing the United States to containing the spread of communism wherever it threatened free peoples. A Communist coup in Czechoslovakia in February 1948 and the beginning of the Berlin blockade in June of that year confirmed for Americans Soviet aggressive intentions. By the time Hiss's second perjury trial ended in January 1950, tensions had escalated further. The Soviets successfully tested a nuclear weapon in August 1949, and shortly thereafter, Communist forces defeated the pro-western Nationalist government in China. These contemporary events had a direct effect on the outcome and impact of the Hiss affair.

For Americans, however, the Cold War threat was not confined overseas. There was also growing evidence of Communist subversion at home that added to feelings of insecurity. In the spring of 1945, the Federal Bureau of Investigation (FBI) raided the editorial offices of the leftist journal *Amerasia* and seized copies of classified State Department documents. Investigators traced these materials to several State Department personnel, including John Stewart Service, a leading expert on Chinese affairs. In early 1946, Igor Gouzenko, a code clerk in the Soviet embassy in Canada, defected with a cache of documents describing an espionage ring active in Canada and indicating that other Soviet agents had infiltrated the U.S. government as well. These revelations reinforced the veracity of former Communists, such as Elizabeth Bentley and Whittaker Chambers, who had been telling their stories to the FBI and congressional committees. The revelations did not stop there. In March 1949, while the attention of the American public was focused on the Hiss case, the FBI arrested Judith Coplon, a clerk in the Justice Department, and her Soviet contact Valentin Gubitchev and charged them with espionage. Their trial unfolded in Washington at the same time that Hiss was defending himself against perjury charges in New York City.

The expanding record of espionage not only made Chambers's charges all the more credible, it also provided ammunition for opponents of the Truman administration. The Republican Party, having captured control of both houses of Congress in the 1946 elections, looked ahead with growing confidence to the 1948 presidential election. Truman seemed vulnerable. His alleged failure to root out subversives complemented charges that he had neglected to adequately confront Soviet expansionism, particularly in Eastern Europe. Republican criticism of the infamous Yalta Conference of 1945, where the United States had bowed to Stalin's demands and purportedly sealed the postwar fate of Poland, resonated in the political arena. Congressional Republicans, particularly in the House Committee on Un-American Activities, led the attack.

Thomas Dewey of New York was the Republican presidential candidate in 1948, but Truman's campaign focused more on the Republican-controlled Congress, in his words the "do-nothing Eightieth Congress." Despite the apparent advantages Dewey and the Republicans enjoyed, Truman's tactics succeeded. He scored an upset victory just weeks before the "pumpkin papers" made headlines. But this electoral defeat failed to quell Truman's opponents. The specter of four more years of Democratic control of the White House redoubled Republican determination to expose the president's failings. Communist subversion became an even more appealing political issue. Truman's defense of Alger Hiss and his description of congressional investigations as a political "red herring," blatant use of the Communist issue to attack his administration and divert attention from more pressing matters, fanned the flames of partisan politics even further.

Despite the president's assertion that all of the concern about spies was a "red herring," his own policies contradicted his words and bore some responsibility for the public frenzy. While he publicly insisted that governmental institutions were not infiltrated with Communists, Truman nonetheless issued Executive Order 9835 in March 1947 establishing his loyalty program. The order called for the establishment of loyalty review boards to investigate government employees and to determine if there were reasonable grounds for believing any to be a security risk for the United States. Anyone determined to be a security risk could be terminated from federal service. The order also called for the attorney general to compile a list of organizations deemed subversive, a list that was subsequently published. Clearly a response to Republican charges and an attempt to demonstrate the administration's vigilance against communism, this program only fed the popular belief that the executive branch faced a problem.[2] As Richard Gid Powers remarked in his study of American anti-communism, the program "was too little too late. The issue of Communist infiltration of the executive branch had given the Republicans a powerful weapon against the administration, and they were not going to let Truman off the hook."[3]

Truman's Justice Department fueled the frenzy even further when it secured a federal grand jury indictment of Eugene Dennis, national secretary of the American Communist Party, and ten other party leaders for violating the 1940 Smith Act, a federal statute that prohibited advocating the overthrow of the U.S. government by force or violence. Bringing these charges against the Communist Party leadership in the short run might have blunted charges that the administration was soft on communism, an advantage for the Democrats in the 1948

election year, but in the long run it contributed to the public's growing concern about Communist subversion. The Dennis case came to
trial in 1949 at the same time and in the same New York City courthouse where Hiss's first perjury case was being heard.

Personal political ambitions went hand-in-hand with this partisan
politics. Exposing Communists could be politically profitable. No
better example exists than the case of freshman Congressman
Richard M. Nixon of California who rode his newfound reputation to
the vice presidency two years after Hiss's conviction. Nixon sat on
HUAC and adopted the Hiss affair as his personal crusade.

International unrest, partisan politics, and political ambition all
contributed to the unsettled atmosphere as the Hiss-Chambers dispute moved from congressional committee rooms to the federal
courts. The case, however, was not only a product of the times, but it
impacted the future direction that the anti-Communist movement
would take. In *The Cold War Comes to Main Street,* Lisle Rose wrote:

> After years of apparently futile alarms and excursions, the issue of
> communist subversion of American liberalism finally seemed about to
> become a central element in the national dialogue. All hinged on the
> outcome of one case. By the end of 1949 much of the country was
> expectantly waiting for the conclusion of the sensational jury trial of
> Alger Hiss. Nixon, using his position on HUAC, had orchestrated the
> whole affair. If Hiss were found innocent, Nixon's fledgling career as a
> Red-hunter, and indeed the entire anticommunist impulse in America,
> might be destroyed. But if Hiss were found guilty, opportunities for a
> comprehensive anticommunist crusade would be limitless.[4]

Hiss was convicted only of perjury in 1950, but the verdict was
tantamount to conviction for espionage. If Hiss was a Soviet agent,
then reason told the American people that there undoubtedly had to
be others. If Hiss's guilt were proven, then conservative and Republican critics of the Democratic Truman administration were right. This
would lead the way for other events that would further the cause of
the anti-Communist crusade. Shortly after Hiss's conviction, on
February 9, 1950, Senator Joseph McCarthy appeared before a
Republican women's group in Wheeling, West Virginia, claiming to
have a list of 205 Communists and fellow travelers in the State
Department. Although the numbers he cited changed in subsequent
versions of his speech, and although his list was never substantiated,
the speech catapulted the obscure senator from Wisconsin to the
forefront in the crusade against Communists in America. He would
ultimately lend his name to this whole period. On February 2, 1950,
Klaus Fuchs, a physicist who had worked on the atomic bomb

project at Los Alamos, New Mexico, was convicted of espionage in England. Investigators followed the espionage trail from Fuchs to Julius and Ethel Rosenberg by July 1950. Overseas, the Cold War turned hot in Asia when North Korea invaded South Korea in June 1950. Americans became increasingly concerned.

These events were not tied directly to Hiss's fate, but his conviction added momentum to the determination to root out Communist infiltration in government. "Without the Alger Hiss case," insisted Earl Latham in a classic study of Communist activity in Washington, "the six-year controversy that followed might have been a tamer affair, and the Communist issue somewhat more tractable."[5]

The Alger Hiss case was as much a product of this age as its outcome contributed to furthering what David Caute called the "great fear" that enveloped America during these post-World War II years.[6] In microcosm, the case encompassed the political and social forces in society that characterized the early Cold War era.

Contemporary Observers Assess the Meaning of the Hiss Case

The trials of Alger Hiss exposed deep political and ideological divisions in the United States during the early Cold War, not only between Republicans and Democrats, but also between conservatives and liberals who kept the debate over Hiss's innocence or guilt alive long after the jury voted to convict. Conservatives, anxious about the expansion of the powers of the federal government wrought by the New Deal and worried that the Roosevelt-Truman administrations had been ineffective in combating the Communist threat, saw the Hiss case as vindication for their legitimate concern about the growing Communist influence.

Congressman Richard Nixon, Hiss's principal antagonist on HUAC, was representative of this perspective. In his memoir *Six Crises,* he devoted an entire chapter to defending his actions during the Hiss episode.[7] According to Nixon, communism presented a serious and immediate threat to American security after World War II. And liberals were particularly guilty of failing to understand this. The case was a "tragedy of history," he maintained, that reflected many disturbing Cold War trends: "[T]he rise, development, and— as some would argue—partial decay of the philosophy called 'liberalism'; the parallel emergence of a liberal heresy called Communism; the assumption of world leadership by two super-powers, America and Russia, each wedded to a competing faith and each strengthened and yet limited thereby; and, finally, the present confrontation of these two faiths and these two super-powers at specific times and places in every part of the world." In his account of the Hiss investigation, he castigated both the Truman and Roosevelt administrations for being blind to the problem of Communist subversion.

In the process of explaining the meaning of the whole case, he pro-moted his role in the affair. Unlike some other government officials at the time, he saw clearly the implications of the events transpiring around him. His efforts involved a crusade with the future of American civilization at stake, not a political event.

Nixon published *Six Crises* after losing the 1960 presidential race to John F. Kennedy. While writing the chapter on the Hiss affair, he said a ques-tion asked by his daughter led him to realize that her generation did not understand the serious issues involved:

> The Hiss case was the first major crisis of my political life. My name, my reputation, and my career were ever to be linked with the decisions I made and the actions I took in that case, as a thirty-five-year-old freshman Congressman in 1948. Yet when I was telling my fifteen-year-old daughter, Tricia, one day about the subjects I was covering in the book, she interrupted me to ask, "What was the Hiss case?"
>
> I realized for the first time that a whole new generation of Americans was growing up who had not even heard of the Hiss case. And now, in retrospect, I wonder how many of my own generation really knew the facts and the implications of the emotional controversy that rocked the nation twelve years ago.[8]

The following excerpt is how he responded to Tricia's question.

SIX CRISES

Richard Nixon

Now, I would like to attempt an answer to the question my daughter, Tricia, asked me.

"What was the Hiss case?"

Whittaker Chambers, with typical insight, perhaps came closest to the truth when he wrote in *Witness* that the situation which involved Alger

Source: From *Six Crises* by Richard M. Nixon, 61–68. Copyright © 1962 by Richard M. Nixon. Used by permission of Doubleday, a division of Random House, Inc.

Hiss and himself was not simply "human tragedy," not just "another fat folder in the sad files of the police," but rather was a "tragedy of history." Here, "the two irreconcilable faiths of our time, Communism and Freedom, came to grips in the persons of two conscious and resolute men."

In this sentence, he compressed whole chapters of world history: the rise, development, and—as some would argue—partial decay of the philosophy called "liberalism"; the parallel emergence of a liberal heresy called Communism; the assumption of world leadership by two superpowers, America and Russia, each wedded to a competing faith and each strengthened and yet limited thereby; and, finally, the present confrontation of these two faiths and these two superpowers at specific times and places in every part of the world. The issue at stake, to put it starkly, is this: whose hand will write the next several chapters of human history?

The Hiss case aroused the nation for the first time to the existence and character of the Communist conspiracy within the United States. It focused attention sharply on the conspiratorial aspects of the Party. The prevailing opinion in the country prior to the Hiss-Chambers case was probably that the Communists were nothing but a handful of noisy but relatively harmless left-wingers attempting to exercise their rights of free speech and political action. A substantial number of Americans believed the investigations of the House Committee on Un-American Activities were "Red-baiting" for partisan purposes only.

The unpopularity of the Committee, whatever the reasons, caused many political leaders and opinion-makers to dismiss without investigation anything the Committee might discover and disclose about Communism in the United States. Upon learning that Communists and fellow-travelers were holding important positions in government, in education, or in labor, many people simply responded—"so what! All they are doing is exercising their legitimate freedom of speech and political opinion." Some went even further and charged that the members of the Committee, and their allies, were really "Fascist agents," bent on denying free expression to "unpopular views."

The Hiss case, for the first time, forcibly demonstrated to the American people that domestic Communism was a real and present danger to the security of the nation.

As Herbert Hoover wrote me after Hiss's conviction, "At last the stream of treason that has existed in our government has been exposed in a fashion all may believe." Chambers testified that his espionage ring was only one of several that had infiltrated the American government. Yet he had turned over to the Committee and the Justice Department hundreds of pages of confidential and secret documents from the State

Department and other government agencies. And he testified that on at least seventy different occasions, the members of his ring had obtained a like number of documents—all of which he had transmitted to Soviet agents.

Hiss was just one of the members of the group from which Chambers obtained government documents. Chambers' contacts included four men in the State Department, two in the Treasury Department, two in the Bureau of Standards, one in the Aberdeen and one in the Picatinny Arsenal, two in the Electric Boat Company, one in the Remington Rand Company, and one in the Illinois Steel Company. The individuals he named, almost without exception, held positions of influence where they had access to confidential and secret information.

But the purpose of the Hiss-Chambers group was not limited to stealing documents and passing information to Soviet agents like common spies. Some, like Hiss, reached positions so high in government that they could influence policy directly. As I said in a speech in the House of Representatives in 1950, this type of activity "permits the enemy to guide and shape our policy; it disarms and dooms our diplomats to defeat in advance, before they go to conferences; traitors in the high councils of our own government make sure that the deck is stacked on the Soviet side of the diplomatic table."

The Hiss case thus demonstrated the necessity of screening federal employees in sensitive positions for loyalty and security—rigorously, fairly, and with sophisticated insight into the many-sided Communist apparatus.

The Hiss case exposed the blindness of the Truman Administration and its predecessors to the problem of Communist subversion in government. It demonstrated the need for congressional investigatory bodies, like the Committee on Un-American Activities, which could expose such laxity and, with the help of a mobilized public opinion, could force the Executive branch to adopt policies adequate for dealing with the problem.

The record of negligence was almost too flagrant to believe. Chambers first made his charges in 1939 and he repeated them to government officials several times thereafter. Yet as far as the public record is concerned, the only action taken on his charges until the Committee started its investigation in 1948, was to promote each of the individuals he named to higher positions of power and influence within the government. The most damning proof of negligence on the part of the Executive branch was that Hiss himself had to be indicted and convicted not for espionage, the crime of which he was originally guilty, but for perjury—for lying when he denied committing espionage. The statute of limitations, requiring prosecution for espionage within three years after the crime had been committed, had already long expired.

The conduct of President Truman in this case was particularly hard to understand. No one would question the tough-minded anti-Communism of the man who had so boldly initiated the program of Greek-Turkish aid and the Marshall Plan. One can understand why he might have felt justified in terming the case a "red herring" when Hiss first testified before the Committee. But he did a disservice to the nation and to his own party by stubbornly maintaining that position as evidence to the contrary piled up. His error was sheer stubbornness in refusing to admit a mistake. He viewed the Hiss case only in its political implications and he chose to handle the crisis which faced his Administration with an outworn political rule of thumb: leave the political skeletons hidden in the closet and keep the door locked. He denied outright the evidence in front of him and he stumped the 1948 political trail flailing away at the "red herring," thus putting himself in a needlessly untenable position on an important issue and—of infinitely graver consequence—leading a large segment of the public away from a deeper understanding of the true threat of the Communist conspiracy in America.

I have no doubt that President Truman personally had just as much contempt for Alger Hiss as I had when the full import of his activities became known to him. An indication of his attitude was a report Bert Andrews gave me shortly after Hiss's indictment. He said Truman was shown copies of the stolen documents by a representative of the Justice Department. As he thumbed through page after page of the incriminating evidence, he muttered, over and over, "Why, the son of a bitch—he betrayed his country!" Yet when asked in his next press conference if he still thought the Committee's investigation of the Hiss case was a "red herring," he replied in the affirmative! When a friend asked him how he could possibly make such a statement in light of the new evidence, his reply was: "Of course Hiss is guilty. But that damn Committee isn't interested in that. All it cares about is politics, and as long as they try to make politics out of this Communist issue, I am going to label their activities for what they are—a 'red herring.'"

President Truman spoke quite properly and effectively of the need for bipartisanship in meeting the threat of Communism abroad. Along with a substantial number of the Republicans in both House and Senate, I responded to his pleas in this respect by voting for and supporting the Greek-Turkish Aid Program and the Marshall Plan. What he did not seem to understand—and here is the really crucial point—was that Communism in America is part and parcel of Communism abroad. The problem, like Communism itself, is indivisible. If, in other words, he had recognized the need for bipartisanship in fighting Communism at home as well as abroad, he would not have persisted in making his "red herring" statements with regard to the Committee investigations. And furthermore, there would have been no need for that investigation to be continued as it was, simply in order to force the Justice Department to take the action demanded by the facts.

Once the FBI was given the green light in its investigation of the Hiss case, it did a magnificent job. The blame for failing to act before that time rests not on the FBI but squarely on those officials of the Executive branch who had full access to FBI reports and who failed or refused to order a full investigation.

The Hiss case taught the nation some major lessons, too, about the most effective methods for fighting Communism in the United States. Communism cannot be fought successfully by brushing off or ignoring the danger because of the small number of Communist Party members, or by concentrating solely on "removing the causes of Communism by making democracy work." The nation finally saw that the magnitude of the threat of Communism in the United States is multiplied a thousandfold because of its direct connection with and support by the massive power of the world Communist conspiracy centered in Moscow.

• • •

These lessons from the Hiss case are important. But more vital still is that we understand why a man like Alger Hiss, with his education and background, joined the Communist Party in the first place.

The tendency too often is to try to find some convenient excuse for his conduct and thereby avoid facing up to the real reasons. But none of the typical excuses fit Alger Hiss. He did not join the Communist Party, accept its rigid discipline, and steal State Department secrets for money, position, or a desire for power, or for psychological reasons stemming from some obscure incident in his early life, or because he had been duped or led astray by his wife. He joined the Communist Party and became a Communist espionage agent because he deeply believed in Communist theory, Communist principles, and the Communist "vision" of the ideal society still to come. He believed in an absolutely materialistic view of the world, in principles of deliberate manipulation by a dedicated elite, and in an ideal world society in which "the party of the workers" replaces God as the prime mover and the sole judge of right and wrong. His morality could be reduced to one perverted rule: anything that advances the goals of Communism is good. Hiss followed his beliefs deliberately and consciously to the utmost logical extreme, and ended up in the area of espionage.

At a less rigorous level—somewhere in a vague area that goes by such names as "positivism" or "pragmatism" or "ethical neutralism"—Hiss was clearly the symbol of a considerable number of perfectly loyal citizens whose theaters of operation are the nation's mass media and universities, its scholarly foundations, and its government bureaucracies. This group likes to throw the cloak of liberalism around all its beliefs. Eric Sevareid's term "liberalists" probably describes them most accurately. They are not Communists; they are not even remotely disloyal; and, give or take a normal dose of human fallibility, they are neither dishonest nor dishonorable. But they are of a mind-set, as doctrinaire as those on the extreme right, which makes them singularly vulnerable to the Communist popular front appeal under the banner of social justice. In the time of the Hiss case they were "patsies" for the Communist line.

The "liberalists" now stand self-accused in all their vulnerability by a most damaging fact. As soon as the Hiss case broke and well before a full bill of particulars was even available, much less open to close critical analysis, they leaped to the defense of Alger Hiss—and to a counterattack of unparalleled venom and irrational fury on his accusers.

Some of the reasons may have been simply political. The New Deal had fallen hard for the popular front tactic and now it was going to be called to account for its past errors—or, perhaps, for its past "innocence." Some thought it had to be defended at any cost. Typical of this attitude was a conversation I had with a New Deal lawyer who had served in the Roosevelt Administration during World War II. The Hiss case was being discussed at a Washington dinner party shortly after the "pumpkin papers" came to public attention. He shouted at me, "I don't give a damn what the facts are. Even if Hiss admits he's guilty, these investigations are dangerous and will have a terrible and disastrous effect on the country—because the net result is to cast reflection on the United Nations and all the other progressive aspects of the Roosevelt-Truman foreign policy."

Nixon was quick to link liberalism with communism and to view the Hiss affair as representative of serious failure on the part of the Roosevelt and Truman administrations to effectively confront the Communist threat. But not all contemporary observers interpreted the Hiss-Chambers confrontation in this way. Alistair Cooke, a British reporter for the *Manchester Guardian,* reported on both perjury trials and saw something different. His take on events is one example of the liberal critique of Hiss's conviction. In *A Generation on Trial,* his account of the two trials published shortly after the guilty verdict, Cooke emphasized the overriding role politics played.[9] To Cooke, not only was Hiss on trial, but a whole "generation" that supported the liberal values of the Roosevelt New Deal era was on trial. Some of these liberals in their idealism had succumbed to Communist blandishments during the 1930s. Now in the charged atmosphere of the Cold War, this threatened to discredit the whole liberal tradition.

To Cooke, Hiss was a victim of this political system. Implicitly questioning why Hiss was on trial in the first place, he faulted Americans for judging the actions of Hiss and others in the 1930s through the hindsight of the 1940s. In the 1930s, he noted, Communists were viewed as moonstruck intellectuals. The New Dealers saw them as useful "minute-men who would alert the countryside to the menace of Fascism." In the 1940s, however, Americans judged their actions during the past decade through the prism of the Cold War.

In Cooke's estimation, HUAC was particularly culpable. Its members persisted in their effort to link the administration of Franklin Roosevelt and his New Deal to Communists essentially for their own political ends. Chambers's charges against Hiss "looked like vindication beyond the dreams of the long-suffering House Committee."

A GENERATION ON TRIAL

Alistair Cooke

In the summer of 1948, when the names of Hiss and Chambers were bannered across the front pages, the United States was convulsed, as at no time since the 1920's, with fear and hatred of the Soviet Union. A Congressional committee, the House Committee on Un-American Activities, had been warning the country for years about the treacherous intentions of Communists when to do so seemed to show a perverse obsession with the lesser of two evils. To most Americans in the 1930's the Communists were moonstruck intellectuals. To the New Dealers, they were useful minute-men, who would alert the countryside to the menace of Fascism. To Catholics, they were anti-Christ. Since this House Committee, once Representative Martin Dies became its chairman, showed a marked allergy for the un-American activity of Communism, and a dogged indifference to the epidemic possibilities of

Source: Alistair Cooke, *A Generation on Trial: U.S.A. v. Alger Hiss* (New York: Alfred A. Knopf, 1950), 7–13. Copyright © 1950, 1952 by Alistair Cooke. Used by permission of Alfred A. Knopf, a division of Random House, Inc.

Fascism,* its investigations were thought mildly absurd during the late thirties and downright egregious in the four years when—however distasteful it may now be to recall—the Soviet Union was embraced as a full fighting ally; an embrace, it is worth saying, that was offered not out of magnanimity but out of a keen preference for survival.

The House Committee, however, persisted in its obsession through the lean years of the New Deal into the fat years of what was called the Cold War, when popular feeling about Russia cooled and soured. In 1948 the Committee was riding a current spy scare with an investigation into espionage. It had been saying for years that the Communists got a sure foothold in the administrations of Franklin Roosevelt. It had never proved it. But in the summer it looked up among others an ex-Communist, one Whittaker Chambers, now a respectable magazine editor, who reminded the Committee of a list of alleged spies and participating fellow travelers he had given nine years before to Mr. Adolf Berle, then an Assistant Secretary of State. It was a list of once young New Dealers who, he said, were expertly organized through the mid-thirties as the official secret underground of the Communist Party in Washington. Some of them had since become fairly prominent in labor circles and two or three of them in Henry Wallace's Progressive Party. One of them had been an adviser to President Roosevelt at the Yalta Conference, which just then the Republicans were making out to be the occasion of a wholesale sell-out to the Russians.

This looked like vindication beyond the dreams of the long-suffering House Committee. It confirmed the worst anxieties of a greatly changed America. It froze the condescension of people who had smiled sympathetically at President Truman's opinion that the House Committee was dragging "a red herring" across the campaign trail of a Presidential election year. The Committee was rewarded with resounding publicity and the grudging admission, from unlikely people, that it was after all perhaps made up of vigilant and patriotic men. The room where it held its hearings was a Roman circus panting for the entrance of dazed Christians. Into this arena walked, of his own volition, one man—the only man on Chambers' astonishing list who wished immediately to deny his accuser. He was Alger Hiss.

Hiss was almost unknown to the public eye, though the subsequent craving for a full-blooded New Dealer transmuted him in no time into the protector of great statesmen, and President Roosevelt's high-policy adviser at Yalta, a fiction that the defense counsel in the fol-

---

*Up to the beginning of the Second World War, the Committee's reports show a preferential concern for Communism over Fascism in the proportion of about 8 to 1.

lowing trials curiously abetted. Hiss was not a policy-maker or ever much more than a devoted and able State Department officer just below the first rank. But he had organized the United Nations Conference on International Organization at San Francisco. He had flown back to Washington, as somebody had to, with the signed Charter. He had gone, in a humble capacity, to the Yalta Conference. His prestige in the Roosevelt Government and the United Nations, or rather the prestige that could be thrust upon him in retrospect, made him a very precious commodity to the House Committee. He became a point of honor and an object of rare suspicion when, of all the underground men named by Chambers, he asked to deny the charge before the Committee, challenged Chambers to repeat it outside the privilege of a Congressional hearing, and, when Chambers obliged, brought suit for defamation of character. Chambers then produced his old State papers.

The Department of Justice took an interest and reopened a grand-jury investigation into espionage that had been sitting on and off for fourteen months in New York. The grand jury called Hiss and Chambers many times and on the last day of its sitting indicted Hiss for perjury, implying that it believed Hiss had passed the State papers to Chambers in 1938. The statute of limitations protected Hiss from an indictment for espionage. But though the count was perjury, the implied charge was espionage. There was a strong desire, in both those who believed Hiss guilty and those who believed him innocent, to make him out to be a more representative Rooseveltian figure than he was. Among the House Committee, which had a Republican majority when the inquiry and the subsequent indictment came about, there was the eager wish to nail the curse of Communism on the coffin of the New Deal and so exorcize the legion of "liberal" and "bureaucratic" spirits that had been loosed on Washington fifteen years before to gibber down two decades and supposedly terrify the country. Among Hiss's supporters there was a defensive reaction to the Republican inference that while Russia was now the cause of all our ills, it was so only because we had been betrayed by the New Deal into diplomatic recognition of the Soviet Union and Heaven knows what exchanges of policy. I have said it is a natural thing to want to make the past consistent with the rationale of our present self-respect, or to want to confess an inconsistency when we have confidently outgrown it. This impulse is very strong in America, where people want the best of everything, believe Time is the Siamese twin of Progress, and refuse to let even experience shake them from their belief that happiness is manageable. If we are now baited in every direction by the Russians, it does not satisfy Americans to say that this is the turn of history. It must mean that somebody entrusted with our welfare betrayed us or blundered. A nation with a religious trust in Progress simply cannot admit that even when the best is done, hard times may follow.

• • •

Those who were for Hiss or against him felt their own pride and past political judgment to be at stake. Many Democrats and old New Dealers felt that Hiss was a gallant protagonist of the younger liberal crowd that went to Washington in the New Deal's first crusade. They feared, as the others hoped, that a verdict against Hiss would be a verdict against the New Deal. Whatever Hiss or his lawyers might say later, the House Committee thus succeeded, before he ever came to trial, in making a large and very mixed public identify Hiss with what was characteristic of the New Deal.

Not all liberals, however, saw Hiss as simply a victim. Leslie Fiedler, a prominent writer and liberal social critic, criticized the liberal defenders of Hiss. To Fiedler, evidence pointed to Hiss's guilt. Hiss had been a naïve follower of the Communist popular front in the 1930s. Like others who had been caught giving assistance to the Kremlin—Judith Coplon, William Remington, and the Rosenbergs—Hiss had been enticed by the appeal of communism. Fiedler contended that Hiss should have admitted this. Liberals, according to Fiedler, had to come to the understanding that "mere liberal principle is not in itself a guarantee against evil." To Fiedler, Hiss was not a personification of liberalism under attack. Many liberals held to the "illusion" of his innocence. They needed to acknowledge his guilt and return to a more responsible liberalism.

"HISS, CHAMBERS, AND THE AGE OF INNOCENCE"

Leslie Fiedler

Alger Hiss is in jail. The last legal judgments have been passed. The decision of the courts stands: guilty as charged—guilty in fact of treason, though technically accused only of perjury. It is time, many of us feel, to forget the whole business: the prison doors have closed; let us consider the question also closed. But history is not so easily satisfied. Like

Source: Leslie Fiedler, "Hiss, Chambers, and the Age of Innocence: Who Was Guilty and of What?" *Commentary* 12 (August, 1951): 109–10, 114, 119. Reprinted by permission. All rights reserved.

some monumental bore, it grabs us by the lapels, keeps screaming into our faces the same story over and over again. The case of Judith Coplon, the case of William Remington, the case of Julius and Ethel Rosenberg, the inevitable case of tomorrow's Mr. X—the names change but the meanings are the same, and we protest that we have long since got the point. But have we? Of what was Alger Hiss guilty anyhow?

The statute of limitations protected Hiss against the charge of having passed secret material from State Department files to his accuser Whittaker Chambers, of having placed in the hands of agents of the Soviet Union documents which, whatever their intrinsic value, enabled our present enemies to break some of our most important codes. The transaction had taken place in 1936 and 1937—a war away, in years we ourselves find it difficult to remember, in years some of us don't want to remember. It is a painful thing to be asked to live again through events ten years gone, to admit one's identity with the person who bore one's name in a by now incredible past. It is hardest of all to confess that one is responsible for the acts of that past, especially when such acts are now placed in a new and unforeseen context that changes their meaning entirely. "Not guilty!" one wants to cry, "that is not what I meant at all!"

And yet the qualifying act of moral adulthood is precisely this admission of responsibility for the past and its consequences, however undesired or unforeseen. Such a recognition Hiss was called upon to make. Had he been willing to say, "Yes, I did these things—things it is now possible to call 'treason'—not for money or prestige, but out of a higher allegiance than patriotism—"; had he only confessed in the name of any of the loftier platitudes for which men are prepared publicly to admit the breaking of lesser laws, he need not even have gone to prison. Why did he lie?

Had Hiss told the truth, the whole meaning of the case might have been different, might have attained that dignity of tragedy for which Alistair Cooke* looks through its dossiers in vain. The defenders of

---

*Alistair Cooke, *A Generation on Trial*. In addition to Mr. Cooke's book, a thorough and scrupulous work, though one with many of whose interpretations I disagree, I have used for this article de Toledano and Lasky's *Seeds of Treason*, which is marred by a journalistic and melodramatic style, but contains much valuable background material and sets the Hiss case in an illuminating context of Communist espionage on two continents. I have also consulted the newspaper accounts of the case, particularly those of the New York *Times*, and the printed hearings of the House Un-American Activities Committee; while for further background, I have turned to the *New Masses* for 1931, and various other official Communist publications. I do not know personally either of the principals in the case, nor have I made any attempt to communicate with them. I have no private or special sources of information. What I have attempted in this piece is an analysis based on publicly available documents, considered in the light of my own experience and knowledge of that world of values and beliefs out of which the incidents of the case arose. It is the lack of such experience and knowledge which makes even Mr. Cooke's careful and subtle book miss what seems to me the essential point.

Hiss, and of the generation they take him to represent, would have been delivered from the intolerable plight that prompted them, during the trials, to declare at one and the same time that (a) Hiss was innocent of the charges, the victim of a malevolent psychopath and (b) even if he was technically guilty, he had the moral right, in those years of betrayal leading to Munich, to give his primary loyalty to the Soviet Union. Why did he lie, and lying, lose the whole point of the case in a maze of irrelevant data: the signature on the transfer of ownership of a car, the date a typewriter was repaired . . . ?

The lie, it is necessary to see, was no mere accident, but was of the essence of the case, a clue to the deepest significance of what was done and to the moral atmosphere that made the deed possible. We can see Hiss's lie now in a larger context, beside William Remington's even more vain denials of Elizabeth Bentley's charges, and the fantastic affirmations of innocence by Julius and Ethel Rosenberg. These were not, after all, common criminals, who plead innocent mechanically on the advice of counsel; these were believers in a new society, for whose sake they had already deceived their closest friends and endangered the security of their country. In the past (and even yet in the present—the Puerto Rican nationalists, for instance) such political idealists welcomed their trials as forums, opportunities to declare to the world the high principles behind their actions, the loyalty to the march of history and the eventual triumph of socialism that had brought them to the bar. They might have been, in some eyes at least, spectacular martyrs; they chose to behave instead, before the eyes of all, like blustering petty thieves.

Not that the avowals of innocence, especially in the case of Hiss, were not affecting. Despite the absurdity of his maunderings about "forgery by typewriter," there was something moving—for a generation brought up on stories of Dreyfus and Tom Mooney, and growing to social awareness through the Sacco-Vanzetti trial and the campaigns to free the Scottsboro boys—in Hiss's final courtroom pose as The Victim. Even now, it is hard to realize how little claim he has to the title. For here was no confessed revolutionary, marked by his avowed principles, his foreign accent, his skin color, as fair game for the frame-up; here was a supereminently respectable civil servant from the better schools, accused by the obvious outsider, the self-declared rebel and renegade, Whittaker Chambers. Hiss seemed to desire both the pathos of the persecuted and the aura of unblemished respectability. His is, as we shall see, the Popular Front mind at bay, incapable of honesty even when there is no hope in anything else.

• • •

Some of the commentators on the case have spoken of the anti-Red "hysteria" that prevailed at the time of the case, as if in such an atmosphere the cards were hopelessly stacked against Alger Hiss. But precisely the opposite is the case. He is just the type that does not normally get caught in the indiscriminate "witch hunt," which tends to pick out those who look like "witches," the visible outsiders. A woman like Assistant Secretary of Defense Anna M. Rosenberg, for instance, foreign-born and a Jew, is much more likely to be haled up without any evidence against her, while a man like Hiss can slip past the ordinary Congressman, to whom Red really means loud-mouth or foreigner or Jew (Rankin, who was on the Committee that examined Hiss, apparently spent his spare time thumbing through *Who's Who in American Jewry*, and turned all his fire on—Chambers!).

The Committee did not want to believe Chambers. They were convinced by his, and his wife's, astonishingly specific memories: though some members of the Committee had been eager to "get the goods" on the New Deal, to catch out the State Department at last, they had apparently found it difficult to put much faith in Chambers. It was impossible to like him, as one instinctively liked Hiss for the boyish charm we think of as peculiarly American. Chambers seems to have worn his unprepossessing air (he is the sort of person of whom one believes immediately quite unfounded stories of insanity and depravity) deliberately, as if he had acquired in his revolutionary days the habit of rebuffing all admiration based on anything but his role in the party.

Every word he spoke declared him an ex-traitor, a present turncoat and squealer, and Hiss, sensing his inestimable advantage in a society whose values are largely set in boyhood when snitching is the ultimate sin, had traded on his role as the honest man confronted by the "rat." Really, Hiss kept insisting, they'd have to call the Harvard Club, say he'd be a few minutes late to dinner—after taking care of this unpleasantness. For a while it came off quite successfully, coming from one who visibly belonged, whose clothes beautifully fitted, whose manners were adequate to all occasions.

We learned later, of course, how much the genteel aspect of Hiss was itself a mask, imposed on a background of disorder and uncertainty not unlike Chambers': the suicide of his father and sister, the undefined psychological difficulties of his stepson, into whose allowance from his actual father, we remember, the Hisses sometimes dipped for contributions to the party. It was as if Alger Hiss had dedicated himself to fulfilling along with his dream of a New Humanity, the other dream his father had passed on to him with his first name—from rags to riches. How strangely the Marxist ideal and the dream of Horatio Alger blended into the motives of his treason. . . .

• • •

American liberalism has been reluctant to leave the garden of its illusion; but it can dally no longer: the age of innocence is dead. The Hiss case marks the death of an era, but it also promises a rebirth if we are willing to learn its lessons. We who would still like to think of ourselves as liberals must be willing to declare that mere liberal principle is not in itself a guarantee against evil; that the wrongdoer is not always the other—"they" and not "us"; that there is no magic in the words "left" or "progressive" or "socialist" that can prevent deceit and the abuse of power.

It is not necessary that we liberals be self-flagellants. We have desired good, and we have done some; but we have also done great evil. The confession in itself is nothing, but without the confession there can be no understanding, and without the understanding of what the Hiss case tries desperately to declare, we will not be able to move forward from a liberalism of innocence to a liberalism of responsibility.

Notes

1. While giving a deposition related to the libel suit Hiss had filed, Chambers turned over sixty-five pages of typed documents on November 17. But the court had prohibited all concerned from divulging this information, so when Chambers produced the "pumpkin papers," for the first time evidence of espionage was made public. Along with the microfilm, he also handed over copies of the sixty-five pages he had earlier surrendered.
2. For a critical examination of how Truman's policies, such as his executive order, fed the anti-Communist concerns that focused on his administration and thus paved the way for Joseph McCarthy, see Athan Theoharis, *Seeds of Repression: Harry S. Truman and the Origins of McCarthyism* (Chicago: Quadrangle Books, 1971).
3. Richard Gid Powers, *Not Without Honor: The History of American Anticommunism* (New Haven: Yale University Press, 1998), 197.
4. Lisle A. Rose, *The Cold War Comes to Main Street: America in 1950* (Lawrence, Kansas: University Press of Kansas, 1999), 60–61.
5. Earl Latham, *The Communist Conspiracy in Washington: From the New Deal to McCarthy* (New York, Atheneum, 1969), 10.

6. David Caute, *The Great Fear: The Anti-Communist Purge Under Truman and Eisenhower* (New York: Simon and Schuster, 1978).

7. Richard M. Nixon, *Six Crises* (Garden City, New York: Doubleday and Company, 1962).

8. Ibid., 1.

9. Alistair Cook, *A Generation on Trial: U.S.A. v. Alger Hiss* (New York: Alfred A. Knopf, 1950).

2

The HUAC Hearings

When Whittaker Chambers first appeared before the House Committee on Un-American Activities in early August 1948, relations between the United States and the Soviet Union were rapidly deteriorating, and a hot war seemed a distinct possibility. Since June, the Berlin blockade had dominated newspaper headlines. As the Hiss episode unfolded, the politically charged presidential election vied with world events for the attention of the public. Partisan political sniping so much a part of the campaign cast shadows of suspicion on the intentions of both Congress and the White House.

HUAC, the committee before which Whittaker Chambers testified, already had a dubious reputation. Over the years, it had been the most persistent of the congressional committees investigating Communists. Both Republicans and Democrats on the committee were recognized critics of the Truman administration. In the committee's ten years of existence, it had captured many headlines, but had consistently come up short on uncovering Communists. Adding to its dubious reputation, its chairman, J. Parnell Thomas, Republican from New Jersey, was under investigation for payroll improprieties involving his congressional staff. The investigation would result in his indictment and conviction.

On July 31, HUAC convened hearings by calling Elizabeth Bentley, the "Red Spy Queen," to testify. Bentley, a confessed Communist agent who already had told her story to the FBI and to Senate investigators, made the same familiar charges she had made in the past. She named figures in the Roosevelt and Truman administrations as Communists—Lauchlin Currie, a top assistant to Roosevelt, and

Harry Dexter White, currently director of the International Monetary Fund, among others. Her revelations on this occasion proved unspectacular. "Although Bentley ranged more widely in her charges before HUAC than during Senate testimony," historian Allen Weinstein wrote, "she offered only her version—her word—and Truman dismissed the accusations as false and politically motivated."[1] Much of the American public shared the president's cynicism.

In an attempt to jump-start the investigation, the committee then turned to Chambers. His appearance triggered a series of events that had major repercussions not only for himself and the man he accused of being a Communist, Alger Hiss, but it ultimately moved the postwar anti-Communist crusade to a new plateau.

CHRONOLOGY: HUAC HEARINGS

1939
September 1: After severing his ties with the Communist Party, Whittaker Chambers met with Assistant Secretary of State Adolf Berle, Jr., and accused Alger Hiss of being a Communist Party member.

1945
May 10: After reviving his charges before State Department officials in the spring, Chambers submitted to an extensive FBI interview.

1946
March 21: Secretary of State James Byrnes informed Hiss that at least two congressional committees were investigating allegations of his Communist affiliation.
March 25: Interviewed by the FBI, Hiss denied Chambers's charges.
December 10: Hiss resigned from the State Department.

1947
February 1: Hiss assumed the presidency of the Carnegie Endowment for International Peace.
June 2: Hiss, interviewed again by the FBI, continued to deny Chambers's accusations and signed an affidavit to that effect.

1948
March 16: Hiss appeared before a grand jury in the Southern District of New York. He repeated the denials he had made to FBI investigators.
August 3: Chambers appeared before the House Committee on Un-American Activities and accused Hiss and other government officials of being Communist Party members in the 1930s.
August 5: Hiss appeared before HUAC to deny Chambers's charges.

August 5: The Hiss affair and other congressional investigations prompted President Harry Truman to characterize this spy scare as a "red herring" at a press conference.

August 7: Chambers appeared before HUAC a second time and provided details of his relationship with Hiss.

August 16: Hiss appeared again before the committee, which attempted to determine the accuracy of Chambers's testimony. Hiss still denied knowing Chambers, but suggested he may have been a man he knew, named George Crosley, who sublet an apartment from him.

August 17: A HUAC subcommittee brought Hiss and Chambers together in a room at New York City's Commodore Hotel. Hiss identified Chambers as George Crosley and challenged Chambers to make his charges in a public forum where he would not be immune from a libel suit.

August 24: Hiss sent an open letter, published in many newspapers, accusing HUAC of prejudging him.

August 25: At an open HUAC session, Hiss and Chambers present their cases publicly for the first time.

August 28: HUAC issued an interim report asserting that perjury had been committed, but it could not determine who was guilty.

Alger Hiss Early Appearance Before Grand Jury

Charges of Alger Hiss's past affiliation with the Communist Party were not new. During 1945 and 1946, while Hiss was still a rising star in the State Department, both FBI and Senate investigators began to take allegations of his Communist ties seriously. Igor Gouzenko, a code clerk in the Soviet embassy in Ottawa, Canada, who had defected and exposed an extensive espionage ring, alluded to an agent who was a leading figure in the State Department. Elizabeth Bentley had told the FBI that she had heard a person name Hiss as a source in the department. Their references were only hearsay, but they revived the FBI's interest in Whittaker Chambers's accusations from as far back as September 1939. Then, in a meeting with Assistant Secretary of State Adolf A. Berle, Jr., Chambers had named Hiss as a leading member of a Communist cell.

In 1946, FBI Director J. Edgar Hoover conveyed his agency's concerns to Secretary of State James F. Byrnes. At the same time, conservative congressmen, some of them recipients of leaked FBI information, prepared to raise the Hiss issue in the halls of Congress. Haunted by these accusations, Hiss left the

State Department in December of that year to assume the presidency of the Carnegie Endowment for International Peace under a cloud of suspicion.[2]

His resignation, however, did not end the investigation. On June 2, 1947, two FBI agents visited his residence and quizzed him extensively regarding his membership in Communist organizations, including the International Juridical Association, a known Communist front organization, and his relationship to various individuals known to be Communists. The agents specifically asked if he knew Whittaker Chambers. Hiss explained his association with the International Juridical Association, denied Communist affiliations, and signed an affidavit to that effect. The Truman Justice Department relayed this information to a federal grand jury in New York, which subpoenaed Hiss to appear on March 16. In this excerpt from the grand jury minutes, Hiss restates the denials he made in his FBI affidavit and explains his association with many figures accused of being Communist. Lacking concrete evidence, the grand jury declined to act at this time.

HISS TESTIMONY BEFORE NEW YORK GRAND JURY, MARCH 16, 1948

Q: Do you recall the names of those two Special Agents?

A: No, I do not, but if you would give me the names I would probably recall them.

Q: Charles Cleveland?

A: I do not recall but I have no doubt it is correct.

Q: Edward L. Grampp?

A: I do remember the second name.

Q: Did you furnish those Special Agents with a signed statement?

A: They asked some of the same questions you have asked, Mr. Donegan, and then themselves sat down and wrote out a statement based upon my answers, which I signed after making a few corrections.

Q: Do you recall the nature or the corrections that were made?

A: Not specifically. They were to make the statements as they had written them more nearly accurate.

Q: If I very quickly read through this, will you tell me whether this is the signed statement?

A: I will tell you to the best of my recollection. It is hard to remember.

Q: Let me put it this way: If you disagree with anything in here that I read, will you call my attention to it?

A: Yes.

Source: Records of U.S. Attorneys and Marshals: Transcripts of Grand Jury in the Alger Hiss Case, Record Group 118, Harry S. Truman Presidential Library, Box 1, 2662–67.

Q: "June 2, 1947. Washington, D. C. I, Alger Hiss, make the following statement to Charles Cleveland and Edward L. Grampp whom I know to be Special Agents of the Federal Bureau of Investigation. No threats or promises of any kind have been made to me to induce me to make this statement. I have been advised that I need not make this statement and I know that it can be used against me in a court of law.

"When I first went to New York City to practice law I became associated with the International Juridical Association. When I became associated this association was a small group which published a pamphlet on labor law mainly. I was one of the editors of the Association's journal. The following men, according to my recollection, contributed to this publication: Jerome Hellerstein, Nathan Witt, Lee Pressman and Isadore Polier, whose wife was Justine Wise. This group was not connected with the International Labor Defense, the National Federation of Constitutional Liberties or the Lawyers Guild to my knowledge. To my belief Earl Browder did not use the International Juridical Association to advertise the "New Masses" or to use the mailing list of the Juridical Association to increase the subscriptions to the "New Masses." I left this association when I came to Washington, D.C. I do not believe that any of the individuals in the Juridical Association were or are Communists but have heard a number of individuals state the belief, since my association with them, that Lee Pressman and Nathan Witt were Communists. I have also heard allegations that Polier was a Communist.

"I have never been a member of or associated with the Committee for Democratic Action or the Young Communist League. I have never been nor am I now a member of the Communist Party. Neither am I personally acquainted with any member of the Communist Party, to my knowledge.

"I can recall only two individuals by the name of Sayre—Francis B. Sayre with whom I was associated in the State Department and Dan Sayre who was formerly with the C.A.B. and is now teaching at Princeton University. To my knowledge neither of these individuals were Communists.

"My brother Donald Hiss, a local lawyer, never worked for Harry Bridges and to my knowledge was never considered for employment for or on behalf of Bridges. I am sure my brother was not and is not now a member of the Communist Party.

"I became acquainted with Harold Ware while I was in the Department of Agriculture. Also I am acquainted with Charles Krivisky, who is now known legally as Charles Kramer, having met him while he was employed at the Dept. of Agriculture. Lee Pressman and I have known each other since my attendance at Harvard Law School. Pressman and I were associated on the Harvard Law Review at which time I wrote a 'note' for the law review on the subject, as well as I can remember, of 'Yellow Dog Contracts.' I have known Henry Collins since childhood and consider him a close personal friend. I cannot recall any person by the name of Nathan Perlow. I knew Alice Mendham quite well when she was running a children's school in 1933 or 1934. Her husband's last name was Powell, but I can't recall his first name. I know no one by the name of Post, in connection with the above individuals, neither do I know Nathan Gregory Silvermaster.

"I have never met with any group at the home of Henry Collins or any other place where government information was discussed when people who had no right to the information were present. Nor do I know of any group of individuals which met together without authority to make government information available, orally or written, for the use of the Soviet Government.

"I first met John Abt at the Agriculture Department in an official capacity. I have never attended any meetings of the foregoing type where John Abt was present, neither have I visited at his apartment."

A: May I stop you there? "Neither have I visited at his apartment"?

Q: Yes.

A: I do not recall any such flat statement. As I recall it, they asked me if I had ever visited at his apartment in New York. I wouldn't be sure when he was in Washington on the Department of Agriculture staff I may not have visited at his apartment, if he had an apartment at that time.

Q: Do you want to change that to New York?

A: Yes; that I think would make it completely accurate.

Q: "I also met Marian Bachrack at the Department of Agriculture through her husband."

A: May I stop you right there? Met her at the Department? I met her while I was connected with the Department. Her husband was employed in the Department.

Q: The sentence, "I also met Marian Bachrack at the Department of Agriculture through her husband," which is contained in the statement of Alger Hiss is, according to Mr. Hiss—is corrected by Mr. Hiss to read, "I also met Marian Bachrack while I was at the Department of Agriculture through her husband." "I have never been known to my knowledge by the name of 'Gene' or 'Eugene'. I know of no individual by the name of 'Gene' or 'Eugene' Hiss having been employed by the State Department.

"I met with Victor Perlo back in 1934 but I can't recall him too well. I have had no further contact with him since approximately that time and do not know of his whereabouts at this time.

"I met Harold Glasser in an official capacity as an official of the Treasury Department. I have never placed Glasser in touch with a Russian representative in order that he might furnish government information to this individual.

"The foregoing represents summaries prepared by Messrs. Cleveland and Grampp of oral answers I had previously given to questions asked orally by them in a call at my office made at this request on June 2, 1947. I have read the foregoing four pages and to the best of my knowledge they are true and correct. I was asked by Agents Grampp and Cleveland if I would give them a signed statement on the information I had given them orally. ALGER HISS. Witnesses: Edward L. Grampp, F.B.I. Charles G. Cleveland, F.B.I." Is that statement correct?

A: Yes, with the minor suggestions I have just made that I believe to be correct.

Chambers's First HUAC Appearance

The grand jury may not have had enough evidence to pursue the case, but that did not deter congressional investigators. On the morning of August 3, the House Un-American Activities Committee met in executive session to hear testimony from Whittaker Chambers. Shortly after he had begun his opening statement, committee members were sufficiently impressed that they stopped him, adjourned, and prepared for him to testify in open session that afternoon. When the committee reassembled, Chambers testified about his experience as a member of the Communist Party during the 1920s and 1930s. A *New York Times* reporter described Chambers as "a quiet, heavy-set man who spoke so softly that at times committee members requested him to repeat what he said." His was "an old story, although it had not come into the open before."[3]

Chambers described his activities as a Communist and explained how he had become disillusioned and left the party in 1937, a date that would later raise questions about his reliability after he himself produced classified State Department materials dated 1938. He identified seven officials he knew to be members of a Communist cell in the federal government at the time. Chambers described his particularly close relationship with one of these men, Alger Hiss. But notably he made no reference to espionage activity. The Communist cells, he insisted, were intended only to extend Soviet influence within the government.

In the following minutes of that session, Robert Stripling, chief HUAC investigator, and committee members question Chambers. The members of the committee in 1948 who would participate in this and later HUAC sessions were Republicans J. Parnell Thomas, New Jersey, chair; Karl E. Mundt, South Dakota; John McDowell, Pennsylvania; Richard Nixon, California; and Richard B. Vail, Illinois. Democratic members included F. Edward Hébert, Louisiana; J. Harden Peterson, Florida; John E. Rankin, Mississippi; and John S. Wood, Georgia.

CHAMBERS'S TESTIMONY, AUGUST 3, 1948

MR. CHAMBERS: Almost exactly 9 years ago—that is, 2 days after Hitler and Stalin signed their pact—I went to Washington and reported to the authorities what I knew about the infiltration of the United States Government by Communists. For years international communism, of which

Source: Congress, House, Committee on Un-American Activities, *Hearings Regarding Communist Espionage in the United States Government*, 80th Cong., 2nd Sess., July–September, 1948, 564–66, 572, 580–82.

the United States Communist Party is an integral part, had been in a state of undeclared war with this Republic. With the Hitler-Stalin pact, that war reached a new stage. I regarded my action in going to the Government as a simple act of war, like the shooting of an armed enemy in combat.

At that moment in history, I was one of the few men on this side of the battle who could perform this service.

I had joined the Communist Party in 1924. No one recruited me. I had become convinced that the society in which we live, western civilization, had reached a crisis, of which the First World War was the military expression, and that it was doomed to collapse or revert to barbarism. I did not understand the causes of the crisis or know what to do about it. But I felt that, as an intelligent man, I must do something. In the writings of Karl Marx I thought that I had found the explanation of the historical and economic causes. In the writings of Lenin I thought I had found the answer to the question, What to do?

In 1937 I repudiated Marx' doctrines and Lenin's tactics. Experience and the record had convinced me that communism is a form of totalitarianism, that its triumph means slavery to men wherever they fall under its sway, and spiritual night to the human mind and soul. I resolved to break with the Communist Party at whatever risk to my life or other tragedy to myself or my family. Yet, so strong is the hold which the insidious evil of communism secures on its disciples, that I could still say to someone at the time: "I know that I am leaving the winning side for the losing side, but it is better to die on the losing side than to live under communism."

For a year I lived in hiding, sleeping by day and watching through the night with gun or revolver within easy reach. That was what underground communism could do to one man in the peaceful United States in the year 1938.

I had sound reason for supposing that the Communists might try to kill me. For a number of years I had myself served in the underground, chiefly in Washington, D.C. The heart of my report to the United States Government consisted of a description of the apparatus to which I was attached. It was an underground organization of the United States Communist Party developed, to the best of my knowledge, by Harold Ware, one of the sons of the Communist leader known as "Mother Bloor." I knew it at its top level, a group of seven or so men, from among whom in later years certain members of Miss Bentley's organization were apparently recruited. The head of the underground group at the time I knew it was Nathan Witt, an attorney for the National Labor Relations Board. Later, John Abt became the leader. Lee Pressman was also a member of this group, as was Alger Hiss, who, as a member of the State Department, later organized the conferences at Dumbarton Oaks, San Francisco, and the United States side of the Yalta Conference.

The purpose of this group at that time was not primarily espionage. Its original purpose was the Communist infiltration of the American Government. But espionage was certainly one of its eventual objectives. Let no one be surprised at this statement. Disloyalty is a matter of principle with every member of the Communist Party. The Communist Party exists for the specific purpose of overthrowing the Government, at the opportune time, by any and all means; and each of its members, by the fact that he is a member, is dedicated to this purpose.

It is 10 years since I broke away from the Communist Party. During that decade I have sought to live an industrious and God-fearing life. At the same time I have fought communism constantly by act and written word. I am proud to appear before this committee. The publicity inseparable from such testimony has darkened, and will no doubt continue to darken, my effort to integrate myself in the community of free men. But that is a small price to pay if my testimony helps to make Americans recognize at last that they are at grips with a secret, sinister, and enormously powerful force whose tireless purpose is their enslavement.

At the same time, I should like, thus publicly, to call upon all ex-Communists who have not yet declared themselves, and all men within the Communist Party, whose better instincts have not yet been corrupted and crushed by it, to aid in this struggle while there is still time to do so.

MR. STRIPLING: Mr. Chambers, in your statement you stated that you yourself had served the underground, chiefly in Washington, D.C. What underground apparatus are you speaking of and when was it established?

MR. CHAMBERS: Perhaps we should make a distinction at the beginning. It is Communist theory and practice that even in countries where the Communist Party is legal, an underground party exists side by side with the open party.

The apparatus in Washington was an organization or group of that underground.

MR. RANKIN: When you speak of the apparatus in Washington you mean the Communist cell, do you not?

MR. CHAMBERS: I mean in effect a group of Communist cells.

MR. RANKIN: A group of Communist cells when you speak of "apparatus"?

MR. CHAMBERS: Yes.

MR. STRIPLING: Was a plan devised by the Communists to infiltrate the Government of the United States for the purpose of using these cells for the benefit of the Soviet Union?

MR. CHAMBERS: I would certainly say that that would be an ultimate objective.

MR. STRIPLING: What about the particular apparatus to which you referred in your statement?

MR. CHAMBERS: Do you mean was it a Soviet agency?

MR. STRIPLING: Was it established for the purpose of causing people in the Government to serve the ultimate objectives of the Soviet Union?

MR. CHAMBERS: I think you could only say that in the extreme sense the American party is an agency which serves the purpose of the Soviet Government.

MR. STRIPLING: Who comprised this cell or apparatus to which you referred?

MR. CHAMBERS: The apparatus was organized with a leading group of seven men, each of whom was a leader of the cell.

MR. STRIPLING: Could you name the seven individuals?

MR. CHAMBERS: The head of the group as I have said was at first Nathan Witt. Other members of the group were Lee Pressman, Alger Hiss, Donald Hiss, Victor Perlo, Charles Kramer—

MR. MUNDT: What was Charles Kramer's correct name?

MR. CHAMBERS: I think his original name was Krevitsky, and John Abt—I don't know if I mentioned him before or not—and Henry Collins.

MR. RANKIN: How about Harold Ware?

MR. CHAMBERS: Harold Ware was, of course, the organizer.

MR. STRIPLING: Harold Ware was the son of Ella Reeve Bloor, the woman Communist?

MR. CHAMBERS: Yes.

MR. STRIPLING: Do you know where in the Government these seven individuals were employed?

MR. CHAMBERS: I did at one time. I think I could remember some of them.

• • •

MR. STRIPLING: When you left the Communist Party in 1937 did you approach any of these seven to break with you?

MR. CHAMBERS: No. The only one of those people whom I approached was Alger Hiss. I went to the Hiss home one evening at what I considered considerable risk to myself and found Mrs. Hiss at home. Mrs. Hiss is also a member of the Communist Party.

MR. MUNDT: Mrs. Alger Hiss?

MR. CHAMBERS: Mrs. Alger Hiss. Mrs. Donald Hiss, I believe, is not.

Mrs. Hiss attempted while I was there to make a call, which I can only presume was to other Communists, but I quickly went to the telephone and she hung up, and Mr. Hiss came in shortly afterward, and we talked and I tried to break him away from the party.

As a matter of fact, he cried when we separated; when I left him, but he absolutely refused to break.

MR. McDOWELL: He cried?

MR. CHAMBERS: Yes, he did. I was very fond of Mr. Hiss.

MR. MUNDT: He must have given you some reason why he did not want to sever the relationship.

MR. CHAMBERS: His reasons were simply the party line.

• • •

MR. NIXON: Mr. Chambers, you indicated that 9 years ago you came to Washington and reported to the Government authorities concerning the Communists who were in the Government.

MR. CHAMBERS: Yes.

MR. NIXON: To what Government agency did you make that report?

MR. CHAMBERS: Isaac Don Levine, who is now the editor of Plain Talk, approached the late Marvin McIntyre, Mr. Roosevelt's secretary, I believe, and asked him what would be the most proper form in which the information I had to give could be brought before President Roosevelt.

    Mr. McIntyre told Mr. Levine that Mr. A. A. Berle, the Assistant Secretary of State, was Mr. Roosevelt's man in intelligence matters.

    I then went to see Mr. Berle and told him much of what I have been telling you.

MR. MUNDT: That was in 1937?

MR. CHAMBERS: That was in 1939 about 2 days after the Hitler-Stalin pact.

MR. NIXON: When you saw Mr. Berle then did you discuss generally the people that were in Government, or did you name specific names?

MR. CHAMBERS: I named specific names, Mr. Hiss among others.

MR. NIXON: Mr. Chambers, were you informed of any action that was taken as a result of your report to the Government at that time?

MR. CHAMBERS: No; I was not. I assumed that action would be taken right away which was, of course, rather naive of me; and it wasn't until a great deal later that I discovered apparently nothing had been done.

MR. NIXON: It is significant, I think, that the report was made 2 days after the Stalin-Hitler pact at the time, in other words, when we could not say by any stretch of the imagination that the Russians were our allies; and yet, apparently, no action was taken.

MR. CHAMBERS: Well, we are here in an area of government which I am not qualified to talk about.

MR. RANKIN: What is that?

MR. CHAMBERS: We are here in an area of government policies I am not qualified to talk about.

MR. NIXON: I understand.

MR. MUNDT: At the time you reported these names to Mr. Berle, you had reason to believe that Communist Russia might well become an active enemy of this country rather than a friend through that Stalin-Hitler Pact?

MR. CHAMBERS: I never supposed Russia at any time was anything but an enemy of this country. It is an enemy of all democratic countries.

• • •

MR. HÉBERT: What was Mr. Berle's attitude when you turned this information over to him?

MR. CHAMBERS: Considerable excitement.

MR. HÉBERT: What did he tell you?

MR. CHAMBERS: I don't know that he made any very sensational comment, but he said among other things that we absolutely have to have a clean Government service because we are faced with the prospect of war. I am paraphrasing that. That is not an exact quotation.

MR. HÉBERT: In view of the statements of Mr. Chambers at this time may I suggest that this committee invite Mr. Berle to come here so we can get the background and also corroborate this testimony. I think it is most important that every chain be linked with the other chain in this situation.

MR. MUNDT: Is he in this country?

MR. HÉBERT: If he is in the country, he should be invited to come. I have every reason to respect the integrity of Mr. Berle.

MR. MUNDT: The Committee will take that up in executive session.

MR. RANKIN: Mr. Berle testified before the committee last year.

MR. HÉBERT: During the discussions on the Mundt-Nixon bill. But the purpose now is to have him corroborate this. What I am most interested in
is that this committee is not witch hunting or Red baiting, but is trying
to get the facts of what is going on. Since this is a public hearing, I think
all these matters should be brought out in full public gaze and for full
public interpretation and appreciation of what we are trying to do; and for
that reason I think every individual mentioned should be brought before
the committee to either corroborate the testimony or impeach it.

Mr. Berle's attention was directed to this matter, and I think it is of
interest to the committee and the people at large to know why methods
were pursued.

MR. NIXON: Mr. Chambers, you indicated a moment ago that it was approximately 4 years after you had spoken to Mr. Berle that you went before
the FBI.

MR. CHAMBERS: That is right.

MR. NIXON: At that time you did give the FBI information concerning
White?

MR. CHAMBERS: White, that is right.

Hiss Refutes Chambers's Accusations

Alger Hiss, understandably upset about the charges made by Chambers,
requested that the committee give him an opportunity to respond. On
August 5, in an open session, he categorically denied that he had ever been
a member of the Communist Party and declared that to the best of his
knowledge the first time he had heard of Whittaker Chambers was when an
FBI agent mentioned his name in 1947. Shown a picture of Chambers, Hiss
said he did not recognize the man, but stated that he would like to see
Chambers in person to definitely determine that he did not know him.

ALGER HISS TESTIMONY, AUGUST 5, 1948

MR. RANKIN: Will you please give your age and place of birth?

MR. HISS: I was born in Baltimore, Md., on November 11, 1904. I am here at
my own request to deny unqualifiedly various statements about me which
were made before this committee by one Whittaker Chambers the day
before yesterday. I appreciate the committee's having promptly granted

Source: Hearings Regarding Communist Espionage in the United States Government, 642–43, 646–47.

PHOTO 2.1   In his first appearance before HUAC on August 5, 1948, Hiss examined pictures of Chambers and declined to definitely say whether he knew him without seeing him in person.

my request. I welcome the opportunity to answer to the best of my ability any inquiries the members of this committee may wish to ask me.

I am not and never have been a member of the Communist Party. I do not and never have adhered to the tenets of the Communist Party. I am not and never have been a member of any Communist-front organization. I have never followed the Communist Party line, directly or indirectly. To the best of my knowledge, none of my friends is a Communist.

As a State Department official, I have had contacts with representatives of foreign governments, some of whom have undoubtedly been members of the Communist Party, as, for example, representatives of the Soviet Government. My contacts with any foreign representative who could possibly have been a Communist have been strictly official.

To the best of my knowledge, I never heard of Whittaker Chambers until in 1947, when two representatives of the Federal Bureau of Investigation asked me if I knew him and various other people, some of whom I knew and some of whom I did not know. I said I did not know Chambers. So far as I know, I have never laid eyes on him, and I should like to have the opportunity to do so.

• • •

MR. MCDOWELL: Mr. Chairman, in that connection so much has been said in the last 4 days that I have forgotten entirely what charge was made by Mr. Chambers. Would the chief investigator enlighten me?

MR. MUNDT: I was going to interrogate the witness about that and I will do that at this time for the benefit of Mr. McDowell.

Have you seen a transcript?

Mr. Hiss: I carefully read the entire transcript of Mr. Chambers' testimony before I came to this committee.

Mr. Mundt: Then I don't have to go into that in so much detail.

Mr. McDowell: I want to find out what was said.

Mr. Mundt: I am getting to it. I want to say for one member of the committee that it is extremely puzzling that a man who is senior editor of Time magazine, by the name of Whittaker Chambers, whom I had never seen until a day or two ago, and whom you say you have never seen—

Mr. Hiss: As far as I know, I have never seen him.

Mr. Mundt: Should come before this committee and discuss the Communist apparatus working in Washington, which he says is transmitting secrets to the Russian Government, and he lists a group of seven people—Nathan Witt, Lee Pressman, Victor Perlo, Charles Kramer, John Abt, Harold Ware, Alger Hiss, and Donald Hiss—

Mr. Hiss: That is eight.

Mr. Mundt: There seems to be no question about the subversive connections of the six other than the Hiss brothers, and I wonder what possible motive a man who edits Time magazine would have for mentioning Donald Hiss and Alger Hiss in connection with those other six.

Mr. Hiss: So do I, Mr. Chairman. I have no possible understanding of what could have motivated him. There are many possible motives, I assume, but I am unable to understand it.

Mr. Mundt: You can appreciate the position of this committee when the name bobs up in connection with those associations.

Mr. Hiss: I hope the committee can appreciate my position, too.

Mr. Mundt: We surely can and that is why we responded with alacrity to your request to be heard.

Mr. Hiss: I appreciate that.

Mr. Mundt: All we are trying to do is find the facts.

Mr. Hiss: I wish I could have seen Mr. Chambers before he testified.

Mr. Rankin: After all the smear attacks against this committee.

• • •

Mr. Stripling: I would like to ask the witness: Mr. Hiss, when did you first hear of these allegations on the part of Mr. Chambers?

Mr. Hiss: May I answer that this way, Mr. Stripling? By saying that the night before he testified a reporter for a New York paper called me and said he had received a tip that Chambers was to testify before this committee the next morning and that he would mention me and would call me a Communist.

Mr. Stripling: You say you have never seen Mr. Chambers?

Mr. Hiss: The name means absolutely nothing to me, Mr. Stripling.

Mr. Stripling: I have here, Mr. Chairman, a picture which was made last Monday by the Associated Press. I understand from people who knew Mr. Chambers during 1934 and '35 that he is much heavier today than he was at that time, but I show you this picture, Mr. Hiss, and ask you if you have ever known an individual who resembles this picture.

MR. HISS: I would much rather see the individual. I have looked at all the pictures I was able to get hold of in, I think it was, yesterday's paper which had the pictures. If this is a picture of Mr. Chambers, he is not particularly unusual looking. He looks like a lot of people. I might even mistake him for the chairman of this committee. [Laughter.]

MR. MUNDT: I hope you are wrong in that.

MR. HISS: I didn't mean to be facetious but very seriously. I would not want to take oath that I have never seen that man. I would like to see him and then I think I would be better able to tell whether I had ever seen him. Is he here today?

MR. MUNDT: Not to my knowledge.

MR. HISS: I hoped he would be.

MR. MUNDT: You realize that this man whose picture you have just looked at, under sworn testimony before this committee, where all the laws of perjury apply, testified that he called at your home, conferred at great length, saw your wife pick up the telephone and call somebody whom he said must have been a Communist, plead with you to divert yourself from Communist activities, and left you with tears in your eyes, saying, "I simply can't make the sacrifice."

MR. HISS: I do know that he said that. I also know that I am testifying under those same laws to the direct contrary.

President Truman Calls HUAC Investigation a "Red Herring"

The Hiss affair was only part of a multifaceted investigation being conducted by HUAC targeting other possible instances of Communist government officials besides Hiss. Much of the information the committee was publicizing had already been referred to a federal grand jury, which had not handed down indictments as yet. But these congressional investigations made headlines and put pressure on the Truman administration, to the delight of committee members. Chambers's August 3 testimony inspired the *New York Times* headline "Red 'Underground' In Federal Posts Alleged by Editor."[4] The next day, the *New York Herald Tribune* quoted acting HUAC chairman, Congressman Karl E. Mundt, who insisted that "even now a spy ring is operating in Washington." Mundt did not substantiate his charge, but it made for the provocative headline "Mundt Asserts Red Spies Are Still Busy in Capital; Truman Assails Inquiry."[5]

As the final part of that headline suggests, President Truman took exception to the congressman's remarks. Confronted at a news conference on August 5, the same day that Alger Hiss was appearing before HUAC, the president attributed all of the charges to politics. He called them a "red herring." The president's comment would come back to haunt him later.

STATEMENT BY PRESIDENT HARRY S. TRUMAN, NEWS CONFERENCE, AUGUST 5, 1948

Q: Mr. President, do you think that the Capitol Hill spy scare is a "red herring" to divert public attention from inflation?

THE PRESIDENT: Yes, I do, and I will read you another statement on that, since you brought it up. [*Laughter*]

[*Reading*] "In response to written requests from congressional groups for information relating to the employment of individuals, the department or agency may forward to the committee all unclassified routine papers, such as Civil Service Form 57, records of promotion, efficiency ratings, letters of recommendation, etc.

"No information of any sort relating to the employee's loyalty, and no investigative data of any type, whether relating to loyalty or other aspects of the individual's record, shall be included in the material submitted to a congressional committee. If there is doubt as to whether a certain document or group of documents should be supplied, the matter should be referred to the White House.

"No information has been revealed by these committees' investigations that has not long since been presented to a Federal grand jury.

"No information has been disclosed in the past few days by the congressional committees that has not long been known to the FBI.

"The Federal grand jury found this information insufficient to justify indictment of the Federal employees involved.

"All but two of the employees involved have left the Federal Government, and these two have been placed on leave without pay before the congressional hearings started.

"The public hearings now under way are serving no useful purpose. On the contrary, they are doing irreparable harm to certain people, seriously impairing the morale of Federal employees, and undermining public confidence in the Government."

And they are simply a "red herring" to keep from doing what they ought to do.

Q: Don't you think the American public is entitled to this information?

THE PRESIDENT: What information?

Source: U.S. Government, *Public Papers of the Presidents of the United States, Harry S. Truman, 1948* (Washington, D.C.: Government Printing Office, 1964), 432–33.

Q: That has been brought out in these investigations?

THE PRESIDENT: What useful purpose is it serving when we are having this matter before a grand jury where action has to take place, no matter what this committee does? They haven't revealed anything that everybody hasn't known all along, or hasn't been presented to the grand jury. That is where it has to be taken, in the first place, if you are going to do anything about it. They are slandering a lot of people that don't deserve it.

Q: Mr. President, could we use a part of the quote there, that last: they are simply a "red herring" etc.?

THE PRESIDENT: Using this as a "red herring" to keep from doing what they ought to do.

Q: Are we going to get copies of that?

THE PRESIDENT: Yes.

Editorial Response to "Red Herring" Remarks

Political observers at the time were uncertain of the significance and meaning of these events, as reflected in the following editorials published in the aftermath of the president's "red herring" remarks. There was clearly serious concern about potential Communist infiltration in the federal government, but there was also skepticism about the motives of both the White House and Congress.

The *New York Herald Tribune* editorial cites assertions by accused Communists Nathan Silvermaster and Lee Pressman that Congress was diverting attention from more serious legislative concerns. But the newspaper said that Truman had no remedies for the infiltration that did exist. The editors, thus, judged that the committee was following the proper course, even though its methods could be questioned.

The *Washington Post* editorial is more skeptical of HUAC's motives. Congressman Mundt said the committee was needling Attorney General Tom Clark to act, a move that the *Post* editors interpreted as a vote of no confidence in the executive. To them, this political activity was violating the separation of powers in the Constitution. Finding the Communist infiltrators was the job of the FBI and the federal grand jury. The newspaper feared that the committee's actions would erode trust in the courts and was "giving example itself of lawlessness by ignoring due process." In contrast to the *New York Herald Tribune,* the *Washington Post* saw no redeeming value in the methods employed by the committee.

"CONCERNING RED HERRINGS"

A red herring is a smoked fish which, by its pungent aroma, can divert a pack of hounds from its proper quarry. It also provided a very apt analogy, particularly useful to politicians. But like most analogies, it can be abused. Since the opening of the current investigation into Communist infiltration in this country, the red herring analogy, in one form or another, has been very much overworked.

Mr. Silvermaster, under questioning by the House Committee on Un-American Activities, said the investigation was "motivated by . . . the necessity to conceal from the American people the failure of Congress to act upon such matters as housing and inflation." Mr. Lee Pressman used similar language, saying that one of the objects of the hearings was "to take the minds of the American people off the real issues before Congress: civil rights, inflation, housing, justice for the heroic people of Israel and the repeal of the infamous Taft-Hartley act." "The Daily Worker" accused both the President and the Republicans of digging up "a mouldy, moth-eaten 'spy scare' " to help them " 'get off the hook' in front of the electorate." And Mr. Truman himself charged that the espionage inquiry was a "red herring" to draw attention from Republican failures in Congress.

Mr. Truman had other complaints to make concerning the investigation. It was going over old ground that had been worked by the Federal Bureau of Investigation and a grand jury without turning up indictments against those accused in the hearings. It was doing "irreparable harm" to some persons innocently involved. Both of these charges are true. The injury to the reputation of certain individuals named in the proceedings was a flagrant violation of elementary rights and a frightening example of what an unfettered inquisition into matters of political opinion can produce. And some of those who may be considered morally reprehensible by their fellow-citizens had committed no indictable offenses, or had covered their tracks too well, But Mr. Truman failed to face up to the real dilemma posed by the investigations. He proposed no remedies except to call the whole thing off.

In other words, Mr. Truman apparently believes that the "spy scare" is a veritable red herring which has drawn public attention on a wholly false trail. It is doubtful whether this notion has much support

Source: New York Herald Tribune, August 6, 1948.

in the country at large. Whatever the shortcomings of the Republicans in Congress, the problem of Communist infiltration does exist. It must be thoroughly studied, and suitable safeguards devised. It is a worthy end of government to examine the manner in which the various wartime loyalty checks operated, and how Communists sought to sidestep them. What the F. B. I. or the grand jury may know of these matters has very little to do with the case, if their information is withheld, as it should be in most instances, from the public. To return to the red herring, the Congressional committees are pursuing a proper quarry in this investigation, and if they are doing so with more riotous behavior and incidental damage than need be, it is the method and not the goal which is open to question.

"MUNDT'S ADMISSION"

Representative Mundt let the tiger out of the bag in his statement about the object of the House spy inquiry of which he is acting chairman. He said the object is to "expose, call attention of the proper authorities to the spying, write letters, make press statements, and try to needle Tom Clark into action." In other words, the committee's action is a vote of no-confidence in the Executive in the discharge of his constitutional duty faithfully to execute the laws. So the House Committee is going over the grounds covered by the grand jury in New York which after a three-year million-dollar investigation returned no indictments against the persons who are being put on the grid in Congress. In effect the committee is usurping the function of a grand jury. We ask, in all seriousness, whether this is the way of a government of powers divided among the executive, the legislature, and the judiciary. Beware, warned Jefferson, of the tyranny of the legislature.

The President calls the inquiry a red herring. To some extent, of course, he is right, as is clear to anybody who listens to the House proceedings. Examples: "He is a Republican, isn't he?" "He is a Democrat, isn't he?" But the presidential ascription does justice neither to the seriousness of the issue of Communist activity in our midst

Source: Washington Post, August 7, 1948. Copyright © 1948, *The Washington Post,* reprinted with permission.

nor to the flagrant disregard of proper procedure in investigating it. Communists, in our opinion, would stop at nothing in serving their Red masters. They are inverted theologians, thoroughly amoral, ever ready to sabotage and destroy. It is the presence of these vipers in our midst, together with our critical relations with Moscow, that accounts for the Red scare and the advantage that the investigators are taking of it.

But it is the purpose of the law to reach out and prosecute termites. And it is the job of the FBI to get the evidence to convict. As to the law, Governor Dewey, in the Dewey-Stassen debate May 17, said "There are 27 acts already that outlaw every conceivable form of subversion." As to the FBI, no institution in the Capital today operates in such favor from the appropriating body. But what the House Committee is doing is telling the American people that neither their courts nor the FBI is giving them protection. This is dangerous procedure—highly dangerous. The legislators' lack of trust in the courts is bound to evoke, if the people take the committee seriously, the same lack of trust in the courts on the part of the people. What is worse, the committee itself is giving an example itself of lawlessness by ignoring due process.

Representative McDowell sought to extract from Mr. Alger Hiss Wednesday an admission that he had had "a fair hearing." Mr. Hiss's reply was to the point:

> Mr. McDowell, I think I have been treated today with great consideration by this committee. I am not happy that I didn't have a chance to meet with the committee privately before there was such a great public press display of what I consider completely unfounded charges against me. Denials do not always catch up with charges.

The answer made an impression which the Representative sought to offset, by what was circumstantially a prevarication. "The committee," he said, "does not know in advance what a witness is going to say." Now, Mr. McDowell! Even if you didn't know, why didn't you make sure by listening to witnesses in camera? The answer is that any such protection for the individual would fly in the face of the declared object of Representative Mundt to let the espionage cases "be decided in the court of public opinion, to let the people determine whether the Committee is right, or Attorney General Tom Clark is right." In other words, if the courts won't convict, then a form of lynch rule must prevail. A fine example to provide for the American people—taught as they are to regard justice as the end of government.

HUAC in Executive Session Probes Chambers for Details of Hiss Relationship

After Hiss's first appearance, HUAC leaned toward dropping the investigation. For Hiss had appeared to be a forthright witness. At this point, Richard Nixon began to assert himself as a major figure in the probe. According to Nixon, he persuaded the other committee members that continuing the investigation would be worthwhile:

> I pointed out my suspicions: that while Hiss had seemed to be a completely forthright and truthful witness, he had been careful never to state categorically that he did not know Whittaker Chambers. He had always qualified his answer by saying that he did not know a man "by the name of Whittaker Chambers." I argued that while it would be virtually impossible to prove that Hiss was or was not a Communist—for that would simply be his word against Chambers'— we should be able to establish by corroborative testimony whether or not the two men knew each other. If Hiss were lying about not knowing Chambers, then he might also be lying about whether or not he was a Communist.[6]

Nixon convinced the committee to continue its probe. He, McDowell, and Hébert formed a subcommittee to question Chambers further in executive session. During this August 7 hearing, Chambers detailed his relationship with Hiss. He described how Hiss had known him only as "Carl," a Communist Party representative who for two or three years collected party dues from him and turned them over to a "Mr. Peters," and how he spent time living in the Hiss residence. Chambers volunteered information about Hiss's personal life that, if verified, could be damning for Hiss—nicknames, hobbies, and much more. In what would later become a particularly valuable piece of information, he described how Hiss once insisted on donating an old 1929 Ford to the Communist Party.

CHAMBERS'S TESTIMONY, AUGUST 7, 1948

    MR. CHAMBERS: I knew Mr. Hiss, roughly, between the years 1935 to 1937.
    MR. NIXON: Do you know him as Mr. Alger Hiss?
    MR. CHAMBERS: Yes.
    MR. NIXON: Did you happen to see Mr. Hiss's pictures in the newspapers as a result of these recent hearings?

Source: Hearings Regarding Communist Espionage in the United States Government, 662–67.

MR. CHAMBERS: Yes; I did.

MR. NIXON: Was that the man you knew as Alger Hiss?

MR. CHAMBERS: Yes; that is the man.

MR. NIXON: You are certain of that?

MR. CHAMBERS: I am completely certain.

MR. NIXON: During the time that you knew Mr. Hiss, did he know you as Whittaker Chambers?

MR. CHAMBERS: No, he did not.

MR. NIXON: By what name did he know you?

MR. CHAMBERS: He knew me by the party name of Carl.

MR. NIXON: Did he ever question the fact that he did not know your last name?

MR. CHAMBERS: Not to me.

MR. NIXON: Why not?

MR. CHAMBERS: Because in the underground Communist Party the principle of organization is that functionaries and heads of the group, in other words, shall not be known by their right names but by pseudonyms or party names.

MR. NIXON: Were you a party functionary?

MR. CHAMBERS: I was a functionary.

MR. NIXON: This entire group with which you worked in Washington did not know you by your real name?

MR. CHAMBERS: No member of that group knew me by my real name.

MR. NIXON: All knew you as Carl?

MR. CHAMBERS: That is right.

MR. NIXON: No member of that group ever inquired of you as to your real name?

MR. CHAMBERS: To have questioned me would have been a breach of party discipline, Communist Party discipline.

MR. NIXON: I understood you to say that Mr. Hiss was a member of the party.

MR. CHAMBERS: Mr. Hiss was a member of the Communist Party.

MR. NIXON: How do you know that?

MR. CHAMBERS: I was told by Mr. Peters.

MR. NIXON: You were told that by Mr. Peters?

MR. CHAMBERS: Yes.

MR. NIXON: On what facts did Mr. Peters give you?

MR. CHAMBERS: Mr. Peters was the head of the entire underground, as far as I know.

MR. NIXON: The entire underground of the Communist Party?

MR. CHAMBERS: Of the Communist Party in the United States.

MR. NIXON: Do you have any other evidence, any factual evidence, to bear out your claim that Mr. Hiss was a member of the Communist Party?

MR. CHAMBERS: Nothing beyond the fact that he submitted himself for the 2 or 3 years that I knew him as a dedicated and disciplined Communist.

MR. NIXON: Did you obtain his party dues from him?

MR. CHAMBERS: Yes, I did.

MR. NIXON: Over what period of time?

MR. CHAMBERS: Two or three years, as long as I knew him.

MR. NIXON: Party dues from him and his wife?

MR. CHAMBERS: I assume his wife's dues were there; I understood it to be.

MR. NIXON: You understood it to be?

MR. CHAMBERS: Mr. Hiss would simply give me an envelope containing party dues which I transferred to Peters. I didn't handle the money.

MR. NIXON: How often?

MR. CHAMBERS: Once a month.

MR. NIXON: What did he say?

MR. CHAMBERS: That was one point it wasn't necessary to say anything. At first he said, "Here are my dues."

MR. NIXON: And once a month over a period of 2 years, approximately, he gave you an envelope which contained the dues?

MR. CHAMBERS: That is right.

MR. NIXON: What did you do with that envelope?

MR. CHAMBERS: I gave it to Peters.

MR. NIXON: In New York?

MR. CHAMBERS: Or Washington.

MR. NIXON: This envelope contained dues of Hiss and other members of the group?

MR. CHAMBERS: Only Hiss.

MR. NIXON: You collected dues from the other members of the group individually?

MR. CHAMBERS: All dues were collected individually.

MR. NIXON: I see. So this money could not have been money from anybody but Hiss?

MR. CHAMBERS: Only from Hiss.

MR. NIXON: Couldn't have been giving you dues for his wife and not for himself?

MR. CHAMBERS: I suppose it is possible, but that was certainly not the understanding.

MR. NIXON: The understanding was it was his dues?

MR. CHAMBERS: The understanding was it was his dues. Not only that, but he was rather pious about paying his dues promptly.

MR. NIXON: Is there any other circumstances which would substantiate your allegation that he was a member of the party? You have indicated he paid dues, you indicated that Mr. Peters, the head of the Communist underground, informed you he was a member of the party before you met him the first time.

MR. CHAMBERS: I must also interpolate there that all Communists in the group in which I originally knew him accepted him as a member of the Communist Party.

MR. NIXON: Referred to him as a member of the party?

MR. CHAMBERS: That doesn't come up in conversation, but this was a Communist group.

MR. NIXON: Could this have possibly been an intellectual study group?

MR. CHAMBERS: It was in nowise an intellectual study group. Its primary function was not that of an intellectual study group. I certainly supplied some of that intellectual study business, which was part of my function, but its primary function was to infiltrate the Government in the interest of the Communist Party.

MR. NIXON: At that time, incidentally, Mr. Hiss and the other members of this group who were Government employees did not have party cards?

MR. CHAMBERS: No members of that group to my knowledge ever had party cards, nor do I think members of any such group have party cards.

MR. NIXON: The reason is—

MR. CHAMBERS: The reason is security, concealment.

MR. NIXON: In other words, people who are in the Communist underground are in fact instructed to deny the fact that they are members of the Communist Party?

MR. CHAMBERS: I was told by Peters that party registration was kept in Moscow and in some secret file in the United States.

MR. NIXON: Did Mr. Hiss have any children?

MR. CHAMBERS: Mr. Hiss had no children of his own.

MR. NIXON: Were there any children living in his home?

MR. CHAMBERS: Mrs. Hiss had a son.

MR. NIXON: Do you know the son's name?

MR. CHAMBERS: Timothy Hobson.

MR. NIXON: Approximately how old was he at the time you knew him?

MR. CHAMBERS: It seems to me he was about 10 years old.

MR. NIXON: What did you call him?

MR. CHAMBERS: Timmie.

MR. NIXON: Did Mr. Hiss call him Timmie also?

MR. CHAMBERS: I think so.

MR. NIXON: Did he have any other nickname?

MR. CHAMBERS: Not that I recall. He is the son, to the best of my knowledge, of Thayer Hobson, who I think is a member of the publishing house of William Morrow here in New York.

MR. NIXON: What name did Mrs. Hiss use in addressing Mr. Hiss?

MR. CHAMBERS: Usually "Hilly."

MR. NIXON: "Hilly"?

MR. CHAMBERS: Yes.

MR. NIXON: Quite often?

MR. CHAMBERS: Yes.

MR. NIXON: In your presence?

MR. CHAMBERS: Yes.

MR. NIXON: Not "Alger"?

MR. CHAMBERS: Not "Alger."

MR. NIXON: What nickname, if any, did Mr. Hiss use in addressing his wife?

MR. CHAMBERS: More often "Dilly" and sometimes "Pross." Her name was Priscilla. They were commonly referred to as "Hilly" and "Dilly."

MR. NIXON: They were commonly referred to as "Hilly" and "Dilly"?

MR. CHAMBERS: By other members of the group.

MR. NIXON: You don't mean to indicate that was simply the nicknames used by the Communist group?

MR. CHAMBERS: This was a family matter.

MR. NIXON: In other words, other friends and acquaintances of theirs would possibly have used these names?

Did you ever spend any time in Hiss' home?

MR. CHAMBERS: Yes.

MR. NIXON: Did you stay overnight?

MR. CHAMBERS: Yes; I stayed overnight for a number of days.

MR. NIXON: You mean from time to time.

MR. CHAMBERS: From time to time.

MR. NIXON: Did you ever stay longer than 1 day?

MR. CHAMBERS: I have stayed there as long as a week.

MR. NIXON: A week one time. What would you be doing during that time?

MR. CHAMBERS: Most of the time reading.

MR. NIXON: What arrangements was made for taking care of your lodging at that time? Were you there as a guest?

MR. CHAMBERS: I made that a kind of informal headquarters.

MR. NIXON: I understand that, but what was the financial arrangement?

MR. CHAMBERS: There was no financial arrangement.

MR. NIXON: You were a guest?

MR. CHAMBERS: Part of the Communist pattern.

MR. NIXON: Did the Hisses have a cook? Do you recall a maid?

MR. CHAMBERS: As nearly as I can remember, they had a maid who came in to clean, and a cook who came in to cook. I can't remember they had a maid there all the time or not. It seems to me in one or two of the houses they did.

In one of the houses they had a rather elderly Negro maid whom Mr. Hiss used to drive home in the evening.

MR. NIXON: You don't recall the names of the maids?

MR. CHAMBERS: No; I don't.

MR. NIXON: Did the Hisses have any pets?

MR. CHAMBERS: They had, I believe, a cocker spaniel. I have a bad memory for dogs, but as nearly as I can remember it was a cocker spaniel.

MR. NIXON: Do you remember the dog's name?

MR. CHAMBERS: No. I remember they used to take it up to some kennel. I think out Wisconsin Avenue.

MR. NIXON: They took it to board it there?

MR. CHAMBERS: Yes. They made one or two vacation trips to the Eastern Shore of Maryland.

MR. NIXON: They made some vacation trips to the Eastern Shore of Maryland?

MR. CHAMBERS: Yes, and at those times the dog was kept at the kennel.

MR. NIXON: You state the Hisses had several different houses when you knew them? Could you describe any one of those houses to us?

MR. CHAMBERS: I think so. It seems to me when I first knew him he was living on 28th Street in an apartment house. There were two almost identical
apartment houses. It seems to me that is a dead-end street and this was
right at the dead end and certainly it is on the right-hand side as you go up.

It also seems to me that apartment was on the top floor. Now, what
was it like inside, the furniture? I can't remember.

MR. MANDEL: What was Mr. Hiss's library devoted to?

MR. CHAMBERS: Very nondescript, as I recall.

MR. NIXON: Do you recall what floor the apartment was on?

MR. CHAMBERS: I think it was on the top floor.

MR. NIXON: The fourth?

MR. CHAMBERS: It was a walk-up. I think the fourth.

MR. NIXON: It could have been the third, of course?

MR. CHAMBERS: It might have been.

MR. NIXON: But you think it was the top, as well as you can recall?

MR. CHAMBERS: I think it was the top.

MR. NIXON: Understand, I am not trying to hold you to absolute accuracy.

MR. CHAMBERS: I am trying to recall.

MR. NIXON: Was there any special dish they served?

MR. CHAMBERS: No. I think you get here into something else. Hiss is a man
of great simplicity and a great gentleness and sweetness of character, and
they lived with extreme simplicity. I had the impression that the furniture in that house was kind of pulled together from here or there, maybe
got it from their mother or something like that, nothing lavish about it
whatsoever, quite simple.

Their food was in the same pattern and they cared nothing about
food. It was not a primary interest in their lives.

MR. MANDEL: Did Mr. Hiss have any hobbies?

MR. CHAMBERS: Yes; he did. They both had the same hobby—amateur
ornithologists, bird observers. They used to get up early in the morning
and go to Glen Echo, out the canal, to observe birds.

I recall once they saw, to their great excitement, a prothonotary warbler.

MR. McDOWELL: A very rare specimen?

MR. CHAMBERS: I never saw one. I am also fond of birds.

MR. NIXON: Did they have a car?

MR. CHAMBERS: Yes; they did. When I first knew them they had a car. Again
I am reasonably sure—I am almost certain—it was a Ford and that it was
a roadster. It was black and it was very dilapidated. There is no question
about that.

I remember very clearly that it had hand windshield wipers. I remember that because I drove it one rainy day and had to work those
windshield wipers by hand.

MR. NIXON: Do you recall any other car?

MR. CHAMBERS: It seems to me in 1936, probably, he got a new Plymouth.

MR. NIXON: Do you recall its type?

MR. CHAMBERS: It was a sedan, a two-seated car.

MR. MANDEL: What did he do with the old car?

MR. CHAMBERS: The Communist Party had in Washington a service station—that is, the man in charge or owner of this station was a Communist—or it may have been a car lot.

MR. NIXON: But the owner was a Communist?

MR. CHAMBERS: The owner was a Communist. I never knew who this was or where it was. It was against all the rules of underground organization for Hiss to do anything with his old car but trade it in, and I think this investigation has proved how right the Communists are in such matters, but Hiss insisted that he wanted that car turned over to the open party so it could be of use to some poor organizer in the West or somewhere.

Much against my better judgment and much against Peters' better judgment, he finally got us to permit him to do this thing. Peters knew where this lot was and he either took Hiss there, or he gave Hiss the address and Hiss went there, and to the best of my recollection of his description of that happening, he left the car there and simply went away and the man in charge of the station took care of the rest of it for him. I should think the records of that transfer would be traceable.

MR. NIXON: Where was that?

MR. CHAMBERS: In Washington, D.C., I believe; certainly somewhere in the District.

MR. NIXON: You don't know where?

MR. CHAMBERS: No; never asked.

MR. NIXON: Do you recall any other cars besides those two?

MR. CHAMBERS: No, I think he had the Plymouth when I broke with the whole business.

HUAC Interrogates Hiss in Executive Session

When Alger Hiss was subpoenaed to testify in executive session, the encounter became increasingly acrimonious. Hiss was indignant that his credibility was being challenged since it was a case of his word against that of a "confessed Communist." He was suspicious of the motives of committee members, especially Congressman Mundt. He was especially upset about newspaper accounts of the developing investigation and worried about the confidentiality of the proceedings. Nixon assured him of the confidential nature of these executive sessions.

In his testimony, Hiss once again hesitated to positively identify Chambers when shown pictures. He admitted a degree of familiarity with the face, but wished to see his accuser face to face before making a positive identification. He suggested that Chambers possibly may have been a man named

"George Crosley," a struggling writer who, with his wife and baby, had sublet an apartment from Hiss around 1934 or 1935. Hiss sketched details of his relationship with Crosley, including information about an old Ford automobile that he had given that individual. Hiss noted that he had parted company with Crosley on a sour note since he had failed to fulfill his agreement to make payments on the apartment. If Chambers was indeed Crosley, these hard feelings might explain why Chambers would be trying to ruin Hiss's reputation. When Hiss answered questions about details of his personal life, it became clear to the committee that, despite some contradictions, Chambers did indeed know Alger Hiss. Asked if he was willing to subject himself to a lie detector test, Hiss expressed doubts about the validity of such an exam and was reluctant to agree. He, however, took it under advisement.

HISS TESTIMONY, AUGUST 16, 1948

MR. STRIPLING: Mr. Hiss, you have previously appeared before the committee in open session. You are here in response to a telegram which was sent you last Friday?

MR. HISS: That is correct. May I make an inquiry?

MR. STRIPLING: Yes, sir.

MR. HISS: I would like to be advised what the arrangements are with respect to a transcript of this particular meeting of the subcommittee. Will I be entitled to receive a copy of the transcript of this meeting?

THE CHAIRMAN: Mr. Hiss, this is an executive session, and that speaks for itself that everything is supposed to be right within these four walls. Therefore, we do not naturally give out the testimony taken in executive session.

MR. NIXON: Mr. Chairman, I think it should be said that in the event the transcript or portions of the transcript are made public you will receive a copy in the event that it is used, but in the event that it is kept confidential and not made public, the custom of the committee is not to furnish a transcript.

THE CHAIRMAN: That is correct.

MR. HISS: That is all.

• • •

MR. NIXON: I am now showing you two pictures of Mr. Whittaker Chambers, also known as Carl, who testified that he knew you between the years 1934–37, and that he saw you in 1939.

I ask you now, after looking at those pictures, if you can remember that person either as Whittaker Chambers or as Carl or as any other individual you have met.

Source: Hearings Regarding Communist Espionage in the United States Government, 935–36, 940–41, 945–49, 952–53, 955–70.

MR. HISS: May I recall to the committee the testimony I gave in the public session when I was shown another photograph of Mr. Whittaker Chambers, and I had prior to taking the stand tried to get as many newspapers that had photographs of Mr. Chambers as I could. I testified then that I could not swear that I had never seen the man whose picture was shown me. Actually the face has a certain familiarity. I think I also testified to that.

It is not according to the photograph a very distinctive or unusual face. I would like very much to see the individual face to face. I had hoped that would happen before. I still hope it will happen today.

I am not prepared to say that I have never seen the man whose pictures are now shown me. I said that when I was on the stand when a different picture was shown me. I cannot recall any person with distinctness and definiteness whose picture this is, but it is not completely unfamiliar.

Whether I am imagining that or not I don't know, but I certainly wouldn't want to testify without seeing the man, hearing him talk, getting some much more tangible basis for judging the person and the personality.

MR. NIXON: Would your answer be any different if this individual were described to you as one who had stayed overnight in your house on several occasions?

MR. HISS: I think, Mr. Nixon, let me say this: In the course of my service in Government from 1933 to 1947 and the previous year 1929–30, and as a lawyer I have had a great many people who have visited in my house.

I have tried to recall in the last week or so anyone who would know my house whom I wouldn't know very well. There are many people that have come to my house on social occasions whom I probably wouldn't recall at all.

As far as staying overnight in my house is concerned—

MR. NIXON: On several occasions.

MR. HISS: On several occasions?

MR. NIXON: On several occasions.

MR. HISS: I can't believe, Mr. Nixon, that anyone could have stayed in my house when I was there—

MR. NIXON: When you were there.

MR. HISS: Overnight on several occasions without my being able to recall the individual; and if this is a picture of anyone, I would find it very difficult to believe that that individual could have stayed in my house when I was there on several occasions overnight and his face not be more familiar than it is.

MR. NIXON—

MR. NIXON: Yes.

MR. HISS: I don't want to suggest any innovations in your procedure, but I do want to say specifically that I do hope I will have an opportunity actually to see the individual.

MR. NIXON: It is going to be arranged. I might say that before arranging the meeting, we want to be certain that there is no question of mistaken identity, as well as possible, and also that we had a clear conflict on certain pieces of testimony that had been given by both sides, and that we are getting right now.

MR. HISS: Yes, sir.

MR. NIXON: I might say this, too: That Mr. Chambers, as you may be aware of newspaper accounts, appeared in executive session before us on Saturday.

MR. HISS: Saturday a week ago, I think.

MR. NIXON: Just 2 days after you appeared.

MR. HISS: I saw the newspaper accounts of that.

MR. NIXON: At that time we went into the situation with him, showed him pictures of you, and he declared without question you were the man.

For that reason we wanted to be sure that you had the same opportunity before we went into open session. Obviously, as you can see, an open session will involve a considerable amount of publicity, and we were thinking that if that could be avoided, that it should be avoided. It is quite apparent now, even so far as we have gone, that eventually that is going to occur, but I wanted to go into a few more questions here first.

• • •

MR. HISS: I have been angered and hurt by one thing in the course of this committee testimony, and that was by the attitude which I think Mr. Mundt took when I was testifying publicly and which it seems to me, you have been taking today, that you have a conflict of testimony between two witnesses—I restrained myself with some difficulty from commenting on this at the public hearing, and I would like to say it on this occasion, which isn't a public hearing.

MR. NIXON: Say anything you like.

MR. HISS: It seems there is no impropriety in saying it. You today and the acting chairman publicly have taken the attitude when you have two witnesses, one of whom is a confessed former Communist, the other is me, that you simply have two witnesses saying contradictory things as between whom you find it most difficult to decide on credibility.

Mr. Nixon, I do not know what Mr. Chambers testified to your committee last Saturday. It is necessarily my opinion of him from what he has already said that I do not know that he is not capable of telling the truth or does not desire to, and I honestly have the feeling that details of my personal life which I give honestly can be used to my disadvantage by Chambers then ex post facto knowing those facts.

I would request that I hear Mr. Chambers' story of his alleged knowledge of me. I have seen newspaper accounts, Mr. Nixon, that you spent the week end—whether correct or not, I do not know—at Mr. Chambers' farm in New Jersey.

MR. NIXON: That is quite incorrect.

MR. HISS: It is incorrect.

MR. NIXON: Yes, sir. I can say, as you did a moment ago, that I have never spent the night with Mr. Chambers.

MR. HISS: Now, I have been cudgeling my brains, particularly on the train coming down this morning, and I had 3 or 4 hours on the train between New York and Washington, as to who could have various details about my family. Many people could.

    Mr. Nixon, I do not wish to make it easier for anyone who, for whatever motive I cannot understand, is apparently endeavoring to destroy me, to make that man's endeavors any easier. I think in common fairness to my own self-protection and that of my family and my family's good name and my own, I should not be asked to give details which somehow he may hear and then may be able to use as if he knew them before. I would like him to say all he knows about me now. What I have done is public record, where I have lived is public record. Let him tell you all he knows, let that be made public, and then let my record be checked against those facts instead of my being asked, Mr. Nixon, to tell you personal facts about myself which, if they come to his ears, could sound very persuasive to other people that he had known me at some prior time.

MR. NIXON: The questions I have asked you to date, Mr. Hiss, if you will recall them, have all been facts that could be corroborated by third parties. Now, the question of whether or not, the question of who your servants were, I will tell you very frankly it is purely for the purpose of corroboration and it will be the intention of the committee, if possible, to find one of the servants to see whether or not they will corroborate the story.

    Now you, of course, are under no compulsion to give the committee the names of the servants, but the purpose is that.

    Now, the second point I wish to make is this. Of course, there is a very serious implication in your statement, and that is that the committee's purpose in questioning you today is to get information with which we can coach Mr. Chambers so that he can more or less build a web around you.

MR. HISS: Mr. Nixon, I meant no such implication.

MR. NIXON: You can be very sure when I say this testimony is going to be in executive session, it will be. The same assurance was given to Mr. Chambers.

MR. HISS: May I please, before that point gets cold—I mean no such implication. You have identified a number of people who are present in the room. A record is being kept. The people in this gentleman's office will process the record, a number of people that none of us here can be sure of now will see this record and will have the information which is contained in it. You are dealing with something, Mr. Nixon, which is very important to you as an official. You are dealing with something which is very important to me not only as a former official and one interested in the security of the United States, but you are also dealing with something which affronts me personally in a way which it does not affect the members of this committee personally.

MR. STRIPLING: May I say something?

Mr. Hiss, I can assure you that as far as the members of the committee I have talked to are concerned, they have a very open mind on this thing and I certainly do, but this testimony you speak of has already been turned over to the United States attorney, including the executive testimony.

Mr. Hiss: Certainly.

Mr. Nixon: Mr. Chambers' testimony has.

Mr. Stripling: We just got this picture. I listened to his testimony in New York and I can assure you that there was no prearrangement or anything else with Mr. Chambers, but here is what he did. He sat there and testified for hours. He said he spent a week in your house and he just rattled off details like that. He has either made a study of your life in great detail or he knows you, one or the other, or he is incorrect.

Mr. Hiss: Could I ask you to ask him some questions?

Mr. Stripling: Here is a larger picture. Let the record show this larger picture taken by the Associated Press photo on August 3, 1948, of Mr. Mundt and Mr. Whittaker Chambers and, as the record previously stated, Mr. Chambers is much heavier now than he was in 1937 or 1938.

Does this picture refresh your memory in any way, Mr. Hiss?

Mr. Hiss: It looks like the very same man I had seen in the other pictures of, and I see Mr. Mundt and him in the same picture. The face is definitely not an unfamiliar face. Whether I am imagining it, whether it is because he looks like a lot of other people, I don't know, but I have never known anyone who had the relationship with me that this man has testified to and that, I think, is the important thing here, gentlemen. This man may have known me, he may have been in my house. I have had literally hundreds of people in my house in the course of the time I lived in Washington.

The issue is not whether this man knew me and I don't remember him. The issue is whether he had a particular conversation that he has said he had with me and which I have denied and whether I am a member of the Communist Party or ever was, which he has said and which I have denied.

If I could see the man face to face, I would perhaps have some inkling as to whether he ever had known me personally.

I have met within the past week a man who said he worked on the same staff in a confidential relationship at San Francisco that I did who definitely knew me, and I have no recollection of ever having seen that man.

The Chairman: May I ask a few questions?

Mr. Nixon: Certainly.

The Chairman: Mr. Hiss, would you be able to recall a person if that person positively had been in your house three or four times, we will say, in the last 10 years?

Mr. Hiss: I would say that if he had spent the night—

Mr. Stripling: Ten years?

Mr. Nixon: Fifteen years.

THE CHAIRMAN: All right.

MR. HISS: I would say if he had spent the night—how many times did you say?

MR. STRIPLING: He spent a week there.

MR. HISS: A whole week at a time continuously?

MR. STRIPLING: Yes.

MR. HISS: And I was there at the same time?

MR. STRIPLING: Yes.

MR. HISS: Mr. Chairman, I could not fail to recall such a man if he were now in my presence.

THE CHAIRMAN: Wait a minute. You are positive then that if Mr. X spent a week in your house in the past 15 years you would recognize him today, assuming that Mr. X looks today something like what he looked then?

MR. HISS: Exactly, if he hadn't had a face lifting.

THE CHAIRMAN: No doubt in your mind?

MR. HISS: I have no doubt whatsoever.

THE CHAIRMAN: Now, here is a man who says he spent a week in your house in the last 15 years. Do you recognize him?

MR. HISS: I do not recognize him from the picture.

MR. NIXON: Did that man spend a week in your house in the last 15 years?

MR. HISS: I cannot say that man did, but I would like to see him.

THE CHAIRMAN: You say you cannot believe, but I would like to have a little more definite answer if you could make it more definite. Would you say he did or did not spend a week in your house?

MR. HISS: Mr. Chairman, I hope you will not think I am being unreasonable when I say I am not prepared to testify on the basis of a photograph. On the train coming down this morning I searched my recollection of any possible person that this man could be confused with or could have got information from about me.

THE CHAIRMAN: Then you are not prepared to testify on this subject from a photograph?

MR. HISS: I am not prepared to testify on the basis of a photograph. I would want to hear the man's voice.

THE CHAIRMAN: If the man himself came in here, you would be able to say yes or no?

MR. HISS: I think I would, sir.

THE CHAIRMAN: You think you would.

MR. HISS: I can't believe a man would have changed as much as that, and I am absolutely prepared to testify that nobody, that man or any other man, had any such conversation with me in my house or anywhere else as he has testified to.

MR. STRIPLING: What conversations did he testify he had with you in your house?

MR. HISS: Mr. Chambers, according to the record that I read, he said that he came to my house and pled with me to break with the Communist Party, and that I refused, and that I had tears in my eyes, and that the reason I gave was something about the Communist Party line.

MR. NIXON: Mr. Hiss, let me explain this. Mr. Chambers, as indicated, did testify that he spent a week in your house. He also testified to other facts concerning his acquaintanceship with you—alleged facts, I should say— and I want to point out that the committee by getting answers to completely objective questions from you will be in a position to go certainly to third parties and to find out whether or not Mr. Chambers has committed perjury.

Now, on one point it is pretty clear that you have indicated that Mr. Chambers must have committed perjury because he said he spent a week in your house.

Now, these other matters to which Mr. Chambers has testified involve the same type of testimony. I want to say when Mr. Chambers appeared, he was instructed that every answer he gave to every question would be material and he was instructed off the record before that that a material question would subject him to perjury. So consequently, as you see, a matter of membership in the Communist Party is one thing because that is a matter which might be and probably would be concealed, but a number of objective items concerning his relationship with you, his alleged relationship with you, can be confirmed in some cases by third parties and that, frankly, is the purpose of these questions.

MR. HISS: May I say one thing for the record?

MR. NIXON: Certainly.

MR. HISS: I have written a name on this pad in front of me of a person whom I knew in 1933 and 1934 who not only spent some time in my house but sublet my apartment. That man certainly spent more than a week, not while I was in the same apartment. I do not recognize the photographs as possibly being this man. If I hadn't seen the morning papers with an account of statements that he knew the inside of my house, I don't think I would even have thought of this name. I want to see Mr. Chambers face to face and see if he can be this individual. I do not want and I don't think I ought to be asked to testify now that man's name and everything I can remember about him. I have written the name on this piece of paper. I have given the name to two friends of mine before I came in this hearing. I can only repeat, and perhaps I am being over-anxious about the possibility of unauthorized disclosure of testimony, that I don't think in my present frame of mind that it is fair to my position, my own protection, that I be asked to put down here of record personal facts about myself which, if they came to the ears of someone who had for no reason I can understand a desire to injure me, would assist him in that endeavor.

MR. NIXON: This man who spent the time in 1933 and 1934 is still a man with whom you are acquainted?

MR. HISS: He is not.

MR. NIXON: And where were you living at that time?

MR. HISS: He was not named Carl and not Whittaker Chambers.

MR. NIXON: Where were you living at that time?

MR. HISS: I have again written down here to the best of my recollection because I have not checked down with leases—this is something I did on the train coming down and the leases are in my house in New York—where I believed I lived from June of 1933 until September 1943.

Again, Mr. Nixon, if I give the details of where I was, it is going to be very easy if this information gets out for someone to say then ex post facto, "I saw Hiss in such and such a house." Actually, all he has to do is look it up in the telephone directory and find where it is.

THE CHAIRMAN: The chairman wants to say this: Questions will be asked and the committee will expect to get very detailed answers to the questions. Let's not ramble all around the lot here. You go ahead and ask questions and I want the witness to answer.

MR. NIXON: Your testimony is that this man you knew in 1933 and 1934 was in one of the houses you lived in?

MR. HISS: I sublet my apartment to the man whose name I have written down.

MR. NIXON: But you were not there at the same time?

MR. HISS: I didn't spend a week in the same apartment with him. He did spend a day or two in my house when he moved in.

MR. NIXON: This was the apartment you lived in between 1933 and 1934?

MR. HISS: It is exactly that apartment—1934 and 1935.

MR. NIXON: Between 1934 and 1935?

MR. HISS: That is right.

MR. NIXON: When you sublet your apartment? There was no other apartment and you can't testify as to what apartment that was?

MR. HISS: I can't testify to the best of my recollection. If this committee feels, in spite of what I have said—

THE CHAIRMAN: Never mind feelings. You let Mr. Nixon ask the questions and you go ahead and answer it.

MR. HISS: I want to be sure Mr. Nixon definitely wants me to answer responsively in spite of my plea that I don't think he should ask me. But if he does—Mr. Nixon also asked me some questions in the public hearing that I didn't want to answer, and I took the same position that if Mr. Nixon insisted on an answer after he knew my position, I will answer. I will give every fact of where I lived.

MR. STRIPLING: Let the record show, Mr. Hiss, you brought up this ex post facto business. Your testimony comes as ex post facto testimony to the testimony of Mr. Chambers. He is already on record, and I am not inferring that you might know what he testified to, but certainly the United States attorney's office has several copies.

MR. HISS: I do not and made no attempt to find out.

• • •

MR. HISS: Apparently for Chambers to be a confessed former Communist and traitor to his country did not seem to him to be a blot on his record. He got his present job after he had told various agencies exactly that. I am sorry but I cannot but feel to such an extent that it is difficult for me to control myself that you can sit there, Mr. Hébert, and say to me casually that you have heard that man and you have heard me, and you just have no basis for judging which one is telling the truth. I don't think a judge determines the credibility of witnesses on that basis.

MR. HÉBERT: I am trying to tell you that I absolutely have an open mind and am trying to give you as fair a hearing as I could possibly give Mr. Chambers or yourself. The fact that Mr. Chambers is a self-confessed traitor—and I admit he is—the fact that he is a self-confessed former member of the Communist Party—which I admit he is—has no bearing at all on whether the facts that he told—or, rather, the alleged facts that he told—

MR. HISS: Has no bearing on his credibility?

MR. HÉBERT: No; because, Mr. Hiss, I recognize the fact that maybe my background is a little different from yours, but I do know police methods and I know crime a great deal, and you show me a good police force and I will show you the stool pigeon who turned them in. Show me a police force with a poor record, and I will show you a police force without a stool pigeon. We have to have people like Chambers or Miss Bentley to come in and tell us. I am not giving Mr. Chambers any great credit for his previous life. I am trying to find out if he has reformed. Some of the greatest saints in history were pretty bad before they were saints. Are you going to take away their sainthood because of their previous lives? Are you not going to believe them after they have reformed?

I don't care who gives the facts to me, whether a confessed liar, thief, or murderer, if it is facts. That is all I am interested in.

MR. HISS: You have made your position clear. I would like to raise a separate point. Today as I came down on the train I read a statement—I think it was in the New York News—that a member of this committee, an unidentified member of this committee believed or had reason to believe from talking to Chambers that Chambers had personally known Hiss, not that Chambers had had the conversation which is the issue here, that Chambers had been in Hiss' house. That is not the issue before this committee. You are asking me to tell you all the facts that I know of people who have been in my house or who have known me whom I would not feel absolutely confident are people I know all about, personal friends, people I feel I know through and through. I am not prepared to say on the basis of the photograph—

MR. HÉBERT: We understand.

MR. HISS:—That the man, that he is not the man whose name I have written down here. Were I to testify to that, what assurance have I that some member of this committee wouldn't say to the press that Hiss confessed knowing Chambers?

In the first place, I have testified and repeated that I have never known anybody by the name of Whittaker Chambers. I am not prepared to testify I have never seen that man.

MR. HÉBERT: You have said that.

MR. STRIPLING: Have you ever seen that one [indicating picture]?

THE CHAIRMAN: What is the question?

MR. STRIPLING: Have you ever seen the individual whose photograph appears there?

MR. HISS: So far as I know; no.

MR. STRIPLING: You have never seen that person?

MR. HISS: No.

MR. HÉBERT: For the record, the issue is whether Chambers did have the conversation with you, that is admitted, but the only way we can establish the fact that Chambers had the occasion to have the conversation with you is we have to establish the fact that Hiss knew Chambers and Chambers knew Hiss, and this is very pertinent.

THE CHAIRMAN: Let's go on with the question.

MR. NIXON: If Chambers' credibility on the question of whether he knew you or not is destroyed, obviously you can see that this statement that he had a conversation with you and that you were a member of the Communist Party, which was made on the basis of knowledge would also be destroyed; and that is exactly the basis upon which this questioning is being conducted, I can assure you, because those are personal matters; whether you are a member of the Communist Party and whether he had a conversation with you individually is something that no third party can corroborate one way or the other. But these other facts are matters which third parties can corroborate. They won't prove, obviously, even if there is agreement on these facts, that this man knew you, but if there is disagreement on these facts, they will prove that Chambers is a perjurer and that is what we are trying to find out. If we prove he is a perjurer on the basis of his testimony now, the necessity of going into the rest of the matter will be obviated.

MR. HISS: But if he is able through my action to make a plausible story of having known me or if he has in fact known me under circumstances very different from those he has testified to, I think in my own self-protection I should have a chance to see him. I think that for me to be asked details that may get back, through no fault of yours—I can only repeat if this committee asks me to go on with this specific line of inquiry, I will certainly do it. I do not feel comfortable about being in a position to protect my own reputation because I don't think knowledge of any individual is the issue here.

• • •

MR. HISS: That is kind of you.

The name of the man I brought in—and he may have no relation to this whole nightmare—is a man named George Crosley. I met him when I was working for the Nye Committee. He was a writer. He hoped to sell articles to magazines about the munitions industry.

I saw him, as I say, in my office over in the Senate Office Building, dozens of representatives of the press, students, people writing books, research people. It was our job to give them appropriate information out of the record, show them what had been put in the record. This fellow was writing a series of articles, according to my best recollection, free lancing, which he hoped to sell to one of the magazines.

He was pretty obviously not successful in financial terms, but as far as I know, wasn't exactly hard up.

MR. STRIPLING: What color was his hair?

MR. HISS: Rather blondish, blonder than any of us here.

MR. STRIPLING: Was he married?

MR. HISS: Yes, sir.

MR. STRIPLING: Any children?

MR. HISS: One little baby, as I remember it, and the way I know that was the subleasing point. After we had taken the house on P Street and had the apartment on our hands, he one day in the course of casual conversation said he was going to specialize all summer in getting his articles done here in Washington, didn't know what he was going to do, and was thinking about bringing his family.

I said, "You can have my apartment. It is not terribly cool, but it is up in the air near the Wardman Park." He said he had a wife and a little baby. The apartment wasn't very expensive, and I think I let him have it at exact cost. My recollection is that he spent several nights in my house because his furniture van was delayed. We left several pieces of furniture behind.

The P Street house belonged to a naval officer overseas and was partly furnished, so we didn't need all our furniture, particularly during the summer months, and my recollection is that definitely, as one does with a tenant trying to make him agreeable and comfortable, we left several pieces of furniture behind until the fall, his van was delayed, wasn't going to bring all the furniture because he was going to be there just during the summer, and we put them up 2 or 3 nights in a row, his wife and little baby.

MR. NIXON: His wife and he and little baby did spend several nights in the house with you?

MR. HISS: This man Crosley; yes.

MR. NIXON: Can you describe his wife?

MR. HISS: Yes; she was a rather strikingly dark person, very strikingly dark. I don't know whether I would recognize her again because I didn't see very much of her.

MR. NIXON: How tall was this man, approximately?

MR. HISS: Shortish.

MR. NIXON: Heavy?

MR. HISS: Not noticeably. That is why I don't believe it has any direct, but it could have an indirect bearing.

MR. NIXON: How about his teeth?

MR. HISS: Very bad teeth. That is one of the things I particularly want to see Chambers about. This man had very bad teeth, did not take care of his teeth.

MR. STRIPLING: Did he have most of his teeth or just weren't well cared for?

MR. HISS: I don't think he had gapped teeth, but they were badly taken care of. They were stained and I would say obviously not attended to.

MR. NIXON: Can you state again just when he first rented the apartment?

MR. HISS: I think it was about June of 1935. My recollection is—and again I have not checked the records—that is, I went with the Nye munitions committee in the early winter of 1934. I don't even remember now when the resolution was passed. In any event, I am confident I was living on Twenty-ninth Street from December 1934 to June 1935 and that coincided with my service with the Nye committee. I say that because one reason we took the apartment was to reduce our living costs, because after I had been on loan from the Department of Agriculture for some months, I thought it would only be a 2-month assignment or so, it became evident that I was to stay on longer if I should complete the job, and my deputy in the Department of Agriculture was doing all my work and not getting my salary and I did not feel it fair, so I resigned from the Department of Agriculture to go on with the Nye committee work at the Nye committee salary and contemplated that and talked it over with my deputy in the Department of Agriculture for some time before I did it. So I am sure, from my recollection, that the Twenty-ninth Street apartment is definitely linked in time with my service on the Nye committee.

MR. STRIPLING: What kind of automobile did that fellow have?

MR. HISS: No kind of automobile. I sold him an automobile. I had an old Ford that I threw in with the apartment and had been trying to trade it in and get rid of it. I had an old, old Ford we had kept for sentimental reasons. We got it just before we were married in 1929.

MR. STRIPLING: Was it a model A or model T?

MR. HISS: Early A model with a trunk on the back, a slightly collegiate model.

MR. STRIPLING: What color?

MR. HISS: Dark blue. It wasn't very fancy but it had a sassy little trunk on the back.

MR. NIXON: You sold that car?

MR. HISS: I threw it in. He wanted a way to get around and I said, "Fine, I want to get rid of it. I have another car, and we kept it for sentimental reasons, not worth a damn." I let him have it along with the rent.

MR. NIXON: Where did you move from there?

MR. HISS: Again my best recollection is that we stayed on P Street only 1 year because the whole heating plant broke down in the middle of the winter when I was quite ill, and I think that we moved from 2905 P Street to 1241 Thirtieth Street about September 1936. I recall that quite specifically though we can check it from the records, because I remember Mr. Sayre, who was my chief in the State Department, who had been my professor at law school, saying he wanted to drive by and see where I was living. I remember the little house on Thirtieth Street which we had just got, a new development, was the little house I drove him by, and it must have been September or October 1936, just after starting to work in the State Department.

MR. NIXON: Going back to this man, do you know how many days approximately he stayed with you?

MR. HISS: I don't think more than a couple of times. He may have come back. I can't remember when it was I finally decided it wasn't any use expecting to collect from him, that I had been a sucker and he was sort of deadbeat; not a bad character, but I think he just was using me for a soft touch.

MR. NIXON: You said before he moved in your apartment he stayed in your house with you and your wife about how many days?

MR. HISS: I would say a couple of nights. I don't think it was longer than that.

MR. NIXON: A couple of nights?

MR. HISS: During the delay of the van arriving.

MR. NIXON: Wouldn't that be longer than 2 nights?

MR. HISS: I don't think so. I wouldn't swear that he didn't come back again some later time after the lease and say, "I can't find a hotel. Put me up overnight," or something of that sort. I wouldn't swear Crosley wasn't in my house maybe a total of 3 or 4 nights altogether.

● ● ●

MR. NIXON: You gave this Ford car to Crosley?

MR. HISS: Threw it in along with the apartment and charged the rent and threw the car in at the same time.

MR. NIXON: In other words, added a little to the rent to cover the car?

MR. HISS: No; I think I charged him exactly what I was paying for the rent and threw the car in in addition. I don't think I got any compensation.

MR. STRIPLING: You just gave him the car?

MR. HISS: I think the car just went right in with it. I don't remember whether we had settled on the terms of the rent before the car question came up, or whether it came up and then on the basis of the car and the apartment I said, "Well, you ought to pay the full rent."

MR. STRIPLING: Are you hard of hearing in your left ear?

MR. HISS: Not to my knowledge.

MR. STRIPLING: I noticed you had your hand up to your ear.

MR. HISS: If I have done that, it is only when I wanted to be sure I was hearing.

MR. STRIPLING: You did that before the committee in open session and did then. If you are having difficulty, we can all move this way.

MR. HISS: I am not aware of it and never heard any doctor say so.

MR. NIXON: I have a few more of these questions, which I feel will help us a great deal if you are willing to answer them.

MR. HISS: I am willing to answer any question you ask.

MR. NIXON: I assure you, as I have before, that as far as the committee is concerned the cold record, Mr. Chambers's testimony, and your testimony are going to have to stand up together.

MR. HISS: We won't go into that question again.

MR. STRIPLING: May I ask another question?

MR. NIXON: Yes.

MR. STRIPLING: When you had this Ford car do you remember where you bought your gasoline?

MR. HISS: No; I don't remember where we bought gas when we were living on Twenty-ninth Street. On O Street I am afraid I don't remember whether I had a regular place. I remember a regular place in recent years, and even earlier, but when we first came down I don't think we had a regular place.

MR. STRIPLING: What kind of car did you get?

MR. HISS: A Plymouth.

MR. STRIPLING: A Plymouth?

MR. HISS: Plymouth sedan.

MR. STRIPLING: Four-door?

MR. HISS: I think I have always had only two-door.

MR. STRIPLING: What kind of a bill of sale did you give Crosley?

MR. HISS: I think I just turned over—in the District you get a certificate of title, I think it is. I think I just simply turned it over to him.

MR. STRIPLING: Handed it to him?

MR. HISS: Yes.

MR. STRIPLING: No evidence of any transfer. Did you record the title?

MR. HISS: That I haven't any idea. This is a car which had been sitting on the streets in snow for a year or two. I once got a parking fine because I forgot where it was parked. We were using the other car.

MR. STRIPLING: Do those model Fords have windshield wipers?

MR. HISS: You had to work them yourself.

MR. STRIPLING: Hand operated?

MR. HISS: I think that is the best I can recall.

MR. NIXON: Do you recall the voice of this fellow Crosley?

MR. HISS: I was trying to recall that this morning. It was a low voice. He speaks with a low and rather dramatic roundness.

MR. STRIPLING: Would you say it is a subdued voice?

MR. HISS: No; I don't particularly think that is so. It is not very loud, but the main thing I have in mind would be a deepness, a lowness.

MR. McDOWELL: A heavy voice?

MR. HISS: Lower voice than I have.

MR. NIXON: Was he a man pretty talkative about his accomplishments, et cetera?

MR. HISS: That is right.

MR. NIXON: There are matters which I wish to go into now to which Mr. Chambers has given categorical answers. I am going to put the questions objectively, as you can see. I am not going to try to lead you one way or the other. It will be very helpful as the two records look together to see how accurate he is in this case.

I want to say first of all, so that it won't come up, that I realize that the matters which are covered are matters which third parties could corroborate, and that is the reason we ask these particular questions.

Again for the purpose of just checking the veracity of Mr. Chambers and your testimony. It will help us to check it again.

What were the nicknames you and your wife had?

MR. HISS: My wife, I have always called her "Prossy."

MR. NIXON: What does she call you?

MR. HISS: Well, at one time she called me quite frequently "Hill," H-i-l-l.

MR. NIXON: What other name?

MR. HISS: "Hilly," with a "y."

MR. NIXON: What other name did you call her?

MR. STRIPLING: What did you say?

MR. HISS: She called me "Hill" or "Hilly." I called her "Pross" or "Prossy" almost exclusively. I don't think any other nickname.

MR. NIXON: Did you ever call her "Dilly"?

MR. HISS: No; never.

MR. NIXON: Never to your knowledge in fun or otherwise?

MR. HISS: Never.

MR. NIXON: What did you call your son?

MR. HISS: "Timmy."

MR. NIXON: "Timmy"?

MR. HISS: Yes; and in the family he is also known as "Moby," M-o-b-y.

• • •

MR. NIXON: What hobby, if any, do you have, Mr. Hiss?

MR. HISS: Tennis and amateur ornithology.

MR. NIXON: Is your wife interested in ornithology?

MR. HISS: I also like to swim and also like to sail. My wife is interested in ornithology, as I am, through my interest. Maybe I am using too big a word to say an ornithologist because I am pretty amateur, but I have been interested in it since I was in Boston. I think anybody who knows me would know that.

MR. McDOWELL: Did you ever see a prothonotary warbler?

MR. HISS: I have right here on the Potomac. Do you know that place?

THE CHAIRMAN: What is that?

MR. NIXON: Have you ever seen one?

MR. HISS: Did you see it in the same place?

MR. McDOWELL: I saw one in Arlington.

MR. HISS: They come back and nest in those swamps. Beautiful yellow head, a gorgeous bird.

• • •

MR. NIXON: Mr. Chambers, of course, as I say, was very convincing in his testimony and you certainly are very convincing in yours.

Now, frankly, the committee has a difficult problem here and I wonder if under the circumstances for the assistance of the committee in this matter you would be willing to take a lie-detector test on this.

I might say before you answer, so you will have full knowledge of what the committee knows, Mr. Chambers was asked that question and said he would take a lie detector test.

Mr. Hiss: Shall I answer now?

Mr. Nixon: Yes.

Mr. Hiss: Mr. Nixon, several days after I testified two members of the press told me that there had been a report that the committee was considering asking various witnesses if they would take a lie-detector test. When I was asked if I had any comment to make on that, I said I didn't think it was appropriate at the time to make any comment.

Since then I have talked about that to several friends who I think are knowledgeable. When I was practicing law actively, quite frankly we had very little confidence in the so-called lie detector tests. I would say that I would rather have you ask me formally if you think lie detector tests are valuable in terms of who would administer it, what expert it is, what type of test, because the people I have consulted—and I think I have consulted knowledgeable people—say there is no such thing; that it is an emotion recording test; that it is not scientific, and that nobody scientifically competent, including the Bureau, regards it as a scientific test.

Mr. Nixon: When you speak of asking you formally, what do you want us to do?

Mr. Hiss: I would like to know who the administrator is, whether this is being done by someone in the Bureau who is an expert or an individual so-called expert, what kind of a test it is. In other words, I don't think I ought to, on the basis of the advice I have had, try to answer it out of hand until I know and you know.

I would be surprised if this committee would want to rely on something that isn't scientific.

Mr. Nixon: Certainly. In answer to your question, the committee has contacted Mr. Leonardo Keeler.

Mr. Hiss: Is he the man from Chicago?

Mr. Nixon: Probably the outstanding man in the country. The test Mr. Keeler has is the polygraph machine. It is the only one, I think, that has any broad acceptance at all.

I might say also that the polygraph machine is one whose accuracy is dependent to a great extent upon the type of operator. In questioning Mr. Keeler about this I said that if we did have the lie detector test, that he would have to operate it. He agreed. I might say we have made no arrangements with Mr. Keeler because it is rather an expensive proposition. When we do make arrangements we will, of course, have a number of witnesses concerning which contradictory testimony has come up. We are putting the question to you officially now and would like for you to give us your answer as soon as you can.

Mr. Hiss: Would it seem to you inappropriate for me to say that I would rather have a chance for further consultation before I gave you the answer? Actually, the people I have conferred with so far say that it all depends on who reads, that it shows emotion, not truth, and I am perfectly willing and prepared to say that I am not lacking in emotion about this business.

I have talked to people who have seen, I think, Dr. Keeler's own test and that the importance of a question registers more emotion than anything else. I certainly don't want to duck anything that has scientific or sound basis. I would like to consult further.

I would like to find out a little more about Dr. Keeler. As I told you, the people I have consulted said flatly there is no such thing, that it is not scientifically established.

MR. NIXON: When could you give a decision on that?

MR. HISS: I would hope to consult in part the same people I consulted last week and anyone they suggested.

MR. NIXON: When could you give a decision?

MR. HISS: When is it important to you to know? Would you like to know tomorrow?

MR. NIXON: Wednesday.

MR. HISS: I will try to let you know Wednesday.

MR. NIXON: Tomorrow might rush you. Could you know by Wednesday?

MR. HISS: I certainly ought to be able to make up my mind on the basis of the questions I ask.

MR. NIXON: If you do decide tomorrow and let us know, it would facilitate things, one way or the other. We have Mr. Keeler more or less standing by. I don't mean he is here, but he has promised to remain available for 3 or 4 days.

MR. HISS: To whom should my reply be addressed?

MR. NIXON: To the chairman of the committee. I might say also that the matter of emotion, of course, as you pointed out, enters into the test. One thing the members of the committee both remarked about is that Mr. Chambers is also a very emotional man.

MR. HISS: Have you ever had any experience with it yourself when you were practicing, Mr. Nixon?

MR. NIXON: No; I have not.

MR. HISS: But you do have confidence in it?

MR. NIXON: Frankly, I have made a study of it in the last week before I put the question. In fact, for the past 2 weeks I have been studying it and have been in correspondence with Mr. Keeler.

MR. HISS: You do have confidence in it as a device?

MR. NIXON: I have. Let me say this: I have confidence that it is a factor which will be helpful in this case. I realize there is no factor which can be conclusive in this case, and I don't pretend that that is the case, but I do have confidence it would be helpful in this case to be weighed with the other facts in the matter.

MR. HISS: I will take that into account.

• • •

MR. HÉBERT: Can you search through your mind, recall or suggest any reason why a man named Whittaker Chambers should give such testimony involving you, and motive?

MR. HISS: I cannot, sir, and I would like to say that this is one of the things I have puzzled and puzzled with.

MR. HÉBERT: Through your connection and association with people on Time and Life, as you undoubtedly have, did you inquire of Chambers?

MR. HISS: On the way down to the public hearing I ran into an editor of Fortune whom I know only slightly, but the man I was with knew him very well, and I asked him because I hadn't found anybody who knew him. I had asked various press people who were asking me for statements if they knew him, and they did not. I have asked various friends who knew people on Time if they could find out more about his personality and what he is like. I haven't heard any reply. This man on Fortune gave an off-hand reaction.

MR. HÉBERT: You didn't just toss it off without trying to find out about Chambers.

MR. NIXON: Was Mr. Crosley a member of the Communist Party?

MR. HISS: Not to my knowledge.

MR. NIXON: Never discussed it?

MR. HISS: No.

MR. NIXON: You feel he might be Whittaker Chambers?

MR. HISS: I find it difficult to believe. I can't identify him from the pictures and can't see any motive.

MR. NIXON: You haven't the slightest idea what became of him?

MR. HISS: No; haven't seen him since 1935.

MR. NIXON: Where was he working at the time you knew him?

MR. HISS: I was working in Washington in the Senate and he was here to get information in order to write articles.

MR. NIXON: For whom did he work? Who was his employer?

MR. HISS: He told me he was a free-lance writer preparing a series of articles which he had no doubt he would be able to market; that he had written for various magazines.

MR. NIXON: What magazines had he written for?

MR. HISS: He told me he had written for American magazine; I think he told me he had written for Cosmopolitan.

MR. NIXON: You are sure about his telling you about writing for American?

MR. HISS: Yes; I am sure of that.

MR. NIXON: Never indicated where he worked or who he worked for?

MR. HISS: He was a free-lance writer.

MR. HÉBERT: Did you ever see his name attached to an article?

MR. HISS: He never sold one of the articles.

MR. HÉBERT: Did you ever see his name attached to an article?

MR. HISS: No.

MR. HÉBERT: Never saw anything he wrote?

MR. HISS: No.

MR. NIXON: Did he pay any rent all the time he was in your house?

MR. HISS: My recollection is he paid $15 or $20, and he gave me a rug, which I have still got.

MR. NIXON: You had hard words when he left?

MR. HISS: Yes, in the sense that I said, "Let's not talk any more about your ever paying back. I don't think you ever intend to, and I would rather forget all of this, and I think you have simply welshed from the beginning."

MR. NIXON: In other words, this wasn't sufficient motive—

MR. HISS: I didn't ask him to leave the house, but I practically did, and haven't seen him since. I made it plain I wouldn't be a sucker.

MR. NIXON: Do you know his middle initial?

MR. HISS: No; If I did I don't remember.

MR. NIXON: Would you say this would be sufficient motive to do what Whittaker Chambers has done?

MR. HISS: No. That is why I say I can't believe it was the same man. I can't imagine a normal man holding a grudge because somebody had stopped being a sucker.

New York Herald Tribune Publishes Account of Hiss Testimony

Despite the fact that Hiss had testified in executive session and been assured of the confidentiality of the proceedings, details of his testimony appeared in a *New York Herald Tribune* article written by Carl Levin. Later evidence clearly indicated that Nixon had leaked the information to the press. Levin was assigned to the newspaper's Washington bureau, which was headed by Bert Andrews, a confidante of Nixon's. In *Six Crises,* Nixon admitted that he had shown Andrews transcripts of the session with Hiss in order "to check the objectivity of [Nixon's] own judgment against the opinions of men [he] respected."[7]

Most disturbing to Hiss was the article's portrayal of his hesitance to agree to a lie-detector test, a test that "heretofore . . . has been limited exclusively to persons charged with crime." The article noted that one of the principals, Hiss and Chambers, had committed perjury. While it correctly stated that evidence did not exist at the time to determine which was guilty, Hiss's reluctance to subject himself to this test clearly left the implication that he had something to hide. The article exacerbated the adversarial atmosphere when Hiss once again appeared before the committee.

"LIE-DETECTOR TEST PROPOSED TO ALGER HISS"

Carl Levin

WASHINGTON, Aug. 16—A lie detector test administered by a prominent Chicago criminologist was proposed today by the House Committee on Un-American Activities to determine whether Alger Hiss, former top State Department official, or his accuser, Whittaker Chambers, is telling the truth about Communist involvement.

The proposal, it was learned, was made by the committee to Mr. Hiss during a three-hour executive session today from which the committee emerged still unable to tell whether the charges of Communist activity against Mr. Hiss are reliable.

Mr. Chambers, self-styled former Communist and now a senior editor of "Time" magazine, who accused Mr. Hiss in public testimony before the committee, already has agreed to undergo the test.

Mr. Hiss, who has denied under oath—a denial which he reiterated today in detail—that he ever knew Mr. Chambers or ever was a Communist, was asked by the committee for an answer by Wednesday morning as to whether he, too, would submit to the lie detector.

DOUBTFUL OF RELIABILITY

Mr. Hiss's immediate reaction to the proposal was that he considers the lie detector an unreliable instrument which measures emotions rather than veracity. However, he agreed to give the committee a formal answer by Wednesday morning. Indications tonight were that under certain conditions he will agree to the test, which would be unique in the history of Congressional investigations.

The spectacle of the former ranking State Department official, now president of the Carnegie Endowment for International Peace, and a senior editor of one of the nation's popular news magazines submitting to a scientific lie test would be, without precedent. It also undoubtedly would be behind closed doors, and would not be a spectacle, which the public would be permitted to witness.

Heretofore use of the lie detector has been limited exclusively to persons charged with crime. In this case no charge of a crime has been

Source: New York Herald Tribune, August 17, 1948.

made, although the crime of perjury has been committed by one or the other of the two men in their conflicting testimony given under oath before the committee.

KEELER CONSULTED

Representative J. Parnell Thomas, Republican, of New Jersey, chairman of the committee, already has consulted Leonarde Keeler, developer of a polygraph, popularly referred to as a lie detector, which records blood pressure, respiration and other physical reactions which may arise in deception tests. Mr. Keeler, considered the leading authority in the nation on this still controversial method of testing a person's truthfulness, has agreed to administer the test in Washington.

Meanwhile, the committee arranged with Mr. Hiss today to have a subcommittee question his wife in New York on aspects of the Chambers' story in which she figured.

Mr. Chambers, as one of the committee's two star witnesses at the current hearings on Communist activities and espionage, has reiterated, since Mr. Hiss's public denial, his original allegation that Mr. Hiss was a member of an "elite" underground Communist group in Washington in the middle 1930s.

Mr. Chambers is also standing on his story that when he renounced communism he went to Mr. Hiss's home here and pleaded with the State Department official to do the same. Mr. Hiss, the witness stated, was so emotionally moved by the plea that he had tears in his eyes, but did not act upon the plea.

Mr. Hiss, publicly before the committee and again today in executive session, has sworn under oath that no such incident ever took place, that he did not know Mr. Chambers and that Mr. Chambers never was in his home.

It is this particular aspect of the diametrically opposed testimony that the committee would seek to resolve through a lie detector test.

Representative Thomas also announced that the committee will bring Mr. Hiss and Mr. Chambers together to face each other at 10:30 a.m., Aug. 25, and will resume its espionage hearings on Sept. 7.

In its prolonged questioning of Mr. Hiss today the committee interrogated him about many bits of testimony which Mr. Chambers has given in private to substantiate his story that he knew Mr. Hiss.

• • •

"From the testimony of the two witnesses," Chairman Thomas announced after today's closed session, "It is impossible at this point to tell which one is telling the truth. The committee is taking every step to determine the true facts. The committee will have the investigative staff check on every possible corroborative detail, this to be implemented by daily executive sessions of two subcommittees meeting in Washington and other places."

"Testimony up to this point has been turned over and will be turned over to the United States Attorney, who is receiving the committee's complete co-operation."

George Morris Fay, United States Attorney for the District of Columbia, obtained the committee's record last week in a move of his own to determine whether perjury had been committed before the committee, and to prosecute if prosecution is warranted.

After today's three-hour session Mr. Hiss emerged from the committee room with a set, determined face, but he refused to answer any of the many questions reporters shot at him as he walked away. One of these was whether he had been asked to submit to a lie detector test.

"Any statement at this time ought to come from the committee," was the youthful-looking witness's only comment.

Hiss and Chambers Meet at the Commodore Hotel, New York City

The face-to-face meeting with Chambers that Hiss had requested came on August 17. A subcommittee of HUAC consisting of Congressmen Thomas, McDowell, Hébert, and Nixon, along with investigator Stripling, traveled to New York City. In Room 1400 of the Commodore Hotel, Hiss and Chambers were brought together.

Hiss was escorted into the room first. In preliminary remarks, he noted that he was not in "the best possible mood." He had just learned of the death of Harry Dexter White, another former New Deal official accused of being a Communist. Furthermore, he was angry that his previous testimony had leaked despite insurances that it was confidential. Nixon, rather disingenuously, denied that the leaks had emanated from members of the committee.

Then Chambers was ushered into the room. After hearing Chambers's voice and questioning him about his teeth, Hiss confirmed that this man was indeed the George Crosley he had known in the mid-1930s. During the proceedings, Hiss challenged Chambers to make his charges in a public venue where he would not be immune from a libel suit, as was the case of his testimony before HUAC. This challenge would later be instrumental in the escalation of the whole affair.

THE HISS-CHAMBERS ENCOUNTER, HOTEL COMMODORE, NEW YORK CITY, AUGUST 17, 1948

MR. STRIPLING: The purpose of the meeting is for the committee to continue to determine the truth or falsity of the testimony which has been given by Mr. Whittaker Chambers. Do you want to proceed, Mr. Nixon?

MR. NIXON: Yes. It is quite apparent at this state in the testimony, as you indicated yesterday, that the case is dependent upon the question of identity. We have attempted to establish the identity through photographs of Mr. Chambers and that has been inadequate for that purpose. Today, we thought that since you had in your testimony raised the possibility of a third party who might be involved in this case in some way and had described him at some length to the committee that it would be well to, at the earliest possible time, determine whether the third party is different from the two parties or the same one, and so consequently we have asked Mr. Chambers to be in New York at the same time so that you can have the opportunity to see him and make up your own mind on that point.

• • •

MR. HISS: I would like the record to show that on my way downtown from my uptown office, I learned from the press of the death of Harry White, which came as a great shock to me, and I am not sure that I feel in the best possible mood for testimony. I do not for a moment want to miss the opportunity of seeing Mr. Chambers. I merely wanted the record to show that.

I would like to make one further comment. Yesterday, I think I witnessed—in any event, I was told that those in the room were going to take an oath of secrecy. I made some comments before I answered certain questions of Mr. Nixon which I had not intended as a reflection on the committee, but which some members of the committee thought implied that. I was referring merely to the possibility of leakage of information. I would like this record to show at this stage that the first thing I saw in the morning paper, the Herald Tribune, was a statement that the committee yesterday had asked me if I would submit to a lie-detector test.

I would also like the record to show at this point that on my way down from my uptown office to keep this appointment after I got Mr. McDowell's telegram, I read in the papers that it was understood that in the course of my testimony yesterday the committee asked me, the subcommittee asked me, if I could arrange to have Mrs. Hiss be examined privately. You will recall, and I hope the record will show, that Mr. Nixon assured me with great consideration that you desired to talk to Mrs. Hiss without any publicity. This was less than 24 hours after you had been so considerate.

Source: Hearings Regarding Communist Espionage in the United States Government, 975–79, 984–89, 991–92.

There were other statements in the press which I read coming down which referred to other bits of my testimony which could only have come from the committee. They did not come from me.

I would like the record to show that is why I asked if I could bring Mr. Dollard, a personal friend, to be with me at this particular time.

MR. NIXON: In that connection, Mr. Hiss, I might suggest that in order to satisfy your own mind as to how that information may have gotten into the press that you get in touch with Mr. Carl Levin, the correspondent for the New York Herald Tribune, who wrote the story.

MR. HISS: I have no reason to get in touch with Mr. Carl Levin. The assurances I had came from the committee.

MR. NIXON: I suggest you do so, because I think you will find that Mr. Levin's information is that he obtained the information from sources outside the committee and outside the committee staff, and I can assure you that no member of this committee or no member of the staff discussed the matter with Mr. Levin at all. That was the only source of this information.

MR. HISS: Mr. Nixon, I didn't say anybody discussed it with Mr. Levin. I said someone must have given information. How Mr. Levin got it, I do not know. I said it did not come from me as a source, either directly or indirectly. I don't want to say any more about it, but like the record to show.

MR. MCDOWELL: The Chair would like to say something. I, too, was greatly disturbed when I read the morning paper. Obviously, there was a leak, because the story that appeared in the various papers I read was part of the activities of yesterday afternoon. I have no idea how this story got out. In my own case, I very carefully guarded myself last night, saw and talked to no one except my wife in Pittsburgh. It is regrettable and unfortunate.

Further than that, I don't know what else to say other than if it was an employee of the committee, and I should discover it, he will no longer be an employee of the committee. As a Member of Congress, there is nothing I can do about that. It is a regrettable thing, and I join you in feeling rather rotten about the whole thing.

MR. HISS: I didn't mean to make any charges but meant to state certain facts which have occurred which I think have a bearing on the reason I made the statements I made to the committee yesterday before I went on with certain parts of my testimony.

MR. MCDOWELL: I want to assure Mr. Dollard he is very welcome.

MR. NIXON: Mr. Russell, will you bring Mr. Chambers in?

MR. RUSSELL: Yes.

(Mr. Russell leaves room and returns accompanied by Mr. Chambers.)

MR. NIXON: Sit over here, Mr. Chambers.

Mr. Chambers, will you please stand?

And will you please stand, Mr. Hiss?

Mr. Hiss, the man standing here is Mr. Whittaker Chambers. I ask you now if you have ever known that man before?

MR. HISS: May I ask him to speak?

Will you ask him to say something?

MR. NIXON: Yes.

Mr. Chambers, will you tell us your name and your business?

MR. CHAMBERS: My name is Whittaker Chambers.

(At this point, Mr. Hiss walked in the direction of Mr. Chambers.)

MR. HISS: Would you mind opening your mouth wider?

MR. CHAMBERS: My name is Whittaker Chambers.

MR. HISS: I said, would you open your mouth?

You know what I am referring to, Mr. Nixon.

Will you go on talking?

MR. CHAMBERS: I am senior editor of Time magazine.

MR. HISS: May I ask whether his voice, when he testified before, was comparable to this?

MR. NIXON: His voice?

MR. HISS: Or did he talk a little more in a lower key?

MR. McDOWELL: I would say it is about the same now as we have heard.

MR. HISS: Would you ask him to talk a little more?

MR. NIXON: Read something, Mr. Chambers. I will let you read from—

MR. HISS: I think he is George Crosley, but I would like to hear him talk a little longer.

MR. McDOWELL: Mr. Chambers, if you would be more comfortable, you may sit down.

MR. HISS: Are you George Crosley?

MR. CHAMBERS: Not to my knowledge. You are Alger Hiss, I believe.

MR. HISS: I certainly am.

MR. CHAMBERS: That was my recollection. (Reading:)

Since June—

MR. NIXON: (interposing) Just one moment. Since some repartee goes on between these two people, I think Mr. Chambers should be sworn.

MR. HISS: That is a good idea.

MR. McDOWELL: You do solemnly swear, sir, that the testimony you shall give this committee will be the truth, the whole truth, and nothing but the truth, so help you God?

MR. CHAMBERS: I do.

MR. NIXON: Mr. Hiss, may I say something? I suggested that he be sworn, and when I say something like that I want no interruptions from you.

MR. HISS: Mr. Nixon, in view of what happened yesterday, I think there is no occasion for you to use that tone of voice in speaking to me, and I hope the record will show what I have just said.

MR. NIXON: The record shows everything that is being said here today.

MR. STRIPLING: You were going to read.

MR. CHAMBERS: (reading from Newsweek magazine)

Tobin for Labor. Since June, Harry S. Truman had been peddling the labor secretaryship left vacant by Lewis B. Schwellenbach's death in hope of gaining the maximum political advantage from the appointment.

MR. HISS: May I interrupt?

MR. McDOWELL: Yes.

MR. HISS: The voice sounds a little less resonant than the voice that I recall of the man I knew as George Crosley. The teeth look to me as though either they have been improved upon or that there has been considerable dental work done since I knew George Crosley, which was some years ago.

I believe I am not prepared without further checking to take an absolute oath that he must be George Crosley.

MR. NIXON: May I ask a question of Mr. Chambers?

MR. HISS: I would like to ask Mr. Chambers, if I may.

MR. NIXON: I will ask the questions at this time.

Mr. Chambers, have you had any dental work since 1934 of a substantial nature?

MR. CHAMBERS: Yes; I have.

MR. NIXON: What type of dental work?

MR. CHAMBERS: I have had some extractions and a plate.

MR. NIXON: Have you had any dental work in the front of your mouth?

MR. CHAMBERS: Yes.

MR. NIXON: What is the nature of that work?

MR. CHAMBERS: That is a plate in place of some of the upper dentures.

MR. NIXON: I see.

MR. HISS: Could you ask him the name of the dentist that performed these things? Is that appropriate?

MR. NIXON: Yes. What is the name?

MR. CHAMBERS: Dr. Hitchcock. Westminster, Md.

MR. HISS: That testimony of Mr. Chambers, if it can be believed, would tend to substantiate my feeling that he represented himself to me in 1934 or 1935 or thereabout as George Crosley, a free lance writer of articles for magazines.

I would like to find out from Dr. Hitchcock if what he has just said is true, because I am relying partly, one of my main recollections of Crosley was the poor condition of his teeth.

MR. NIXON: Can you describe the condition of your teeth in 1934?

MR. CHAMBERS: Yes. They were in very bad shape.

MR. NIXON: The front teeth were?

MR. CHAMBERS: Yes; I think so.

• • •

MR. STRIPLING: Mr. Hiss, you say that person you knew as George Crosley, the one feature which you must have to check on to identify him is the dentures.

MR. HISS: May I answer that my own way rather than just "Yes" or "No"?

MR. STRIPLING: Well, now, I would like to preface whatever you are going to say by what I say first.

I certainly gathered the impression when Mr. Chambers walked in this room and you walked over and examined him and asked him to open his mouth, that you were basing your identification purely on what his upper teeth might have looked like.

Now, here is a person that you knew for several months at least. You knew him so well that he was a guest in your home.

MR. HISS: Would you—

MR. STRIPLING: I would like to complete my statement—that he was a guest in your home, that you gave him an old Ford automobile, and permitted him to use, or you leased him your apartment and in this, a very important confrontation, the only thing that you have to check on is this denture; is that correct?

There is nothing else about this man's features which you could definitely say, "This is the man I knew as George Crosley," that you have to rely entirely on this denture; is that your position?

MR. HISS: Is your preface through? My answer to the question you have asked is this:

From the time on Wednesday, August 4, 1948, when I was able to get hold of newspapers containing photographs of one Whittaker Chambers, I was struck by a certain familiarity in features. When I testified on August 5 and was shown a photograph by you, Mr. Stripling, there was again some familiarity features. I could not be sure that I had never seen the person whose photograph you showed me. I said I would want to see the person.

The photographs are rather good photographs of Whittaker Chambers as I see Whittaker Chambers today. I am not given on important occasions to snap judgments or simple, easy statements. I am confident that George Crosley had notably bad teeth. I would not call George Crosley a guest in my house. I have explained the circumstances. If you choose to call him a guest, that is your affair.

MR. STRIPLING: I am willing to strike the word "guest." He was in your house.

MR. HISS: I saw him at the time I was seeing hundreds of people. Since then I have seen thousands of people. He meant nothing to me except as one I saw under the circumstances I have described.

My recollection of George Crosley, if this man had said he was George Crosley, I would have no difficulty in identification. He denied it right here.

I would like and asked earlier in this hearing if I could ask some further questions to help in identification. I was denied that.

MR. STRIPLING: I think you should be permitted—

MR. HISS: I was denied that right. I am not, therefore, able to take an oath that this man is George Crosley. I have been testifying about George Crosley. Whether he and this man are the same or whether he has means of getting information from George Crosley about my house, I do not know. He may have had his face lifted.

MR. STRIPLING: The witness says he was denied the right to ask this witness questions. I believe the record will show you stated "at this time." I think he should be permitted to ask the witness questions now or any other motion should be granted which will permit him to determine whether or not this is the individual to whom he is referring.

MR. HISS: Right. I would be very happy if I could pursue that. Do I have the Chair's permission?

MR. McDOWELL: The Chair will agree to that.

MR. HISS: Do I have Mr. Nixon's permission.

MR. NIXON: Yes.

MR. McDOWELL: Here is a very difficult situation.

MR. NIXON: The only suggestion I would make in fairness to Mr. Chambers is that he should also be given the opportunity to ask Mr. Hiss any questions.

MR. McDOWELL: Of course.

MR. HISS: I will welcome that.

MR. NIXON: Mr. Chambers, do you have any objection?

MR. CHAMBERS: No.

MR. HISS: Did you ever go under the name of George Crosley?

MR. CHAMBERS: Not to my knowledge.

MR. HISS: Did you ever sublet an apartment on Twenty-ninth Street from me?

MR. CHAMBERS: No; I did not.

MR. HISS: You did not?

MR. CHAMBERS: No.

MR. HISS: Did you ever spend any time with your wife and child in an apartment on Twenty-ninth Street in Washington when I was not there because I and my family were living on P Street?

MR. CHAMBERS: I most certainly did.

MR. HISS: You did or did not?

MR. CHAMBERS: I did.

MR. HISS: Would you tell me how you reconcile your negative answers with this affirmative answer?

MR. CHAMBERS: Very easily, Alger. I was a Communist and you were a Communist.

MR. HISS: Would you be responsive and continue with your answer?

MR. CHAMBERS: I do not think it is needed.

MR. HISS: That is the answer.

MR. NIXON: I will help you with the answer, Mr. Hiss. The question, Mr. Chambers, is, as I understand it, that Mr. Hiss cannot understand how you would deny that you were George Crosley and yet admit that you spent time in his apartment. Now would you explain the circumstances? I don't want to put that until Mr. Hiss agrees that is one of his questions.

MR. HISS: You have the privilege of asking any questions you want. I think that is an accurate phrasing.

MR. NIXON: Go ahead.

MR. CHAMBERS: As I have testified before, I came to Washington as a Communist functionary, a functionary of the American Communist Party. I was connected with the underground group of which Mr. Hiss was a member. Mr. Hiss and I became friends. To the best of my knowledge, Mr. Hiss himself suggested that I go there, and I accepted gratefully.

MR. HISS: Mr. Chairman.

MR. NIXON: Just a moment. How long did you stay there?

MR. CHAMBERS: My recollection was about 3 weeks. It may have been longer. I brought no furniture, I might add.

MR. HISS: Mr. Chairman, I don't need to ask Mr. Whittaker Chambers any more questions. I am now perfectly prepared to identify this man as George Crosley.

MR. NIXON: Would you spell that name?

MR. HISS: C-r-o-s-l-e-y.

MR. NIXON: You are sure of one "s"?

MR. HISS: That is my recollection. I have a rather good visual memory, and my recollection of his spelling of his name is C-r-o-s-l-e-y. I don't think that would change as much as his appearance.

MR. STRIPLING: You will identify him positively now?

MR. HISS: I will on the basis of what he has just said positively identify him without further questioning as George Crosley.

MR. STRIPLING: Will you produce for the committee three people who will testify that they knew him as George Crosley?

MR. HISS: I will if it is possible. Why is that a question to ask me? I will see what is possible. This occurred in 1935. The only people that I can think of who would have known him as George Crosley with certainty would have been the people who were associated with me in the Nye Committee.

● ● ●

MR. NIXON: Mr. Hiss, another point that I want to be clear on, Mr. Chambers said he was a Communist and that you were a Communist.

MR. HISS: I heard him.

MR. NIXON: Will you tell the committee whether or not during this period of time that you knew him, which included periods of 3 nights, or 2 or 3 nights, in which he stayed overnight and one trip to New York, from any conversation you ever had any idea that he might be a Communist?

MR. HISS: I certainly didn't.

MR. NIXON: You never discussed politics?

MR. HISS: Oh, as far as I recall his conversations—and I may be confusing them with a lot of other conversations that went on in 1934 and 1935— politics were discussed quite frequently.

May I just state for the record that it was not the habit in Washington in those days, when particularly if a member of the press called on you, to ask him before you had further conversation whether or not he was a Communist. It was a quite different atmosphere in Washington then than today. I had no reason to suspect George Crosley of being a Communist. It never occurred to me that he might be or whether that was of any significance to me if he was. He was a press representative and it was my duty to give him information, as I did any other member of the press.

It was to the interest of the committee investigating the munitions industry, as its members and we of its staff saw it, to furnish guidance and information to people who were popularizing and writing about its work.

I would like to say that to come here and discover that the ass under the lion's skin is Crosley. I don't know why your committee didn't pursue this careful method of interrogation at an earlier date before all the publicity. You told me yesterday you didn't know he was going to mention my name, although a lot of people now tell me that the press did know it in advance. They were apparently more effective in getting information than the committee itself. That is all I have to say now.

MR. McDOWELL: Well, now, Mr. Hiss, you positively identify—

MR. HISS: Positively on the basis of his own statement that he was in my apartment at the time when I say he was there. I have no further question at all. If he had lost both eyes and taken his nose off, I would be sure.

MR. McDOWELL: Then, your identification of George Crosely is complete?

MR. HISS: Yes, as far as I am concerned, on his own testimony.

MR. McDOWELL: Mr. Chambers, is this the man, Alger Hiss, who was also a member of the Communist Party at whose home you stayed?

MR. NIXON: According to your testimony.

MR. McDOWELL: You make the identification positive?

MR. CHAMBERS: Positive identification.

(At this point, Mr. Hiss arose and walked in the direction of Mr. Chambers.)

MR. HISS: May I say for the record at this point, that I would like to invite Mr. Whittaker Chambers to make those same statements out of the presence of this committee without their being privileged for suit for libel. I challenge you to do it, and I hope you will do it damned quickly.

I am not going to touch him [addressing Mr. Russell]. You are touching me.

MR. RUSSELL: Please sit down, Mr. Hiss.

MR. HISS: I will sit down when the chairman asks me.

Mr. Russell, when the chairman asks me to sit down—

MR. RUSSELL: I want no disturbance.

MR. HISS: I don't—

MR. McDOWELL: Sit down, please.

MR. HISS: You know who started this.

MR. McDOWELL: We will suspend testimony here for a minute or two, until I return.

(Short recess.)

MR. HISS: Mr. Chairman, would you be good enough to ask Mr. Chambers for the record his response to the challenge that I have just made to him?

MR. McDOWELL: That has nothing to do with the pertinency of the matter that the committee is investigating, and I don't feel I should.

MR. HISS: I thought the committee was interested in ascertaining truth.

MR. STRIPLING: What is the challenge?

MR. McDOWELL: That he, Mr. Chambers, would make those statements he has made before the committee in public where they would not be privileged under congressional immunity. That I would take it would be strictly a matter up to Mr. Chambers and Mr. Hiss, but I don't feel the committee has any proper or parliamentary right to ask such a question.

MR. STRIPLING: I don't think it is necessary that he do so. He has made those statements many times to the Government, and that is not privileged.

MR. HISS: I am advised by counsel that they were probably privileged. Are you a lawyer?

MR. STRIPLING: After a fashion.

MR. NIXON: I am a lawyer.

MR. HISS: It is your opinion they are not privileged?

MR. NIXON: It is my opinion if a statement is made to an investigative officer not under subpena, but voluntarily, voluntarily by the witness, that the statement would not be privileged. If the statement is made in this hearing, of course, it is privileged.

   If we subpoena Mr. Chambers, it is privileged, but if Mr. Chambers goes to somebody in the Government, we will say, on his own, and makes certain charges concerning you, I don't think you certainly would claim they are privileged.

● ● ●

MR. NIXON: You never knew this man under the name of Carl?

MR. HISS: I did not.

MR. NIXON: You never paid this man any money for Communist Party dues?

MR. HISS: I certainly did not.

MR. NIXON: This is the man you gave the car to?

MR. HISS: The car?

MR. NIXON: Yes.

MR. HISS: C-a-r—yes.

MR. CHAMBERS: May I ask a question?

MR. NIXON: Yes.

MR. CHAMBERS: Did you ever pay dues to J. Peters?

MR. HISS: I certainly did not.

MR. CHAMBERS: To Henry Collins?

MR. HISS: I certainly did not; not even for the Audubon Society did I pay dues to Henry Collins.

MR. NIXON: Did you ever discuss your hobby, ornithology, with this man?

MR. HISS: I may very likely have. My house has pictures very similar to that [indicating picture on wall]. This is an appropriate hearing room.

MR. McDOWELL: It was a complete coincidence.

MR. HISS: Anyone who had ever been in my house would remark that I had an interest in birds.

MR. NIXON: Do you know if this man you knew as Crosley was an ornithologist?

MR. HISS: Not to my knowledge.

MR. NIXON: You have never given Crosley anything you recall besides the car?

MR. HISS: I have no such recollection. I don't consider I gave him the car, but threw it in with the whole transaction.

MR. NIXON: I understand you had it sublet for $225 and gave him the car.

MR. HISS: May I say I resent the implication of the statement. I take it it was not a question.

MR. NIXON: That is all. Mr. McDowell?

MR. McDOWELL: Mr. Hiss, did you ever have a dinner or a meal with George Crosley?

MR. HISS: I think we fed him when he was in the house for a couple of days. That is my custom with people staying under my roof.

MR. McDOWELL: You are not sure?

MR. HISS: I know I have had lunch with him, because it was my practice, and still is, that if someone wants to talk to me about a matter that requires relatively lengthy discussion, a luncheon discussion has a termination. If they come to see you in your office, it is not quite so easy to terminate it at your own convenience.

MR. McDOWELL: Did this fellow have any characteristics or habits that you can recall now?

MR. HISS: No; not of significance, except his bad teeth.

MR. McDOWELL: Would you know whether—aside from his bad teeth, would you know whether he was a heavy drinker or modest drinker, or nondrinker?

MR. HISS: I have no information about that.

MR. McDOWELL: Did you ever take a walk with him?

MR. HISS: That I couldn't be sure. I certainly must have walked to lunch if we went to lunch from the Senate Office Building. You had to walk quite a distance to get to any restaurant from the Senate Office Building.

MR. McDOWELL: It would appear to me, Mr. Hiss, of all the newspaper men that you were in contact in your highly important jobs with the Nye committee that you must have formed some sort of an affection for this man to go through all of the things that you did to try to occupy your home, take over your lease, and give him an automobile.

New York Herald Tribune Again Reveals Committee Proceedings

Once again, there were leaks. Bert Andrews, writing in the *New York Herald Tribune,* detailed what had happened in the New York hotel room and praised Nixon for his "bulldog tenacity" and determination to root out the liar. The article noted that the committee was hopeful to get answers that thus far had eluded the Federal Bureau of Investigation and the federal grand jury. This was particularly important because of the 1948 presidential campaign and Truman's insistence that the whole investigation was a "red herring."

Andrews's piece also provided background information that fanned suspicions in the Hiss camp that Chambers and the committee were collaborating. Chambers, mistakenly believing this session was to be held in Washington, took the same train to New York as did the committee members.

"ALGER HISS NOW ADMITS HE KNEW CHAMBERS, BUT NOT BY HIS OWN NAME"

Bert Andrews

WASHINGTON, Aug. 17—The two most prominent antagonists in the Congressional investigation of espionage came face to face tonight in a room in the Commodore Hotel in New York City and the dramatic and far-reaching results were:

1. Alger Hiss, who went to his present job as president of the Carnegie Endowment for International Peace after ten years in the State Department, admitted he knew—under another name—Whittaker Chambers, who had accused him of being one of a seven-man Communist underground "apparatus" that operated in Washington.
2. Mr. Hiss, who had twice previously denied knowing Mr. Chambers by that name or as "Carl," which Mr. Chambers said was his Communist cover name, said he had known him under the name of George Crosley.
3. Mr. Chambers, who went to "Time" magazine after he broke with the Communist party and is now a senior editor of the magazine, reiterated earlier testimony that Mr. Hiss knew him as "Carl," knew full well that "Carl" was a Communist functionary, and was, himself, a "dedicated" Communist worker who paid dues and toiled secretly for the party.
4. Mr. Hiss, with his job and reputation at stake, just as Mr. Chambers' job and reputation are at stake, repeated his denial that he is or ever was a Communist and told the committee that his relationship with Mr. Chambers was entirely innocent.

CONGRESSMEN ARE PRESENT

The dramatic confrontation came in a hotel room in which the onlookers were Representative J. Parnell Thomas, Republican, of New Jersey; Representative John McDowell, Republican, of Pennsylvania, Representative Richard M. Nixon, Republican, of California, and a stenographic reporter, W. P. Bannister.

The Hiss-Chambers meeting—and the startling disclosures—were, primarily, the result of the bulldog tenacity of Mr. Nixon, who

Source: New York Herald Tribune, August 18, 1948.

had hammered away at this particular phase of the investigation after other committee members were inclined to give up and say: "Somebody's lying, but we can't tell who."

Mr. Nixon, it was clear to anybody who had read the testimony taken before the committee when Mr. Hiss and Mr. Chambers appeared separately in open session, took the position that the stories were so diametrically opposite that some one just had to be lying—and that there had to be some way of showing it.

Mr. Nixon tried to show it.

It was a difficult task.

If the committee could show it, it would be something more tangible than the Federal Bureau of Investigation and the Federal grand jury in New York City had been able to show after long inquiries into all the talk of espionage.

If the committee could show it—and then prove it—it would play a part in the 1948 national political campaign, inasmuch as President Truman has termed the whole investigation a red herring and Republicans have disputed it.

Mr. Nixon persuaded the other committee members to advance the confrontation a week.

DID NOT RECOGNIZE PHOTO

He and the others had this knowledge:

1. That Mr. Hiss, in open session, had denied knowing "a man named Whittaker Chambers" and, when shown a photograph, had said he didn't recognize it as any one he knew, Mr. Hiss was not asked specifically whether he knew "Carl" and so did not answer it.
2. That Mr. Hiss, in executive session yesterday said he knew a George Crosley, that he once sublet an apartment in Washington to him, that he "threw in" an automobile he had, that he never collected any rent from "Mr. Crosley" and that he broke with "Mr. Crosley" because the latter was a deadbeat and no good.
3. Mr. Hiss again denied, at the executive session, that he knew "Carl" and that he, Hiss, was a Communist. He said he did not recognize the pictures of Mr. Chambers—he was shown them again—as any one he knew. But he was not positive.
4. Mr. Nixon and the other committee members who were in Washington yesterday and today got to thinking things over. Was there a connection between "Crosley" and Chambers or "Carl?"

The upshot was that the committee notified Mr. Chambers and Mr. Hiss that it wanted to see them in New York.

Mr. Chambers, on his job in New York, misunderstood. He thought he was wanted in Washington.

He came to Washington and walked up to one of the House office buildings just as the three committee members were leaving it.

The committee members, Mr. Chambers and Mr. Bannister, the reporter, boarded a train.

Now, the committee members have become very sensitive to criticism and to leaks.

Pro-Hiss people have suggested that members have "leaked" stuff to Mr. Chambers. Pro-Chambers people have suggested that members have "leaked" stuff to Mr. Hiss.

And so, for most of the train trip, the three committee members sat by themselves. Mr. Chambers and Mr. Bannister, the reporter, sat in the club car

So it was, with Mr. Bannister as a companion of Mr. Chambers most of the way, and present when he sat down for a snack with the others, that the committee protected itself against charges that it aided or abetted Mr. Chambers so he could accuse Mr. Hiss.

ROOM AT THE COMMODORE

When the train arrived in New York City, the party went to Room 1400 in the Commodore Hotel.

The six—Mr. Hiss, Mr. Chambers, Mr. Thomas, Mr. McDowell, Mr. Nixon and Mr. Bannister were there slightly more than an hour and a half.

Only a formal announcement was issued of what went on—an announcement followed by the revelation that the two men would again have a chance to tell all in a public hearing in Washington on Aug. 25—a week hence.

It was known, that Chairman Thomas would tell the two antagonists something like this:

"Look, we know some one's lying. You two will have to agree to that. And so, Mr. Hiss, we ask you if you have ever laid eyes on this man under any name."

This reporter has reason to believe Mr. Hiss's story was something like this:

1. He did recognize the man face to face, where had not recognized him by photographs (He had been shown three photographs in all at two previous sessions.) or by the names of "Chambers" or "Carl."

2. He recognized him as a free-lance writer that he and Mrs. Hiss had known back in 1934 and 1935. Also as a man they sublet the

apartment to for a brief period of time. Also as a man who did not pay the rent or reimburse him for the car that he "threw in."

3. But, Mr. Hiss did not know that "Mr. Crosley" was a Communist, did not see how it affected his basic testimony before the committee, and adhered to the fact that he was never a Communist and never gave away any secrets.

4. Mr. Hiss, in the belief his first testimony in open session should have been enough to convince the committee, was obviously disturbed at the session in the Commodore Hotel and was particularly burned at Mr. Chambers.

VERSION OF CHAMBERS'S STORY

This reporter has reason to believe that Mr. Chambers was also disturbed, too, and that he took a stand along these lines:

1. What motive could he, Mr. Chambers, have for lying about Mr. Hiss and the others he named as members of the Communist "apparatus" in Washington?

2. What motive, inasmuch as it might be deemed a foregone conclusion that he'd lose his $30,000-a-year job with "Time" magazine if he were proved a liar?

3. He doesn't ever remember using the name Crosley in Washington. He insists he was known to Mr. Hiss—and Mrs. Hiss— as Carl, and he thinks they came to know what his real name—Chambers—was.

4. He is willing to submit to a lie detector test on his testimony. (Mr. Hiss, reports said yesterday, may be similarly willing but will not announce his decision until tomorrow—Wednesday.)

5. He was a Communist courier between 1934 and 1937 and he visited Mr. and Mrs. Hiss at their homes many times.

Mr. Nixon, after the confrontation today, said:

"Mr. Hiss gave the impression to the public that he had never known this man at all under any name. This identification is a direct contrast with that impression. We were trying to see if there was—or could possibly be—a mistake in identity.

"We have tried to be scrupulously fair in all this.

"All we want is the truth.

"That is all, in my opinion, that the public wants.

"Now that we have the stories, we will have the public hearing.

"The committee will question them as to every single phase of their relationship.

"Between now and then, the committee is going to question every last witness mentioned in the hearings.

"We are going to get the truth—and the whole truth."

Mr. Chambers, in previous testimony, had said Mr. Hiss was a member of an "elite" Communist underground group that operated in Washington prior to 1937. It was a group, he said, made up of people selected because the Communist party thought they would rise in influence.

Mr. Chambers testified that when he left the party after the Russian-German alliance he tried to take Mr. Hiss with him: He described a visit to Mr. Hiss's home where, he said, he begged Mr. Hiss to get out of the party, too. He said Mr. Hiss broke into tears but declined.

Mr. Hiss, for his part, denied such a scene ever took place with anyone.

Hiss Open Letter to HUAC, August 24, 1948

HUAC's investigation proceeded expeditiously. Soon sufficient evidence had been gathered that committee members scheduled an open meeting for August 25, where Hiss and Chambers could publicly confront each other. On August 24, the day before the long-awaited encounter, Hiss sent an open letter to HUAC pleading his case and airing his grievances. He accused the committee of bias and decried not only the attacks on him personally, but also the committee's denigration of the achievements of the Democratic administrations that he had served. He singled out Congressman Mundt as particularly guilty. He chronicled the achievements of his fifteen years in government service and cited a long list of prominent figures, both Republican and Democrat, who would attest to his integrity.

TEXT OF HISS OPEN LETTER TO CHAIRMAN J. PARNELL THOMAS OF HUAC, AUGUST 24, 1948

Tomorrow will mark my fourth appearance before your committee. I urge, in advance of that hearing, that your committee delay no longer in penetrating to the bedrock of the facts relevant to the charge which you have publicized—that I am or have been a Communist.

Source: Washington Post, August 25, 1948. Copyright © 1948, *The Washington Post*, reprinted by permission.

This charge goes beyond the personal. Attempts will be made to use it, and the resulting publicity, to discredit recent great achievements of this country in which I was privileged to participate.

Certain members of your committee have already demonstrated that this use of your hearings and the ensuing publicity is not a mere possibility, it is a reality. Your acting chairman himself was trigger-quick to cast such discredit. Before I had a chance to testify, even before the press had a chance to reach me for comment, before you had sought one single fact to support the charge made by a self-confessed liar, spy, and traitor, your acting chairman pronounced judgment that I am guilty as charged, by stating that the country should beware of the peace work with which I have been connected.

I urge that these committee members abandon such verdict-first-and-testimony-later tactics along with dramatic confrontations in secret sessions, and get down to business.

First my record should be explored. It is inconceivable that there could have been on my part, during 15 years or more in public office, serving all three branches of the Government, judicial, legislative, and executive, any departure from the highest rectitude without its being known. It is inconceivable that the men with whom I was intimately associated during those 15 years should not know my true character far better than this accuser. It is inconceivable that if I had not been of the highest character, this would not have manifested itself at some time or other, in at least one of the innumerable actions I took as a high official, actions publicly recorded in the greatest detail.

During the period cited by this accuser, I was chief counsel to the Senate Committee Investigating the Munitions Industry, at a great many public hearings, fully reported in volumes to be found in libraries in every major American city. During my term of service under the Solicitor General of the United States, I participated in the preparation of briefs on a great many of the largest issues affecting the United States. Those briefs are on public file in the United States Supreme Court, in the Department of Justice, and in law libraries in various American cities.

As an official of the Department of State, I was appointed Secretary General, the top administrative officer, of the peace-building international assembly that created the United Nations. My actions in that post are a matter of detailed public record. The same is true of my actions at other peace-building and peace-strengthening international meetings in which I participated—at Dumbarton Oaks and elsewhere in this country, at Malta, at Yalta, at London and in other foreign cities. All my actions in the executive branch of the Government, including my work in the AAA on farm problems are fully recorded in the public records.

In all this work I was frequently, and for extensive periods, under the eye of the American press and of the statesmen under whom or in association with whom I worked. They saw my every gesture, my every movement, my every facial expression. They heard the tones in which I spoke, the words I uttered, the words spoken by others in my presence. They knew my every act relating to official business, both in public and in executive conference.

Here is a list of the living personages of recognized stature under whom or in association with whom I worked in the government (there may be omissions which I should like to supply in a supplemental list):

1. Men now in the United States Senate:
   Senate Tom Connally, a United States Delegate to the San Francisco Conference which created the United Nations, and to the first meeting of the General Assembly of the United Nations in London.
   Senator Arthur Vandenberg, a member of the Senate Committee Investigating the Munitions Industry, and a member of the San Francisco Conference and London General Assembly delegations.
2. Men now in the House of Representatives:
   Representative Sol Bloom, a member of both the San Francisco and the London delegations.
   Representative Charles Eaton, also a member of both the San Francisco and the London delegations, although his health kept him from making the trip to London.
3. Former Secretaries of State Cordell Hull, Edward Stettinius, James Byrnes.
4. Former Undersecretaries of State Joseph Grew, also a member of the Dumbarton Oaks delegation: Dean Acheson, William Clayton.
5. United States Judges:
   Stanley Reed, Associate Justice of the United States Supreme Court, who as Solicitor General was my immediate superior during my service in the Department of Justice.
   Homer Bone and Bennett Clark, former Senators and members of the Munitions Committee.
   Jerome Frank who as General Counsel of the Agricultural Adjustment Administration was my immediate chief in the Department of Agriculture.

6. Men Formerly in Congress:

Former United States Senator Gerald Nye, chairman of the Munitions Committee, who appointed me as the chief attorney of that committee.

Former United States Senator James Pope, a member of the Munitions Committee and now a director of TVA.

Former United States Senator John Townsend, a member of the London Delegation.

7. Others at international conferences where I assisted their labors to build the peace:

Isaiah Bowman, member of Dumbarton Oaks Delegation, President of Johns Hopkins University.

John Foster Dulles, a chief adviser to the San Francisco delegation and a member of each delegation to the meetings of the General Assembly.

Lieut. Gen. Stanley Embick, a member of the Dumbarton Oaks delegation.

Charles Fahy, former legal adviser of the Department of State and member of the United States delegation to the General Assembly.

Gen. Muir Fairchild, Air Force, member of the Dumbarton Oaks delegation.

Henry Fletcher, former Assistant Secretary of State and member of the Dumbarton Oaks delegation.

Green Hackworth, former legal adviser of Department of State and a member of the Dumbarton Oaks delegation, now a judge of the international court of justice.

Admiral Arthur Hepburn, member of the United States delegation at Dumbarton Oaks.

Stanley Hornbeck, member of the Dumbarton Oaks Delegation, later our Ambassador to the Hague, and earlier, as chief Far Eastern expert of the Department of State, my immediate superior from the fall of 1939 until the early winter of 1944.

Breckinridge Long, former Assistant Secretary of State, and member of the Dumbarton Oaks Delegation.

Mrs. Eleanor Roosevelt, member of the San Francisco Delegation and also of each United States Delegation to the meetings of the General Assembly.

Harold Stassen, member of the United States Delegation to the San Francisco Conference.

Rear Admiral Harold Train, member of the Dumbarton Oaks Delegation.

Frank Walker, former Postmaster General and member of the Delegation to the London meeting of the General Assembly.

Edwin Wilson, my predecessor as director of the office for United Nations affairs and my last immediate superior in the Department of State, who was also a member of the Dumbarton Oaks Delegation, now our Ambassador at Ankara.

8. Other superiors to whom I reported:

Chester Davis, Administrator of the Agricultural Adjustment Administration, and now president of the Federal Reserve Bank of St. Louis.

Francis Sayre, my first direct superior in the Department of State, former Assistant Secretary of State and United States High Commissioner to the Philippines, now United States Representative to the Trusteeship Council of the United Nations and member of the United States Delegation to the General Assembly.

These are the men whom I was honored to help in carrying out the finest and deepest American traditions. That is my record. I too have had a not-insignificant role in the magnificent achievements of our Nation in recent times.

These men I have listed are the men with whom and under whom I worked intimately during my 15 years in Government service—the men best able to testify concerning the loyalty with which I performed the duties assigned me. All are persons of unimpeachable character, in a position to know my work from day to day and hour to hour through many years. Ask them if they ever found in me anything except the highest adherence to duty and honor.

Then the committee can judge, and the public can judge, whether to believe a self-discredited accuser whose names and aliases are as numerous and as casual as his accusations.

The other side of this question is the reliability of the allegations before this committee, the undocumented statements of the man who now calls himself Whittaker Chambers.

Is he a man of consistent reliability, truthfulness and honor? Clearly not. He admits it, and the committee knows it. Indeed, is he a man of sanity?

Getting the facts about Whittaker Chambers, if that is his name, will not be easy. My own counsel have made inquiries in the past few days and have learned that his career is not, like those of normal men, an open book. His operations have been furtive and concealed. Why? What does he have to hide?

I am glad to help get the facts.

At this point I should like to repeat suggestions made by me at preceding hearings with respect to the most effective method of getting facts so far as I can supply them. The suggestions I made beginning with the very first time I appeared before your committee were not then accepted, and the result has only been confusion and delay. Let me illustrate by recalling to your minds what I said when you asked me to identify the accuser, not by producing him under your subpena power but by producing only a newspaper photograph taken many years after the time when, by his own statements, I had last seen him. I said to you on the occasion of my first appearance:

"I would much rather see the individual . . . I would not want to take oath that I have never seen that man. I would like to see him and I would be better able to tell whether I had ever seen him. Is he here today? . . . I hoped he would be. . . ."

Let me add one further example of how the procedures followed have caused confusion and delay. In your secret sessions, you asked me housekeeping and minor details of years ago that few, if any, busy men could possibly retain in their memories with accuracy. I told you, and one of your own members acknowledged, that you or I should consult the records. I warned you that I had not checked them and that I doubted if I could be helpful under those circumstances.

I am having a check made of the records and will furnish the results to you.

One personal word. My action in being kind to Crosley years ago was one of humaneness, with results which surely some members of the committee have experienced. You do a favor for a man, he comes for another, he gets a third favor from you. When you finally realize he is an inveterate repeater, you get rid of him. If your loss is only a loss of time and money, you are lucky. You may find yourself caluminiated in a degree depending on whether the man is unbalanced or worse.

Hiss and Chambers Before HUAC

On August 25, the American people had an opportunity to judge for themselves. As the following *Washington Post* account indicates, interest was high. The *Post* estimated the overflow crowd to number about twelve thousand. Newsreel and television cameras recorded the proceedings. John Chabot Smith in his study of the Hiss case described this session as "a show ballyhooed into a circus, with a sellout audience packed into the big

PHOTO 2.2 On August 25, 1948, Hiss appeared with Chambers in a public hearing. Here Hiss, standing on the left, identifies Chambers, standing on the right, as the "George Crosley" he had known in the 1930s.

caucus room, radio broadcasters, klieg lights, motion picture cameras for the movie newsreels, and that still new invention, television cameras."[8]

In a marathon session that lasted nearly ten hours, the witnesses and the committee revisited the ground covered in the previous executive hearings. The *Post* reporter sensed that the committee was aligned against Hiss. The former government official with the stellar credentials testified for six hours, while Chambers had to endure less than two hours of examination. Chambers's recollections of apartment leases and particularly Hiss's disposal of the old Ford automobile proved more accurate and verifiable than Hiss's. Congressman Mundt—who had been a particular target of Hiss's scorn—noted that much of Chambers's allegations "stands unchallenged." As for Hiss's defense, some of the evidence had been "clearly refuted," while other parts were "clouded by a strangely deficient memory."

"HISS CONFRONTS CHAMBERS; EACH CALLS OTHER LIAR"

Alger Hiss and Whittaker Chambers, together under the glaring lights of a Congressional hearing room, remained worlds apart last night in their stories of who they were and what they did together in the mid '30s.

Source: Washington Post, August 26, 1948. Copyright © 1948, *The Washington Post,* reprinted by permission.

What will be the next move on Chambers' charge that Hiss was a dues-paying member of an elite Communist underground apparatus in the Federal Government here will be considered by the House Committee on Un-American Activities today. The committee will meet in executive session at 10:30 a.m. Chairman J. Parnell Thomas (R., N.J.) said there would be no further public hearing today.

Hiss, slender, serious former State Department official, now president of the Carnegie Endowment for International Peace, was questioned steadily by the committee for six hours. Chambers, thickset avowed former Communist writer and underground worker, now a senior editor for Time Magazine, was on the stand for about an hour and 40 minutes before the hearing ended at 8 p.m.

"DAMNEDEST LIAR"

Each heard the other call him a liar. Each heard a committee member, Representative F. Edward Hébert (D., La.), declare one of them was the "damnedest liar" ever to appear on the American scene, and the one that was lying was "the greatest actor" ever seen in this country.

Some 12000 persons crowded the hearing room, and other hundreds lined up outside in the corridor as the hearing opened. The room stayed packed most of the day. Movie and television lights glared through the session.

Hiss was called to the stand shortly after 10:30 a.m. With him was Attorney John F. Davis of 1700 1st, nw. After preliminaries, Chief Investigator Robert E. Stripling called on Hiss to stand up.

Then Chambers, also called by Stripling, stood up a few feet away, beyond a press table to Hiss' right, near the curving committee bench.

Hiss identified Chambers as George Crosley, whom he knew in 1934 and 1935 and thought he had last seen in 1935.

Chambers identified Hiss as the Alger Hiss he thought he had first met in 1934 and whom he had last seen about 1938. The two sat down.

While Hiss testified, Chambers sat quietly, sometimes with folded arms, sometimes with eyes fixed on the ceiling. While Chambers was on the stand, Hiss sat behind him at the second press table back, taking notes steadily.

Committee reaction made clear it was Hiss who was having the uphill fight in the dramatic face-to-face showdown on who was telling the truth. At the outset Chairman Thomas gave a blunt warning that one of the two certainly would be tried for perjury. Near the close of Hiss' testimony, Representative Karl E. Mundt (R., S.Dak.) told Hiss while the latter sat erect looking at the speaker that "on every point on which we have had verifiable evidence, Mr. Chambers' testimony has stood up and it stands unchallenged." In contrast, he said, some of Hiss' testimony had been "clearly refuted" and on other points it was "clouded by a strangely deficient memory."

Hiss replied he was not then making a final answer to Mundt's "so-called summation" of the testimony. He said the "man who calls himself Chambers" for ten years had been "peddling" to Government agencies the report that Alger Hiss was a Communist. He said Chambers had had ample time to check on the details he gave in testimony. He said he would try to produce witnesses who knew Chambers as Crosley. "So far as I know, you only have his (Chambers') unsupported testimony that he was a Communist."

SUBPOENA FOR PETERS

A strong suggestion of one future course the hearings may take came with Chambers' testimony that "J. Peters" was one of those who introduced him to Hiss in a Washington restaurant in the '30s. Peters, identified by Chambers as onetime head of the Communist underground in the United States and in that position when he knew Hiss as a member of the underground, is to be subpoenaed by the House committee in New York Monday. At that time Peters is to be produced by his lawyer for a deportation hearing. He is now free on $5000 bond.

In the windup of his bout on the witness stand, Hiss dramatically called upon the committee to put to Chambers a series of 10 questions. For one thing he wanted to know if Chambers had ever been treated for a mental illness.

Representative Hébert said he had asked Chambers that question in an executive hearing in New York and had received a negative answer. Hébert said it was a typical Communist smear to charge a witness as a mental case. He said Chambers had added that he was not an alcoholic. Hiss said he raised the question because he had second-hand hearsay reports that Chambers had received treatment as a mental case.

"I have never been treated for a mental illness, period," Chambers told the committee. "Nor have I ever been in a mental institution."

In another tense exchange, Representative Richard M. Nixon (R., Calif.) asked Chambers why he had gone to Hiss to persuade the latter to break from the Communist Party in 1938.

"I was very fond of Hiss," said Chambers. "He was certainly the closest friend I ever had in the Communist Party."

Nixon asked what his motive had been for accusing Hiss as a Communist.

"The story is spread that I am working out some old motives of revenge or hatred," Chambers replied. "I don't hate Mr. Hiss. We were friends. But we are caught in a tragedy of history. Hiss represents the concealed enemy against him with remorse and pity."

As he went on Chambers' voice slowed close to choking, and he appeared struggling to hold back tears. Behind him, Hiss looked up, head shaking as if in amazement.

"In a moment of historical jeopardy in which this Nation now stands, so help me God, I could not do otherwise," Chambers concluded. He reached for a paper cup of water and sipped it.

The passage brought into new focus previously secret testimony by Chambers about his association with Hiss, presented to the committee in executive session August 7, and made public yesterday.

Chambers then testified he knew that Chambers was a member of the Communist Party, because he was told it by Peters, head of the Red underground in this country. He said Hiss had submitted himself for the two or three years of their acquaintance as a "dedicated and disciplined Communist." He recalled Hiss as prompt in party dues-paying, but said that in the Communist group which included Hiss none of the members had party cards for reasons of security and concealment.

In that session he was asked about whether the Hiss family had served any special dish at mealtimes, and Chambers gave this reply:

"No. I think you get here into something else. Hiss is a man of great simplicity and a great gentleness and sweetness of character, and they (referring to Hiss and his wife) lived with extreme simplicity. I had the impression that the furniture in that (the Hiss) house was kind of pulled together from here and there, maybe got it from their mother or something like that. Nothing lavish about it whatsoever, quite simple. The food was in the same pattern, and they cared nothing about food. It was not a primary interest in their lives."

Reaction to the Hearings

However impressed committee members were with Chambers's testimony, the public hearing failed to resolve the debate about who to believe. Editorials castigated all parties involved and for the most part insisted that the important questions about Communist infiltration in government had not been answered.[9] Many still cynically sensed that partisan politics was the driving force for the investigation. James Reston in his syndicated column exemplified the ambivalence Americans felt. He detected HUAC's hostility toward Hiss. He acknowledged that there were deficiencies in Hiss's testimony, but criticized the "prosecutor's attitude" the congressmen brought to their questioning. The committee as much as Hiss was being judged. While some felt that the committee's procedure had brought out valuable facts, others believed that in the committee's quest to show that it had been misled by Hiss, it had failed to prove his "disloyalty."

JAMES RESTON, "QUESTIONERS SEEM UNIMPRESSED AS HISS TRIES TO REFUTE CHAMBERS"

WASHINGTON, Aug. 25—At the end of the Hiss-Chambers hearing on Capitol Hill today, there seemed to be general agreement among objective observers on one point: That the most prominent and outspoken members of the House Un-American Activities Committee were unimpressed by the testimony of Alger Hiss, and seemed to some to adopt a prosecutor's attitude toward him.

Mr. Hiss, former chief of the United Nations section of the State Department, was on the stand for six hours today. He is a tall, well-groomed, handsome young man, adroit in manner, diplomatic in his speech.

From beginning to end of his testimony, however, he was hard pressed and openly challenged not only by his accuser, Whittaker Chambers, but by members of the committee themselves.

In particular, Representative Karl E. Mundt, Republican, of South Dakota; Richard M. Nixon, Republican, of California; Chairman J. Parnell Thomas, Republican, of New Jersey, and F. Edward Hebert, Democrat, of Louisiana, directly and by inference questioned the validity of some of his past and present testimony.

When Mr. Hiss stated that he could not remember whether he had sold a car to Mr. Chambers fourteen years ago or given it to him, Mr. Nixon said he was "amazed."

When Mr. Hiss was vague about the details of this transaction, Mr. Mundt said that it was "inconceivable" that the former State Department official should not remember how he had disposed of his property. When Mr. Hiss asked the committee in a formal statement to seek evidence of his integrity from a long list of officials with whom he had worked—including three former Secretaries of State, two prominent Senators and several judges—Mr. Hebert commented that these people could not possibly offer testimony as to whether Mr. Hiss was a Communist.

Near the end of the six hours on the stand, in fact, Mr. Mundt stated directly that Mr. Hiss' testimony at a previous meeting of the committee on how he had disposed of his car, had been "refuted" by documentary facts; accused him of having a "strangely deficient memory" about his relations with men accused by Mr. Chambers of being Communists; and bluntly informed him that the testimony of Mr. Chambers against Mr. Hiss—which Mr. Hiss had not yet seen in detail—stood up to the committee's scrutiny.

Mr. Nixon consulted repeatedly with Robert E. Stripling, the chief investigator of the Un-American Activities Committee, and his questions, like those of Mr. Stripling, were detailed and often acid.

By the end of the hearing tonight, the issue of the committee's procedure was hotter than ever. There were many persons in the House caucus room who felt that the questions had brought out facts which lent credence to the charge that Mr. Hiss had, at one time, been associated with Communists in the capital.

At the same time, there were others who were citing the committee's questioning today in support of the contention that it was more concerned to prove that Mr. Hiss had misled the committee than to discover whether he had been a disloyal servant of the Government.

Those who felt this way were saying tonight that there was a marked difference between the attitude of leading members of the committee toward Mr. Chambers when he finally took the stand tonight than toward Mr. Hiss.

Mr. Chambers was far less hesitant in his replies, far less diplomatic in his language than Mr. Hiss. He is a short, round jowly little man who looks vaguely like Charles Laughton. He was dressed in a gray suit and black tie. His hair, once blond, was now gray and he talked well with just a trace of hoarseness and lisp.

All of Mr. Hiss' story about renting him his apartment and selling him his car, he maintained, was the bunk. He and Hiss were old Communist comrades and Hiss had given him the use of the apartment and the car and paid over his Communist dues, as good comrades invariably do.

HUAC Issues Interim Report

On August 27, HUAC issued an interim report. The investigation appeared to have been stalled. Absent new information, it was just the word of Hiss against that of Chambers. So the committee tried to summarize the progress it had made in order to justify its actions. Stung by criticism of its methods and wary of accusations of political motivations, the report began by explaining the committee's failure to come to definite conclusions.

In the sections addressing the Hiss-Chambers issue specifically, the report did not answer the key question of Hiss's Communist Party affiliation, but it criticized him on four major points. Hiss admitted that he had associated with Communists, had not been forthright with the committee when he initially could not affirm his familiarity with Chambers, failed to tell the whole truth about the disposal of the old Ford, and had been the only person the committee could identify who knew Chambers as "George Crosley."

Finally, the report charged the Truman administration with failing to cooperate in the committee's investigation. The White House, the document argued, hampered rather than helped get to the answers. The committee called upon the attorney general to become more aggressive in enforcing existing laws.

INTERIM REPORT, AUGUST 27, 1948

REASONS FOR PUBLIC HEARINGS

Questions are sometimes raised both by chronic critics of this committee and by sincere observers as to whether holding public hearings on questions of loyalty, espionage, and Communist conspiracy ever serves the public interest. These people hold that our committee should screen witnesses carefully in secret executive sessions and sift the testimony, releasing to the public only such portions as the committee decides it should see or hear.

It is argued by those adhering to this position that this committee, in its zeal to protect the reputations and feelings of innocent people whose names may occasionally be injected into public hearings, should operate in large part after the manner of a grand jury and in utmost

Source: Hearings Regarding Communist Espionage in the United States Government, 1348–49, 1352–54.

secrecy, withholding from the public the steps by which evidence is accumulated and its decisions made. This committee yields to nobody in its earnest desire to protect the innocent and to expose the guilty.

It is the established policy of this committee to protect in every feasible manner the reputations and the sensibilities of innocent citizens. It is also an established fact that in conducting public hearings—and this committee deplores the use of star-chamber, secret sessions unless public necessity requires them—an occasional mention of some innocent citizen in connection with a nefarious practice will inevitably occur. When it does, we provide every opportunity for those mentioned to clear themselves of all suspicion in the same forum before the same publicity media as in the case of the original allegations. In addition we have frequently inserted memoranda in our files to protect those innocently accused elsewhere from unjust attack or suspicion.

At times, however, your committee is confronted with the necessity of running the risk that a few innocent people may be temporarily embarrassed or the risk that 140,000,000 innocent Americans may be permanently enslaved. When necessary to resolve the relative merits of two such risks as that, your committee holds to the position that its primary responsibility is to that great bulk of our American population whose patriotic devotion to our free institutions deserves the greatest diligence in being protected against those who would utilize our Bill of Rights and our American freedoms to destroy permanently these great safe-guards of personal liberty and human dignity.

There is another very vital and important reason why public hearings such as are held by this committee provide an indispensable supplement to the off-the-record investigations and activities of such institutions as the FBI and the grand jury. It is illustrated most recently by the controversial features of the Chambers-Hiss testimony. Despite the fact that Alger Hiss had been interrogated as to his connections with communism and Communists by at least two outstanding Americans, Secretary of State Byrnes and John Foster Dulles, acting independently, and by other Government officials, none of these interrogatories had established the relationship of Hiss and Chambers until our committee held its public hearings on this case. In fact, it was not until our public hearings had proceeded for some time that it was definitely established that Alger Hiss and Whittaker Chambers knew each other personally and rather intimately during the precise period of time that Whittaker Chambers testified that their associations took place. Mr. Hiss testified that he knew Whittaker Chambers by the name of "George Crosley" but he positively identified the man known today as Whittaker Chambers as the man he knew. He testified unequivocally that he not only knew Chambers (by name of Crosley) but that he let him use his apartment without ever receiving payment for it, that he loaned Chambers money, that he loaned or gave him an automobile, and that he had even kept Mr. and Mrs. Chambers and their baby in his own home overnight on one or more occasions. Thus the connection between Alger Hiss and Whittaker Chambers, as a man-to-man relationship, stands without challenge confirmed by the testimony of both men and the public hearings held by this committee. This fact had never been established by other investigations.

It should also be noted that the stark fact that Alger Hiss and Whittaker Chambers, a self-confessed paid Communist functionary and espionage agent, were acquainted with each other and did have numerous transactions and associations together, is of far greater significance under the circumstances than whether Chambers was known to Hiss by the name of "Carl" or of "George Crosley." This fact has been established without challenge for the record by the public hearings of this committee, although through the years it had been established by no other investigation.

Hiss will be given every opportunity to reconcile the conflicting portions of his testimony, but the confrontation of the two men and the attendant testimony from both witnesses has definitely shifted the burden of proof from Chambers to Hiss, in the opinion of this committee. Up to now, the verifiable portions of Chambers' testimony have stood up strongly; the verifiable portions of the Hiss' testimony have been badly shaken and are primarily refuted by the testimony of Hiss versus Hiss, as the complete text of the printed hearings will reveal.

• • •

HISS-CHAMBERS TESTIMONY

One of the most difficult problems which has faced the committee has been that of resolving the conflict between the testimony submitted by Whittaker Chambers and Alger Hiss. Chambers testified on August 3 that Hiss was a member of a Communist underground group of Government workers during the period 1934–37 when Chambers was serving as a Communist Party functionary in Washington. On August 5 Hiss categorically denied the charges of Chambers that he was or ever had been a member of the Communist Party, and furthermore denied ever having known Chambers or "having laid eyes upon him." As a result of exhaustive investigation by the committee's staff and of hours of executive session testimony from Hiss, Chambers, and all others who had information concerning the conflicting stories, Hiss finally admitted on August 17 for the first time that he actually had known Chambers as George Crosley, during the period in question.

As a result of the hearings and investigations which have been conducted by the committee to date, these facts have been clearly established: (1) There is no doubt whatever but that Chambers from 1931 to 1938 was a paid functionary of the Communist Party and that from 1934 to 1937 he operated as a member of the Communist underground among Government workers in Washington. (2) The refusal of Nathan Witt, John Abt, Henry Collins, Lee Pressman, and Victor Perlo to answer any questions concerning their activities as members of this group on the ground of self-incrimination and to answer as to whether or not they were members of the Communist Party during that period is in itself strong corroborative evidence for Chambers' story. (3) By his own admission Hiss knew Chambers for a period of at least 10 months during the period in question and possibly longer. It is also clear that Hiss knew Chambers very well as indicated by his admission that he sublet his furnished apartment to him, that he met him on various occasions for lunch, that on at least one occasion he gave him a ride to New York from Washington, that for several days the Chambers family visited in the Hiss home and that he loaned money to Chambers, and that he gave him an automobile. (4) While admitting that he knew Chambers, Hiss still denies that he knew that Chambers was a Communist, and that he, Hiss, was a member of the Communist Party at any time.

Hiss testified on August 16 and 17 that at the time that he leased his apartment to Chambers he gave him a 1929 Ford automobile. In his testimony in the public session on August 25, however, when confronted with documentary evidence which committee investigators produced, that he actually had transferred the car in 1936 to the Cherner Motor Co. who the same day transferred it to one William Rosen, Hiss changed his position on the car and testified in a manner which to the committee seemed vague and evasive. He stated that he could not recall whether or not he gave the car to Chambers or whether he loaned it to him. He could not recall whether he gave it to him at the same time he sublet the apartment to him or whether he did so several months later after Chambers had left the apartment. He had no recollection whatever of having transferred the car to the Cherner Motor Co. although he admitted that the signature on the transfer of title was his own. He said that it was possible that he could have given the car to Chambers and that Chambers could have given it back to him, and that he later could have transferred it to the Cherner Motor Co. but that he could not recall what happened.

This much concerning the testimony in regard to the car can definitely be concluded. Hiss stated on August 16 and 17 that he sold or gave the car to Crosley (Chambers) at the same time that he sublet the apartment to him and that at the time that he did this he had another car which he himself was using. A check of the records by the committee staff showed that Hiss did not acquire another car until several months after the apartment transaction was concluded and that he actually transferred the car over a year later to the Cherner Motor Co.

His vague and evasive testimony on this transaction raises a doubt as to other portions of his testimony. In this connection it should be observed that on 198 occasions Hiss qualified his answers to questions by the phrase "to the best of my recollection" and similar qualifying phrases, while Chambers, on the other hand, was for the most part forthright and emphatic in his answers to questions.

For example, Chambers testified on August 7 that Hiss had expressed a desire to transfer the automobile in question to a Communist Party worker and that he effected this transfer by taking the car to a used-car lot which was operated by a Communist sympathizer, who in turn was to turn it over to a Communist organizer. To date the committee's investigations of the car transaction tend to bear out Mr. Chambers' version of what happened rather than Hiss' version. The only evidence of the transfer of the car is of the transfer to the Cherner Motor Co. in 1936 and to William Rosen to whom the car was transferred by Cherner. When questioned by the committee, Rosen refused to answer any questions concerning the car or concerning whether he was a member of the Communist Party on the ground of self-incrimination. The committee will continue to pursue its investigations of this transaction.

In summary, the developments of the Hiss-Chambers controversy to date warrant the following conclusions:

1. Despite his denial that he has ever been a member of the Communist Party or had any friends who were Communists, Hiss has admitted knowing and associating with Harold Ware, Nathan Witt, John Abt, Henry Collins, Lee Pressman, and Whittaker Chambers, all of whom are either known or admitted members of the Communist Party, or who have refused to answer the question as to whether they were members of the Communist Party on the ground of self-incrimination. It stretches the credulity of the committee to believe that Hiss could have known these people, including Chambers, as well as he did without at some time suspecting that they were members of the Communist Party.

2. The committee believes that Mr. Hiss was not completely forthright in his testimony before the committee on August 5 when he failed to tell the committee that he noted a familiarity about the features of Whittaker Chambers when a picture of Chambers was shown to him. He has since admitted that he told several friends before the hearing of his noting this familiarity but when shown a picture of Chambers he deliberately created the impression that the face meant nothing to him whatever. It is hard to believe that Hiss could have known Chambers as well as he admits he knew Crosley without being able to recognize the picture which was shown him during the hearing of August 5.

3. Hiss has either failed or refused to tell the committee the whole truth concerning the disposition of his 1929 Ford automobile. It is inconceivable that a man would not remember whether he had given a car away twice or at all and it is just as inconceivable that he would not recall whether a person to whom he had given the automobile had later returned it to him.

4. Despite the fact that Hiss says he knew Chambers under the name of Crosley, a thorough investigation by the committee has failed to date to find any person who knew him by that name during the period in question. The committee believes that the burden is upon Hiss to establish that Chambers actually went under the name of Crosley at the time he knew him and that Hiss knew Crosley as a free-lance writer rather than as the admitted Communist functionary which Chambers actually was during that period.

OBSTRUCTIVE TACTICS BY WHITE HOUSE

The committee's investigation of espionage among Government workers has been hampered at every turn by the refusal of the executive branch of the Government to cooperate in any way with the investigation due to the President's loyalty freeze order. Not only have the executive agencies refused to turn over to the committee the loyalty files of the suspected members of the spy rings but they have even gone so far as to refuse to turn over the employment records of these individuals. The committee can see no excuse whatever for such arbitrary action since it is obvious that turning over employment records would in nowise involve disclosing sources of information or confidential data. Had the executive agencies of the Government cooperated with the committee in its investigation, there is no question but what the public would now have full information concerning all the ramifications of the espionage rings. The committee has proceeded to obtain this information in every way possible and eventually will see that it is presented to the public, but the committee deplores the fact that the executive branch of the Government will in no way aid the committee in its efforts to protect the national security from those who are doing everything they can to undermine and destroy it.

RESPONSIBILITY OF THE ATTORNEY GENERAL

The committee again calls upon the Attorney General of the United States to vigorously enforce the existing espionage and other laws against those who are participating in the Communist conspiracy. These laws should be enforced without regard to partisan or political considerations because the very security of the Nation is at stake. The failure of the Attorney General to enforce the laws as vigorously as he should has been in large part responsible for the growth and power of the Communist conspiracy in the United States.

The committee again calls upon the Attorney General to forward to the Congress at the earliest possible date recommendations for strengthening the espionage laws so that they will be adequate to deal with the Communist conspiracy. As long ago as February 5 the Attorney General appeared before the Legislative Subcommittee of the Un-American Activities Committee and declared that amendments to the espionage laws were essential in order to meet the new techniques which had been developed by the Communists and other foreign agents. He assured the committee that his recommendations would be forwarded to the Congress at an early date. Members of this committee have repeatedly requested the Attorney General since that time to give the Congress his recommendations for needed changes of the espionage laws, and as yet have received no response whatever as to what changes are needed.

The Attorney General has from time to time inferred that those who participated in the Bentley spy ring might be immune from prosecution under present laws because of the inadequacy of those laws. This investigation has shown clearly that a well-organized and dangerous espionage ring operated in the Government during the war; and if present laws are inadequate, as the Attorney General has inferred, to prosecute the members of this ring, it is the solemn responsibility of the Attorney General to forward to the Congress immediately his recommendations for needed changes in the espionage laws so that the national security can be protected.

It is also imperative that the Attorney General proceed promptly to call the New York special grand jury back into session to consider his recommendations on the disposition of the evidence he has placed before it. The public has the clear right to have this proceeding concluded by indictments where indicated, by a no true bill where warranted, and by a full report by the Attorney General on his disposition of the case.

Notes

1. Allen Weinstein, *Perjury: The Hiss-Chambers Case* (New York: Random House, 1997), 4.
2. Ibid., 307–8, 316–33.
3. "Red 'Underground' in Federal Posts Alleged by Editor," *New York Times*, August 4, 1948.
4. *New York Times*, August 4, 1948.
5. *New York Herald Tribune*, August 6, 1948.
6. Richard M. Nixon, *Six Crises* (Garden City, New York: Doubleday and Company, 1962), 10–11.
7. Ibid., 20. John Chabot Smith, *Alger Hiss: The True Story* (New York: Holt, Rinehart, and Winston, 1976), 215–16, points out that Levin worked under Andrews in the Washington bureau.
8. Smith, *Alger Hiss: The True Story*, 232–33.
9. See "The Confrontation," *New York Herald Tribune*, August 26, 1948; "Hiss vs. Chambers," *Washington Post*, August 27, 1948.

3
The Indictment

When the House Committee on Un-American Activities issued its interim report, the issues surrounding the Hiss-Chambers controversy were at a stalemate. In fact, some questioned the relevance of the Hiss matter to the expressed purpose of the probe—to investigate espionage in the United States government. Chambers to this point had accused Hiss only of Communist Party membership, not spying for the Soviet Union. The public heard the word of a respected former government official and current president of the Carnegie Endowment for International Peace being challenged by a confessed former Communist. It was obvious that one was lying. But absent further evidence, there was no way to determine the guilty party. When HUAC turned over its findings to the Justice Department, the attorney general concluded on October 15 that there were no grounds for bringing charges at the time.[1]

Lacking new evidence, the affair appeared to be simply part of the expected political in-fighting between the Republican Congress and the Democratic president, particularly in an election year. Nevertheless, if the Republicans could keep this issue alive and instill suspicion among the electorate that the Truman administration was infiltrated by Communists, this would bode well for the chances of the Republican Party and its presidential candidate, Thomas E. Dewey, in November.

Not to be ignored in the political scheme of things was the growing notoriety of Congressman Richard Nixon. A relative unknown when Chambers first accused Hiss, Nixon quickly assumed a leading role. But at the end of August, it seemed that his pursuit of the facts was at a dead end. That soon changed. By the end of the year, classified State Department documents surrendered by Chambers not only vindicated the efforts of the committee, but also enhanced Nixon's reputation even further. Both Hiss and the Truman administration were forced on the defensive.

CHRONOLOGY: HISS INDICTMENT

1948

August 27: On the day before HUAC issued its interim report, Whittaker Chambers appeared on the radio program "Meet the Press." No longer protected by immunity from libel suits afforded by the congressional committee, he responded to Hiss's challenge by repeating his charges in a public forum.

September 27: Hiss filed a slander suit in U.S. District Court in Baltimore, Maryland, seeking $50,000 in damages. On October 8, the suit was amended to seek $75,000.

October 15: The Justice Department, which had received the material on the Hiss case from HUAC, determined that there was insufficient evidence to bring charges at that time.

November 5: During a pretrial deposition hearing, Chambers stated that he had read classified State Department documents supplied by Hiss, but denied receiving material for transfer to the Soviet Union.

November 17: Chambers altered his testimony and produced documents he said were State Department materials received from Hiss.

November 18: Libel suit attorneys turned the documents over to the Justice Department.

December 2: When HUAC served Chambers a subpoena demanding any additional documents in his possession, he led committee investigators into a pumpkin patch on his Maryland farm, where he had hidden five rolls of microfilm.

December 6–15: Both Chambers and Hiss appeared before the New York grand jury.

December 10: Chambers resigned as an editor of *Time* magazine.

December 7–14: HUAC reconvened to probe Chambers's new evidence.

December 13: Hiss submitted his resignation as president of the Carnegie Endowment for International Peace. The board of trustees voted not to accept it, but rather granted him a three month leave of absence.

December 15: The New York grand jury indicted Hiss on two counts of perjury—that he lied when he said that he had no contact with

Chambers after January 1, 1937, and when he denied turning government documents over to Chambers.

Whittaker Chambers Appears on "Meet the Press"

On the day before HUAC issued its interim report, Whittaker Chambers accepted Alger Hiss's challenge to make his charges in a forum other than before the committee, where he was shielded by immunity from prosecution. Chambers appeared on the radio program "Meet the Press" and in answer to questions from a panel of reporters publicly accused Hiss of being a Communist Party member. Pressed for more information, he was evasive and declined to charge Hiss with anything more.

In these excerpts from the show's transcript, the panelists—moderator James Reston of the *New York Times*, Tom Reynolds of the *Chicago Sun-Times*, Nat Finney of Cowles Publications, Edward Folliard of the *Washington Post*, and Lawrence Spivak of the *American Mercury*—question Chambers.

"WHITTAKER CHAMBERS MEETS THE PRESS," AUGUST 27, 1948

FOLLIARD: Mr. Chambers, in the hearings on Capitol Hill you said over and over again that you served in the Communist Party with Alger Hiss. Your remarks down there were privileged; that is to say, you were protected from lawsuits. Hiss has now challenged you to make the same charge publicly. He says if you do he will test your veracity by filing a suit for slander or libel. Are you willing to say now that Alger Hiss is or ever was a Communist?

CHAMBERS: Alger Hiss was a Communist and may be now.

•   •   •

FINNEY: I thought you left it a little unclear as to whether you are certain in your mind if Alger Hiss is now a member of the Communist Party or not.

CHAMBERS: I would not presume to say whether Mr. Hiss now is or is not a member of the Party.

FINNEY: Do you mean to say that you have not made a check whether he, as you, has recanted?

Source: American Mercury 68 (February, 1949): 153, 155, 157–59. Reprinted by permission of the Enoch Pratt Free Library of Baltimore in accordance with the terms of the will of H. L. Mencken.

CHAMBERS: I have no possibility of making such a check. The House Committee on Un-American Activities subpoenaed me to tell what I knew about the Communist Party at the time Mr. Hiss was a member. I have testified to that. I have not presumed to testify what he is now.

FOLLIARD: Mr. Chambers, to go back to that opening question, you accepted Alger Hiss' challenge and publicly said that he had been at least a member of the Communist Party. Does that mean that you are now prepared to go into Court and answer to a suit for slander or libel?

CHAMBERS: I do not think Mr. Hiss will sue me for slander or libel.

REYNOLDS: Would you charge Alger Hiss with an overt act as a Communist, as you said he was? Did Alger Hiss at any time, to your knowledge, do anything that was treasonable or beyond the law of the United States? That, I believe, brings you the opportunity to accept the Hiss challenge.

CHAMBERS: Whether or not it brings me the opportunity to accept the Hiss challenge, I am quite unprepared to say whether he did or did not. I am not familiar with the laws of treason.

• • •

REYNOLDS: Are you prepared at this time to say that Alger Hiss was anything more than, in your opinion, a Communist? Did he do anything wrong? Did he commit any overt act? Has he been disloyal to his country?

CHAMBERS: I am only prepared at this time to say he was a Communist.

REYNOLDS: It seems to me, then, sir, if I may say so, that in some respects this may be a tempest in a teapot. You say that he was a Communist, but will not accuse him of any act that is disloyal to the United States.

CHAMBERS: I am not prepared legally to make that charge. My whole interest in this business has been to show that Mr. Hiss was a Communist.

REYNOLDS: Would you be prepared, for instance, to put on the record the testimony that you gave during the three or four or five interrogations by the FBI?

CHAMBERS: The gist of that testimony is already on the record in the Un-American Committee.

REYNOLDS: I am not interested in the gist. But I presume that there were assertions that overt acts were committed. Are you willing to put on the record, so that it can be tested in Courts under the laws of evidence, that this man did something wrong?

CHAMBERS: I think that what needs clarification is the purpose for which that group was set up to which Mr. Hiss belonged. That was a group, not, as I think is in the back of your mind, for the purpose of espionage, but for the purpose of infiltrating the government and influencing government policy by getting Communists in key places.

FINNEY: It was not, then, by definition, conspiracy?

CHAMBERS: No, it was not.

SPIVAK: Mr. Chambers, when you were a member of the underground, was there anything of particular importance or significance to the Russians that you yourself did or accomplished, or were you just a member of an underground that kind of played around Washington?

CHAMBERS: Well, I would hesitate to say that an underground which was able to place people in the Treasury and the State Department in positions of such importance was "playing around." They certainly were not doing anything directly for the Russians.

SPIVAK: You didn't place them there necessarily for spying, but rather to influence policy?

CHAMBERS: That is true; which is something very much more important than spying.

SPIVAK: Have you any idea whether Mr. Hiss, in any of the jobs he had, had any real influence on our policy? For example, do you know specifically or exactly what he did when he went to Yalta with the President?

CHAMBERS: No, I can't say that I do.

FINNEY: Mr. Chambers, was Mr. Hiss not in charge of the United Nations section of the State Department precisely at the time when our policy changed to a firm policy against the Soviet Union?

CHAMBERS: I do not know.

REYNOLDS: I was in Washington at the time that the Soviet Union was recognized by the United States. Liberalism, so called, was the fashion and the fad. Oliver Wendell Holmes was the god of such young people as Mr. Alger Hiss. Mr. Alger Hiss was a leftist in the Holmes pattern. Did he have to go far to the left to be guilty of whatever you are accusing him of, which I am not quite sure of?

CHAMBERS: I am accusing him of membership in the Communist Party. I am not even accusing him of that. I am simply saying that he *was* a member of the Party.

Chambers's Deposition in Hiss Slander Suit, November 5, 1948

Once Chambers had made his charges on "Meet the Press," Hiss filed a slander suit on September 27, 1948, in U.S. District Court, Baltimore, Maryland. Deposition proceedings began on November 4. During the first day of questioning by Hiss's lawyers, led by Baltimore barrister William L. Marbury, Chambers repeated his account of his relationship with Hiss. At the end of that day, Marbury asked Chambers "to produce tomorrow, if he has any, any correspondence, either typewritten or in handwriting, or anything of that sort, from any member of the Hiss family, letters from Mr. Alger Hiss, or Mrs. Hiss, or from Mr. Donald Hiss [Hiss's brother, whom Chambers had also accused of Communist activity], or from Mrs. Donald Hiss, which he has received at any time, or anything of that sort, any papers signed by Mr. Hiss which may be in his possession."[2]

When the proceedings reconvened the following day, Chambers's attorney, William D. Macmillan, informed Marbury that his client at that time had nothing to hand over, but stated that Chambers "has not explored all of the sources where some conceivable data might be found." Macmillan assured Marbury that, in the event that such documents were discovered, they would be turned over.[3] Marbury then proceeded to question Chambers.

During this session, Chambers expanded on Hiss's Communist Party activities. In particular, he described how on many occasions Hiss had allowed him to examine State Department documents in Hiss's apartment. Pressed for details, Chambers described the contents of some of these documents. He recalled seeing information about a Bulgarian rug dealer in the Soviet Union who was spying for Great Britain and a Phantom Red Cosmetics Company that was a front for Communist activity. He also recalled some trade reports from Austria.[4] But Chambers insisted that Hiss had never turned these documents over to him. Chambers, therefore, only made "verbal transmissions" to his Soviet handlers.

CHAMBERS'S DEPOSITION, NOVEMBER 5, 1948

Q: No, I am afraid I will have to press you for an answer to the question. Is there anything else that should be added to the list that you have just made? I want you to tell us everything which you know which indicated any activity on Mr. Hiss' part, other than his association with you, which is consistent with his having been a Communist during the period in which you knew him, in addition to those we have just listed.

A: He occasionally gave the Communist Party bits of information which he thought might be useful to them.

Q: Now, will you tell us about that, just what information, and when?

A: I will try. I remember an occasion when there had been a round-up of Soviet people in England, I believe, and the English apparatus had some kind of a connection in America, as so often happens with international apparatuses, and Mr. Hiss was able to tell us that there was some danger threatening what was known as the Phantom Red Cosmetics Company, and a furniture store on Madison Avenue, which was evidently a cover for the activities of this apparatus.

Q: This is a British apparatus?

A: This is presumably a Russian or a Soviet or an international apparatus, Communist, of course, whose main activity was in England—

Q: I see.

Source: Stenographic Transcript in the Case of Alger Hiss v. Whittaker Chambers, U.S. District Court for the District of Maryland, Baltimore, Maryland, November 5, 1948, 306–7, 310–17.

A: —and which was rounded up in England, or disposed of in some way.

Q: Where was Mr. Hiss employed at this time?

A: Mr. Hiss was in the State Department at that time.

• • •

Q: What other information did he ever convey to you?

A: He told us about a Bulgarian who was operating in Moscow, I think for the British Government, and a man who had formerly been in Italy, I think in Milan—I have forgotten the details of this affair, but, anyway, he was in Moscow at that time, and he felt that that might be interesting.

Q: Well, now, what did he tell you about it?

A: He just gave us the fact that this man was operating in Moscow.

Q: You mean he reported to you that a man—

A: A Bulgarian.

Q: —that a Bulgarian—

A: Who, if I remember correctly, had been a rug dealer in Milan, Italy.

Q: What do you mean by operating in Moscow?

A: Engaged in espionage in Moscow.

Q: On whose behalf?

A: The British, I believe.

• • •

Q: Do you know how he got the information about the surveillance of the Phantom Red people?

A: Yes, I do, he got that from a document.

Q: What document?

A: A State Department document.

Q: Well, can't you be more specific than that? What kind of document?

A: Well, I don't know what kind of document it could be other than a State Department document. I am not familiar with categories, or I don't understand what you mean.

Q: Well, was it a secret report of some sort?

A: Oh, I don't know whether it was secret. I presume it was confidential.

Q: Was it an Intelligence report, or what?

A: I think, if I remember correctly, it was a State Department report, not an Intelligence report. It was a report within the State Department, within the Diplomatic Service.

Q: A report within the Diplomatic Service?

A: I believe so, but I could be mistaken.

Q: Well, now, you said it was a document. You know no more about it than he said it was document?

A: No, I saw that one.

Q: Well, what did you see?

A: Just what I have told you.

Q: Well, tell me now. Certainly, if you saw the document, you ought to be in a position to describe it. You mean he handed you a document?

A: I frequently read State Department documents in Mr. Hiss' house.

• • •

Q: Now, what other State Department documents did you see? You say you frequently saw State Department documents?

A: Yes, Mr. Hiss very often brought a briefcase with documents home, and I used to read those that were interesting. They were not very interesting, most of them I think they were chiefly on trade agreements, and one thing and another. The most interesting ones were Mr. Messerschmidt's reports from Vienna, which were rather long and talky.

• • •

Q: Well, what documents that were of interest to the Communist Party or to the Soviet Government, if you please, did you ever obtain from Mr. Hiss other than this Phantom Red business?

A: I would not say that I ever obtained any documents from him, but the only documents that I remember which were of interest to the Communist Party were connected with that Phantom Red business and the Bulgarian in Moscow. Now, there may have been a few others, but those are the ones that stay in my mind.

Q: Those two documents?

A: Yes.

Q: You say there may have been others?

A: There may have been one or two others.

Q: Wouldn't you remember those if they did come to you?

A: Not necessarily.

Q: At any rate, at present you cannot recollect any others, or the subject matter of any others?

A: I don't at the moment, no.

Q: All right. I will appreciate it if you will search your memory on that point, because I think it is vital to know what papers of interest to the Communist Party other than this Messerschmidt report that you have told us about.

A: The others I have told you were chiefly accounts of trade agreements, or commercial figures of one kind or another relating to exports and imports, and this and that.

Q: Those were of no interest to you?

A: They were of no interest. I simply read most of them out of curiosity, to see what kind of things were written about in such places.

Q: Now, can you tell us of any other activities of Mr. Hiss, or, by the way, you said you did not obtain any documents. And I take it you mean by that that he only handed you the documents or copies, he only handed you the originals or copies of the originals, but you were permitted to read them—is that what you mean by that, saying that you never obtained any?

A: I mean by never obtained any that I never transmitted a State Department document from Mr. Hiss to the Communist Party.

Q: Did you ever transmit the contents of any State Department documents to the Communist Party?

A: The instances I recall, which were verbal transmissions, I think were the two that I have mentioned—the Phantom Red Cosmetics, and the Bulgarian.

Chambers Produces Documents, November 17, 1948

Chambers gradually began to fear that the case was developing to his disadvantage. According to Allen Weinstein, two factors led him to conclude that he had to produce more evidence or risk losing the suit. First, Chambers worried that Marbury was intent on destroying both his and his wife's reputations. His anxiety became particularly acute after the aggressive treatment his wife endured during her deposition on November 16 and 17. Second, Chambers feared that, should he lose the libel suit, the grand jury would then indict him, not Hiss, for perjury.[5]

Therefore, on November 14 he traveled to Brooklyn, New York, to recover an envelope he had left with his wife's nephew, Nathan Levine, in 1938. He and Levine went to Levine's mother's house, where they retrieved a large envelope from an unused dumbwaiter. When Chambers opened the envelope, he was surprised at the amount of material it contained. Over the years, he had forgotten what specifically he had left with Levine. He had apparently expected to find only a few pieces of paper with Hiss's handwriting. But the envelope actually contained four small notes written by Hiss, sixty-five typewritten documents, four sheets of yellow paper with Harry Dexter White's handwriting, two strips of developed film, three cans of undeveloped film, and one other small piece of paper.[6]

Chambers described his reaction to his examination of these materials in this way:

> In his [Levine's] absence, I opened the envelope and drew part way out the thick batch of copied State Department documents. At a glance, I saw that, besides those documents, and Hiss's handwritten memos, there were three cylinders of microfilm and a little spool of developed film (actually two strips). By a reflex of amazement, I pushed the papers back into the envelope. Then I held on to the edge of the table, for I had the feeling that the floor was swinging around me and that I was going to fall to it. That passed in an instant. But I continued to grip the edge of the table in the kind of physical hush that a man feels to whom has happened an act of God.[7]

On the afternoon of November 17, he presented the four pages with Hiss's handwriting and the sixty-five typed documents to Hiss's lawyers. He then proceeded to describe how J. Peters, a spymaster and Comintern representative in the United States, introduced him to a man named "Peter," later identified as spymaster Colonel Boris Bykov. Chambers in turn introduced Peter to Hiss, who began to regularly provide typewritten copies of State Department documents, materials that often had been eagerly copied by his wife.

CHAMBERS'S DEPOSITION, NOVEMBER 17, 1948

MR. MACMILLAN: Let me say this, Mr. Marbury, that Mr. Chambers desires to make a statement at this time in connection with certain testimony that has been given by him heretofore in this deposition.

MR. MARBURY: Very well, go ahead.

THE WITNESS. In response to your request to produce papers from Mr. Hiss, I made a search, and I have certain papers in Mr. Hiss' handwriting and certain other papers.

In testifying from the beginning, I have faced two problems.

My first problem was to paralyze and destroy in so far as I was able the Communist conspiracy.

My second problem was to do no more injury than necessary to the individuals involved in that operation.

I was particularly anxious, for reasons of friendship, and because Mr. Hiss is one of the most brilliant young men in the country, not to do injury more than necessary to Mr. Hiss.

Therefore, I have carefully avoided testifying to certain activities of Mr. Hiss at any place or any time heretofore.

I found when I looked at the papers which I had put by certain documents which I had forgotten I had put by. I thought I had destroyed them. I supposed that the documents I had put away were the handwriting specimens of Mr. Hiss. The documents I refer to reveal a kind of activity, the revelation of which is somewhat different from anything I have testified about before. I first saw those documents last Sunday evening. I first brought them to the attention of my counsel on Monday. I was incapable of deciding at that time whether or not to present them in evidence. My counsel very strongly urged me, in the nature of the case, that I had practically no other choice. But I left them on Monday not strongly convinced, but without having reached a decision. And I waited until Tuesday to finally make up my mind. That is why I was unable to depose on Tuesday. The result of my turmoil, which is merely

Source: Stenographic Transcript in the Case of Alger Hiss v. Whittaker Chambers, November 17, 1948, 717–20, 738–43.

the last act of the turmoil that has been going on for a decade, was the decision to give you the material.

MR. MARBURY: May we have it, sir.

MR. MACMILLAN: There it is. (Indicating)

   Let it be known that we have the original documents that Mr. Chambers has just referred to, and we also have had photostats taken thereof, because we don't want the originals to leave our possession. We are prepared, however, to leave with you a photostatic set of the various documents.

● ● ●

MR. MACMILLAN: Now, I would like the privilege of inquiring of the witness whether or not he does not have more to say as part of the statement which he desired to make at the outset of this afternoon's session.

MR. MARBURY: I was going to ask him that myself.

MR. MACMILLAN: All right.

MR. MARBURY: I was going to ask him to explain what these papers are which have been identified.

MR. CLEVELAND: I think the point might be made that this testimony today is an amplification of answers to questions you have previously asked him.

THE WITNESS: May I explain in my own words?

MR. MARBURY: Go ahead.

THE WITNESS: I have been very careful to make a distinction in testifying as to Mr. Hiss' activities with the Communist Party, but in the year 1937 a new development took place in the Washington apparatus, which I was—

Q: (By Mr. Marbury) Excuse me one minute. You said a distinction. A distinction between what?

A: Between Mr. Hiss' activities prior to that date and afterwards. Sometime in 1937, I think about the middle of the year, J. Peters introduced me to a Russian who identified himself under the pseudonym Peter, I presume for purposes of confusion between his name and J. Peters. I subsequently learned from Walter Krivitsky that the Russian Peter was one Colonel Bykov—B-y-k-o-v, I believe it is spelled, and I propose to refer to him as Bykov hereafter, to avoid the confusion between his pseudonym and the name J. Peters. Colonel Bykov was extremely interested in the Washington apparatus about which he questioned me endlessly. J. Peters was extremely interested that Colonel Bykov should not know too much about the Washington apparatus, not out of any Communistic disloyalty, but due to a proprietary sense, I think, that the Russians were moving in on the apparatus, which he had, at least, had a large share in creating. He, of course, did not tell me in so many words, "Do not help Bykov," but he gave me to understand that the less I told him about the Washington apparatus the better. Nevertheless, it proved impossible not to tell him about the details of the apparatus. He then having learned presently of the group, raised the question of procuring documents through them. I should think in August or the early fall of 1937

I arranged a meeting between Alger Hiss and Colonel Bykov. For that purpose, Mr. Hiss came to New York, where I met him. I have forgotten where our rendezvous was held, but I believe it was somewhere near the Brooklyn Bridge. We then proceeded by the elevated train to a movie house quite a distance out in Brooklyn, which I cannot locate, but which I believe I could easily find. Alger and I waited on a bench on the mezzanine, and presently Bykov emerged from the body of the theatre. I introduced them. We left the theatre and went for a long walk, and by various conveyances, we went back to New York City and had supper, the three of us together, at the Port Arthur Restaurant in Chinatown. Colonel Bykov spoke no English, or refused to speak English. He spoke German with a very bad Yiddish accent. He raised the question of procuring documents from the State Department, and Mr. Hiss agreed.

Q: What?

A: Mr. Hiss agreed. Colonel Bykov also raised the question of Donald Hiss' procuring documents. Alger Hiss said that he was not sure that his brother was sufficiently developed yet for that function—and perhaps I should say right here that Donald Hiss never at any time procured any documents. Nevertheless, he was a member of the apparatus which I headed. Following that meeting Alger Hiss began a fairly consistent flow of such material as we have before us here. The method was for him to bring home documents in his brief case which Mrs. Hiss usually typed. I am not sure that she typed all of them. Alger Hiss may have typed some of them himself. But it became a function for her and helped to solve the problem of Mrs. Hiss' longing for activity, that is, Communist activity. Nevertheless, there occasionally came to Mr. Hiss' knowledge, certain things, or he saw certain papers which he was not able to bring out of the Department for one reason or another, either because they merely passed through his hands quickly, or because he thought it inadvisable, but notations, in his handwriting are notes of such documents, such information, which he made and brought out in that form.

Would you like to ask questions at that point?

Q: You say this began in 1937?

A: I believe so.

Q: Can you place the meeting any more closely than that?

A: As to months?—No, I am not sure, but it seems to me that the weather was not very severe, so I presume it had to be late spring, or the summer or fall—early fall.

Q: Now, may I ask, did I understand you to say that you had not testified as to this activity of Mr. Hiss before?

A: I have never to my knowledge testified as to this activity.

Q: Did you inform the Senate Committee of this activity?

A: I have never informed any one of this activity.

Q: You never informed the FBI?

A: I have never informed any one of this activity. I said before my desire was to destroy the Communist activities, but to preserve in so far as possible the very fine people who are engaged in them. Any informing of such matters was bound to injure them, but there are degrees of injury. And I did not think that it was proper to inflict that injury on Alger Hiss, partly because I am not without compassion, and partly because I was once a Communist. It was given me to find the strength to break with the Communist Party. And there is always a possibility that others who are still Communists will also find that strength. Time is of the essence of such matters. And that was an important factor for me to keep this information to myself. I am perfectly satisfied as to what I have done both with respect to trying to smash the conspiracy, and to try to shield such people as Alger Hiss from the most extreme consequences.

Q: In other words, your view of the matter is that although Mr. Hiss passed directly to the Russian—

A: Mr. Hiss passed this information to me. I gave it to Colonel Bykov.

Q: He knew where it was going?

A: Both Mr. Hiss and I knew where it was going.

Microfilm in the Pumpkin Patch

The next day Hiss's attorneys with the concurrence of the judge in charge of the libel suit turned the material over to the Justice Department. Chambers had always been suspicious of the Justice Department and the grand jury proceedings, particularly because of Hiss's connections in high places within the Democratic administration. He had, therefore, withheld part of the material he had recovered in order to protect his interests. His apprehensions seemed justified when the Justice Department suppressed the documents and forbade anyone to reveal the contents under threat of contempt of court. As weeks passed, Chambers began to fear even more that he, not Hiss, would be the target of a perjury indictment since he had in past testimony explicitly denied any espionage activity.

Meanwhile, alerted by rumors of the suppressed evidence, Nixon and Stripling visited Chambers at his Maryland farm on December 1. During their discussion, Chambers confirmed the existence of the documents and revealed that he had more. After this meeting, Nixon ordered Stripling to seek a subpoena for the material, which Stripling did on December 2. The congressman then left for a previously planned vacation in Panama. Allen Weinstein has speculated that Nixon did not delay his vacation because he wanted to distance himself from the proceedings should the whole affair blow up in his face.[8] Besides, if the documents proved valuable, summoning him from his vacation would publicly demonstrate his personal importance in the whole matter.

On December 2, when served the subpoena, Chambers led HUAC investigators to a pumpkin patch on his farm where he pulled two developed

Photo 3.1 Nixon dramatically flew back to the United States from his vacation in Panama when he received word of the discovery of the microfilm in the hollowed-out pumpkin.

Associated Press

and three undeveloped rolls of microfilm from a hollowed-out pumpkin. He also gave them photostatic copies of the documents in the possession of the Justice Department.

On December 3, Stripling sent a navy plane to bring Nixon back to Washington and called a news conference to announce the discovery. The following is the *New York Herald Tribune*'s account of Stripling's press conference. Note Stripling's exaggerations, particularly his contention that the documents were "three or four feet high" when in actuality the Baltimore documents and the microfilm combined comprised approximately 106 pages of material, which made only about a one-inch stack. Also note Nixon's prominent place in the whole account.

"CHAMBERS'S MICROFILMS INDICATE HE GOT STATE DEPT.-NAVY SECRETS WHILE IN SERVICE OF COMMUNISTS"

WASHINGTON, Dec. 3—Microfilms brought out of their hiding place in a hollowed-out pumpkin on his Maryland farm have been produced by Whittaker Chambers, it was revealed tonight, and they strongly indicate that highly secret State and Navy

Source: New York Herald Tribune, December 4, 1948.

Department information was obtained by him in the days when he was a Communist.

The evidence, some of which has been seen by this reporter, is by far the most startling that has been yet brought to light as a result of the celebrated controversy involving Mr. Chambers, a senior editor of "Time" magazine, and Alger Hiss, former State Department official and now president of the Carnegie Endowment for International Peace.

It is evidence that overshadows Mr. Chambers's charge—and Mr. Hiss's denial—that Mr. Hiss was a member of a Communist "apparatus" in Washington while a Federal employee in the mid-1930s.

EVIDENCE RAISES QUESTIONS

It is evidence that gives rise to the larger questions:

Was treason committed?

Can espionage be proved?

It is evidence that will be placed before a New York Federal grand jury, probably next Wednesday, and will most certainly give the jury reasons to ponder these additional questions:

Who fed the information—including plans of technical instruments highly valuable in war—to Mr. Chambers?

Was it transmitted to Soviet Russia?

Did it give away secret codes used by the State Department and the Navy Department—and, for that matter, other departments, if it turns out from complete examination that documents from other departments are pictured in the microfilms?

No word or hint was given tonight, however, as to the person or persons in the State Department and the Navy Department who supplied the microfilmed documents to Mr. Chambers.

One illustration of how "hot" the microfilms are lies in the fact that letter-sized reproductions made of them—of some of them, in fact, since the job of enlarging them is still going on—make a stack three to four feet high.

Other illustrations are these:

1. Representative Karl E. Mundt, Republican of South Dakota, is flying back from his home in Madison, S.D., to bring the facts to light as a member of the House Committee on Un-American Activities.

    Informed in detail in an hour-long telephone conversation with Robert E. Stripling, chief committee investigator, Mr. Mundt, who will be a Senator in the next Congress, said: "These documents are of such startling and significant importance and reveal such a vast network of Communist espionage within the

State Department that they far exceed anything yet brought before the committee in its ten-year history."

Mr. Stripling was asked: "Will anybody be subpoenaed in the investigation?" He replied emphatically: "Yes, indeed."

2. Mr. Mundt sent a wireless message to Representative Richard M. Nixon, Republican of California, vacation-bound to Panama on the liner Panama. Mr. Mundt asked Mr. Nixon to leave the ship by plane if possible and fly back. Mr. Nixon, all reporters in Washington know, has been more responsible than any other member of the committee for bringing Hiss-Chambers facts into the open. It was Mr. Nixon, in fact, who ordered a subpoena served on Mr. Chambers—and who got a pumpkin and its contents.

3. The microfilms supplement documents turned over two weeks ago by Mr. Chambers in Baltimore at a pre-trial examination in the libel suit brought against him by Mr. Hiss for his charge that Mr. Hiss was a Communist once. It was learned tonight that at that examination Mr. Chambers, asked by Mr. Hiss's attorney if he had any documentary proof, "stopped the show" by saying, "only these." By his words "only these" he meant more than sixty documents which were in document and not in microfilm form. They were so important that Federal Judge W. Calvin Chestnut was called in. So was Alexander M. Campbell, Assistant Attorney General in charge of the criminal division of the Department of Justice. The upshot was that the documents were sealed in the interests of national security and given into Mr. Campbell's custody.

SUBPOENA ISSUED

4. Mr. Nixon, presumably acting on the theory that if Mr. Chambers had some undisclosed documents he might have others, issued a subpoena calling for anything and everything pertinent that Mr. Chambers had.

5. Mr. Hiss, who was not present when Mr. Chambers was questioned but who read today that the documents of the pre-trial hearing were under study, issued a statement in New York tonight saying: "During the course of the examination by counsel of Mr. Chambers in the libel action which I have brought against him in Baltimore, Mr. Chambers produced certain documents which I considered of such importance that I directed my attorney to place them at once before the Department of Justice. This has been done and I have offered my full co-operation to the Department of Justice and to the grand jury in a further investigation of this matter."

Other persons have said that the decision to call in the Department of Justice was reached after consultation of the attorneys for Mr. Hiss and Mr. Chambers with Judge Chestnut, and without Mr. Hiss being present.

6. Thomas J. Donegan, special Assistant Attorney General, came from New York to Washington, did a lot of hurried conferring about the case, and went back by train to New York, presumably to get ready to present the whole case to the Federal Grand Jury there on Wednesday.

7. It was learned incontrovertibly that the Department of Justice had studied for two weeks the information given by Mr. Chambers in the pre-trial examination in Baltimore. Nothing had been done or announced by the department.

There were many other points that could be numbered but the outstanding fact was that Representative Nixon, because of his belief that Mr. Chambers might have other untold information, gave Mr. Stripling some strong instructions on Wednesday night.

Mr. Nixon was to leave—and did leave—on Thursday afternoon for Panama.

Mr. Nixon requested Mr. Stripling to get up early in the morning on Thursday and take a blanket subpoena to Mr. Chambers on his farm in Westminster, Md.

Mr. Stripling did.

The microfilm was brought out of the pumpkin by Mr. Chambers in the presence of Mr. Stripling and two other committee agents, William A. Wheeler and Donald Appell.

Messrs. Stripling, Wheeler and Appell came back to Washington.

Mr. Stripling fired off a wireless message to Mr. Nixon but didn't receive an answer fast enough.

Mr. Stripling got Representative Mundt on the telephone and after many microfilms had been developed, told him about them and about the more than sixty documents of the libel suit pre-trial examination.

Mr. Mundt dictated a statement.

It stressed that the microfilms and documents would be kept under twenty-four-hour guard.

It said the existence of the microfilms had been suspected and the microfilms sought for more than ten years.

It said they all offered definite proof of "one of the most extensive espionage rings in the history of the United States."

It said there was "conclusive proof" that secret documents were fed out of the State Department to Mr. Chambers at a time when he was acting as a Washington contact for the Communist underground in America.

STRIPLING DISPLAYS FILMS

(Mr. Mundt talked before he knew there were Navy Department as well as State Department documents in the microfilms.)

Mr. Stripling held a press conference tonight.

"Here is a case of film, unopened," he said. He showed a metal cylinder about an inch in diameter and two and a half inches long. He said there were many cylinders, but did not say how many.

"Reproduced the ones we have developed so far make a stack of letter-sized documents three or four feet high," he reported.

He said that presumably the documents were returned to the departmental files after being microfilmed.

How important they were was shown by the top few lines on one. (Mr. Stripling steadfastly refused to allow publication of the contents of any of the documents.) But the top lines on one read: "This telegram must be closely paraphrased before being communicated to any one."

It was dated June 13, 1938, was received at the State Department at 3:15 P.M. that day, was addressed to the Assistant Secretary of State, and was from Former Ambassador William C. Bullitt, in Paris. The Bullitt message related details of a conversation with a high Chinese official in Paris who had previously been stationed in Moscow. It confirmed the prospects of Russia entering into a war against Japan.

The significance of the order to paraphrase it was this:

1. If it were released or made known as it was sent, it would give any good code-breaker a chance to reverse matters and see what the code used was.
2. If the code used was broken on the one message, it could be readily used to translate other messages.
3. It was in effect, the equivalent of the war-time top-secret warning on highly confidential matters.

Another such message in the microfilms bore the same preface and the additional words in capital letters: "Strictly confidential for the Secretary."

This was peace-time equivalent of topping top-secret stuff.

Another bore in long-hand the notation: "Handed to the German Ambassador by Mr. Welles." It was dated 7/21/37. Summer Welles, former Under Secretary of State, was still with the department then.

Mr. Stripling's press conference produced a lot of questions:

"Why didn't Mr. Chambers bring all this out before?" (The questioner meant during the House committee investigation of the Hiss-Chambers story, the Federal Grand Jury's investigation, and the libel pre-trial quizzing.)

Mr. Stripling said he had no comment.

"Would he be legally culpable for possessing such information?"

Mr. Stripling would not comment, but, said the House committee would seek all the facts.

"How many tubes of microfilm were found?"

"Enough," said Mr. Stripling.

"Were the documents—or microfilms—actually turned over to Soviet Russia?"

Mr. Stripling had no comment. One reporter spoke up to say he guessed it was possible to make more than one microfilm copy of a single document and to retain a copy while sending one elsewhere. Mr. Stripling didn't disagree.

STATE DEPARTMENT NOT CONSULTED

"Have you talked to the State Department about this?"

"No," Mr. Stripling said.

"To the Justice Department?"

"No."

"What if the Justice Department demands jurisdiction over the material you have subpoenaed?"

"That will be a matter for the committee to decide," Mr. Stripling said.

"Is Alger Hiss's name mentioned in any of the documents reproduced from the film?"

"We have not analyzed all of them yet," he replied.

"Is the Justice Department seeking Mr. Chambers?"

"I don't know," Mr. Stripling said. "I think the most important thing is—who made these things available to Mr. Chambers."

"Is there any evidence, other than the testimony of Mr. Chambers, that he got anything from Mr. Hiss?"

Mr. Stripling said he had no comment.

"Has Mr. Hiss been re-subpoenaed as yet?"

Mr. Stripling replied; "Not as yet."

TEXT OF MUNDT'S STATEMENT

The text of the statement by Representative Mundt as telephoned to Washington tonight from his home in Madison, S.D., follows:

"Documents secured by subpoena last night from Whittaker Chambers indicate that a final conclusion is imminent in the long-discussed Hiss-Chambers espionage case with which the House Committee on un-American Activities has been concerned since before the special session of the Eightieth Congress.

"There is now in the possession of the committee, under twenty-four-hour guard, microfilmed copies of documents of tremendous importance, which were removed from the offices of the State Department and turned over to Chambers for the purpose of transmittal to Russian Communist agents. These documents are of such startling and significant importance, and reveal such a vast network of Communist espionage within the State Department, that they far exceed anything yet brought before the committee in its ten-year history.

"These microfilms have been the object of a ten-year search by agents of the United States government and provide definite proof of one of the most extensive espionage rings in the history of the United States.

"On the basis of evidence now before the committee, it appears that conclusive proof has been established that secret documents of direct significance to our national security were fed out of the State Department by a member of the Communist underground to Whittaker Chambers, who at that time was operating as one of the Washington contacts for the Communist underground operating in America.

"As the chairman of the subcommittee handling this entire matter, I shall proceed to Washington as soon as possible.

"I have radioed Congressman Nixon to fly back to Washington, if possible, and am getting in touch with other members of the subcommittee to ascertain the earliest possible date for a public hearing. The evidence before us is so shocking that I do not feel justified in delaying action a day longer than required."

The Baltimore Documents and the Pumpkin Papers

The documents clearly pointed to espionage activity between the middle of 1937 and the spring of 1938. The Baltimore documents were sixty-five typed pages of copies of State Department communications plus four small notes in Hiss's own handwriting. All but one of the documents had been typed on the same typewriter. Three of the five rolls of microfilm taken from the pumpkin were light-struck and blank. The two rolls of developed film contained fifty-eight reproductions of State Department communications and reports. Three of these "pumpkin papers," totaling ten pages, were incoming telegrams initialed by Hiss. Five others, totaling forty-eight pages, dealt with the negotiation of a trade agreement with Germany.

PHOTO 3.2   Document a: One of the Baltimore documents, a note in Hiss's handwriting summarizing a report on French military sales to China.

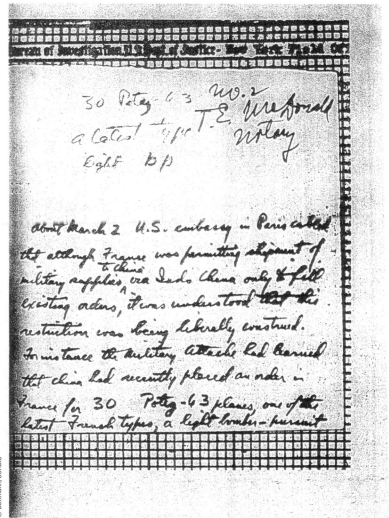

PHOTO 3.3 Document b: One of the Baltimore documents, retyped summaries of cables sent in January 1938 by Ambassador William C. Bullitt in Paris to the State Department detailing events as Europe moved toward World War II.

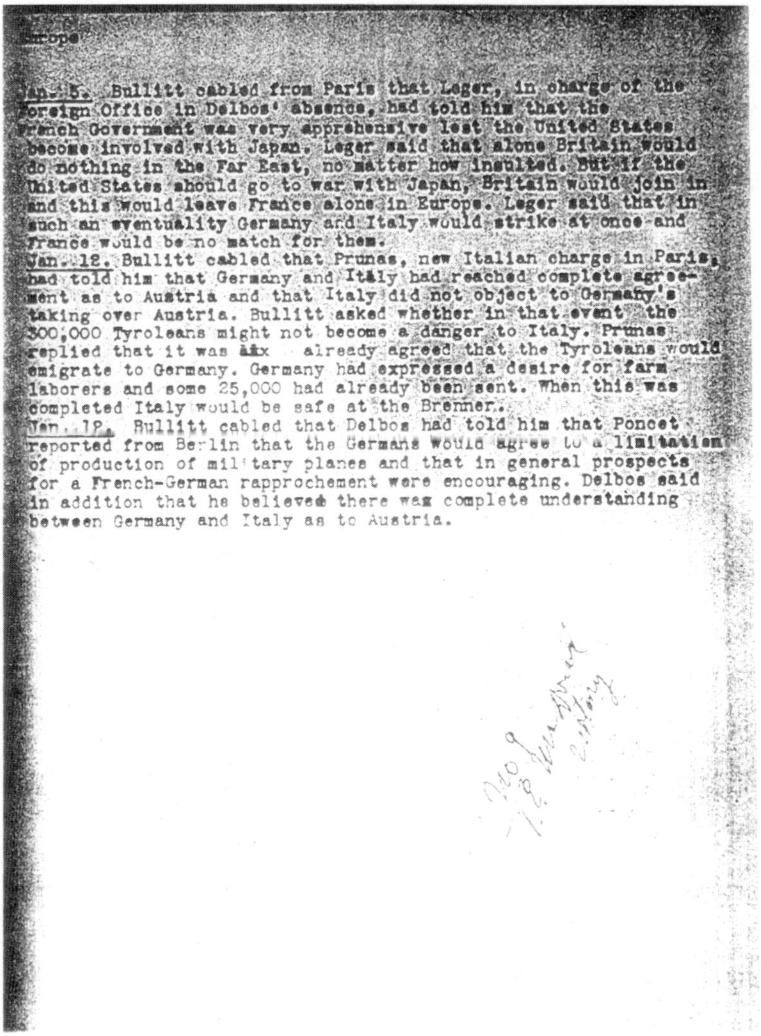

Europe

Jan. 5. Bullitt cabled from Paris that Leger, in charge of the Foreign Office in Delbos' absence, had told him that the French Government was very apprehensive lest the United States become involved with Japan. Leger said that alone Britain would do nothing in the Far East, no matter how insulted. But if the United States should go to war with Japan, Britain would join in and this would leave France alone in Europe. Leger said that in such an eventuality Germany and Italy would strike at once and France would be no match for them.
Jan. 12. Bullitt cabled that Prunas, new Italian charge in Paris, had told him that Germany and Italy had reached complete agreement as to Austria and that Italy did not object to Germany's taking over Austria. Bullitt asked whether in that event the 300,000 Tyroleans might not become a danger to Italy. Prunas replied that it was already agreed that the Tyroleans would emigrate to Germany. Germany had expressed a desire for farm laborers and some 25,000 had already been sent. When this was completed Italy would be safe at the Brenner.
Jan. 12. Bullitt cabled that Delbos had told him that Poncet reported from Berlin that the Germans would agree to a limitation of production of military planes and that in general prospects for a French-German rapprochement were encouraging. Delbos said in addition that he believed there was complete understanding between Germany and Italy as to Austria.

PHOTO 3.4 Document c: Another Baltimore document, a retyped January 7, 1938, report on activities of the members of the Anti-Comintern Pact, particularly in Asia.

Reliable source reports that since signing the tripartite Anti-Comintern Pact an agreement has been reached whereby complete Italian and German military aircraft engineering and designing data, plus the services of technical advisers, are made available to Japan.

A "Shanghai Mail" report states that German experts on ordinance and airplane matters are now in Japan.

American military attache at Hangkow paints gloomy picture of China's present military plight. States that a Chinese counter-offensive is unthinkable and he doesn't believe a force that can offer serious resistance can now be created.

Japanese are reported to be moving 80,000 fresh troops from Japan via Mukden. First of these troops arrived at Mukden on December 17th. Believes they are destined for the northern frontier. Barracks with a capacity of 50,000 troops are reported to have been erected at Chaimussu and Poli in northeast Manchuria. Other barracks with capacities for 100,000 troops are reported to be located between railroads which are rapidly being pushed to the Mongolian and northeast frontiers. Japanese agents are reported to be fomenting action by Mohammedans in Ninghsia and Chenghi to harrass the Urunchi-Lanchow Road.

PHOTO 3.5 Document d: One of the pumpkin papers, a photostat of January 13, 1938, telegram from Ambassador William C. Bullitt in Paris to the State Department, detailing developments in China.

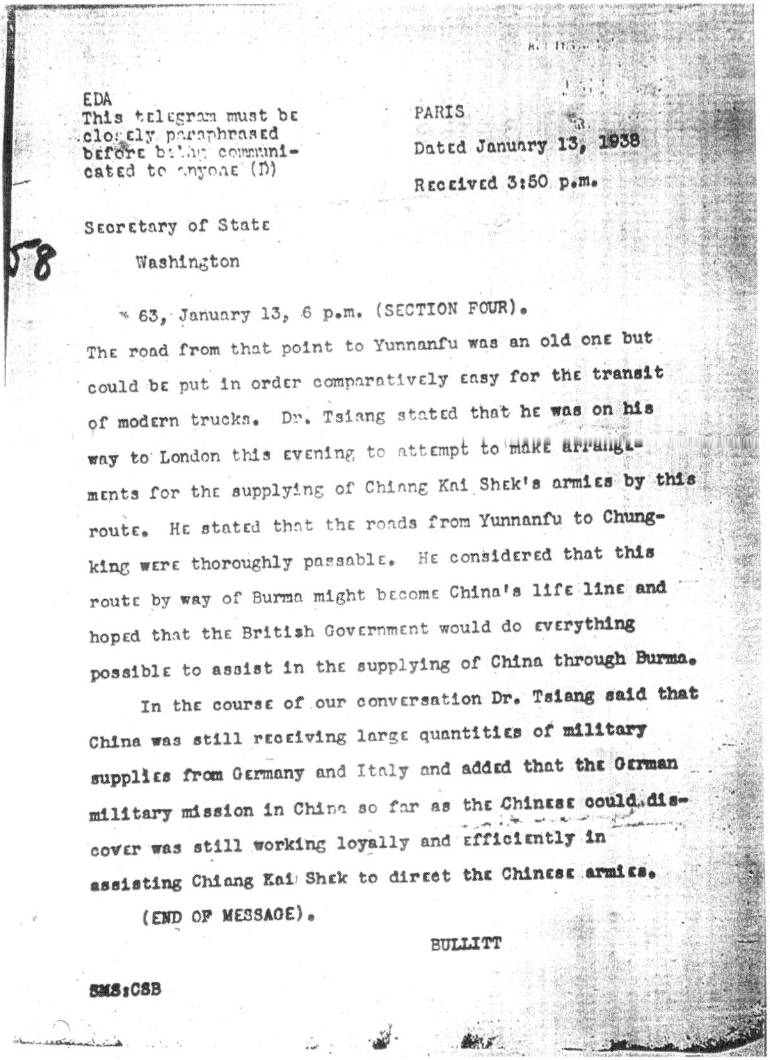

EDA
This telegram must be closely paraphrased before being communicated to anyone (D)

PARIS
Dated January 13, 1938
Received 3:50 p.m.

Secretary of State
Washington

58

63, January 13, 6 p.m. (SECTION FOUR).

The road from that point to Yunnanfu was an old one but could be put in order comparatively easy for the transit of modern trucks. Dr. Tsiang stated that he was on his way to London this evening to attempt to make arrangements for the supplying of Chiang Kai Shek's armies by this route. He stated that the roads from Yunnanfu to Chungking were thoroughly passable. He considered that this route by way of Burma might become China's life line and hoped that the British Government would do everything possible to assist in the supplying of China through Burma.

In the course of our conversation Dr. Tsiang said that China was still receiving large quantities of military supplies from Germany and Italy and added that the German military mission in China so far as the Chinese could discover was still working loyally and efficiently in assisting Chiang Kai Shek to direct the Chinese armies.

(END OF MESSAGE).

BULLITT

SMS:CSB

Nixon Identifies Hiss as Chambers's State Department Contact

Nixon quickly took the lead in exposing Hiss as the man who had provided the State Department documents to Chambers. As this account in the *New York Herald Tribune* records, HUAC made public Chambers's sworn testimony in Hiss's libel suit where he identified Hiss as the source of the material. Nixon divulged that experts had identified Hiss's handwriting on some of the material. Underlining the seriousness of the espionage, Nixon refused to release the documents for security reasons.

"CHAMBERS CHARGES HISS COPIED SECRET PAPERS FOR RED COLONEL; SOME REPORTED IN HISS'S WRITING"

Washington, Dec. 6—The House Committee on Un-American Activities announced today that Whittaker Chambers has produced copies of confidential State Department documents, which the committee said are in the handwriting of Alger Hiss, to support his direct charge

PHOTO 3.6   Nixon and Stripling examine some of the microfilm taken from the pumpkin.

© Bettmann/CORBIS

Source: New York Herald Tribune, December 7, 1948.

that Mr. Hiss had relayed a "consistent flow" of such information to Communist agents.

The relaying of this information was done, Mr. Chambers asserted, at the solicitation of a Russian colonel who was identified by the committee as the director of Soviet military intelligence in the United States at the time.

This sensational development came as both men were telling their stories again—and in secret—in New York before the special grand jury which for eighteen months has been investigating Communist espionage in the United States.

DIRECT LINK ASSERTED

The House committee asserted that it has established the first direct evidence of a link between Mr. Chambers—a self-styled courier for the Communist underground in Washington in the mid-1940s—and Mr. Hiss—then a top-level official of the State Department—as it revealed:

1. That Mr. Chambers in sworn testimony has flatly accused Mr. Hiss of turning over to him a "fairly consistent flow" of secret State Department documents beginning in 1937 with full knowledge that Mr. Chambers would relay them to Russian espionage agents.
2. That three of sixty-five documents produced by Mr. Chambers to back up this charge are in the handwriting of Mr. Hiss. Mr. Chambers alleged, the committee revealed, that Mr. Hiss had prepared these three papers in the form of notes on State Department documents which he was unable to remove from the department to have copied for delivery to Communist agents.

NIXON MAKES DISCLOSURES

These disclosures were made by Representative Richard M. Nixon, of California, who has taken the leading role in the committee's investigation of the Hiss-Chambers case for many months.

Mr. Nixon made public excerpts from sworn testimony given by Mr. Chambers two weeks ago in Baltimore in making a pre-trial deposition in the $75,000 libel suit filed against him by Mr. Hiss.

In New York Mr. Hiss issued the following statement tonight: "I am advised that the Committee on Un-American Activities has released to the press certain portions of the testimony given by Mr. Chambers in depositions taken in my libel action against him in Baltimore. I deny without qualification the accusations made in that testimony. Inasmuch as this matter is now before the grand jury, I do not feel it appropriate to comment further at this time."

• • •

Mr. Nixon said that Mr. Chambers had produced at the Baltimore pre-trial hearing sixty-five copies of such documents or notes on documents which he said Mr. Hiss had delivered to him to be relayed to Colonel Bykov.

Mr. Nixon said that the committee had possession of these documents and three of them were "in Mr. Hiss's handwriting."

He added that a government handwriting "expert" had examined these three and had informed the committee "conclusively, without qualification, that they are in the handwriting of Mr. Hiss."

Asked if it was not possible for Mr. Hiss to have written these three papers in question as part of his State Department duties and for departmental purposes, Mr. Nixon replied:

"From reading the documents it is apparent that the form and context is such that they were obviously not intended just to be part of the State Department's records."

Mr. Nixon flatly refused to discuss the contents of the documents, declared that he considered them of such importance that even now, eleven years after they were removed from the State Department, he would "vote against" having the committee make them public. He called the documents "confidential," "restricted," and "important," and said that, in some cases, they contained "military information."

ACCUSES ADMINISTRATION

Before making these revelations, Mr. Nixon fired a barrage of serious charges at the Truman administration and the Department of Justice for the handling of the Hiss-Chambers case. They were:

1. That the Administration had shown more interest in "concealing from the American people facts which might be embarrassing to certain individuals still in the Administration" than in investigating the Hiss-Chambers case.
2. That the Department of Justice has shown an "apparent lack of interest" in "getting to the real crux of the case."
3. That the department has "almost frantically" attempted to pin all the blame in the case on Mr. Chambers rather than to find out whether secret documents had been stolen from the State Department and who was responsible.

• • •

TO LIMIT DISCLOSURES

Mr. Nixon left no doubt that he was irate that the Department of Justice had "stolen" the committee's key witness and at the attitude of the Administration in general toward the Hiss-Chambers case.

He emphasized that the committee would make "no disclosure of any information from the documents which in the judgment of responsible State Department officials and the judgment of the committee would in any way impair the national interest in the United States."

"I am not speaking of the apparent interest of the Administration in concealing from the American people facts which might be embarrassing to certain individuals still in the Administration," he continued. "The committee will make public all information in the case without regard to embarrassment of any individual, but not any information which might be embarrassing to the American people.

"The committee is concerned at the apparent lack of interest of the Department of Justice in getting to the real crux of the case. The Department of Justice has been almost frantically attempting to find a method of placing the blame of having these documents in his possession on Mr. Chambers.

"That is not debatable. Mr. Chambers admits having the documents in his possession and is prepared to take the consequences, if any.

"The real issues, which concern the committee and which should concern the Justice Department, are determining who in the State Department furnished this information to Mr. Chambers. This committee is directing its entire investigation to establish beyond doubt who the person or persons were."

CHAMBERS TESTIMONY READ

Mr. Nixon then noted that the committee had obtained the stenographic transcript of Mr. Chambers's pretrial deposition in Baltimore and was prepared to make portions of it public.

"There has been considerable interest as to what charge Mr. Chambers has made as to the source of the materials he has turned over," he said. "In that connection, since Mr. Chambers's testimony was taken under oath and under very strict cross-examination by Mr. Hiss's attorney on that very point, it is time that the public be apprised of Mr. Chambers's allegation in that regard."

He proceeded to read from the Chambers testimony, explaining that it had been placed formally in the committee record so that it would be "privileged"—thus exempting publication of his charges from libel action.

Editorial Response to the New Evidence

The focus of the investigation now was on the New York grand jury, which would examine the evidence and decide whether to indict. But Nixon and his HUAC colleagues were not ready to abandon this opportunity to expose the failures of the Truman administration. Between December 7 and 14, the committee held hearings to follow up on the new evidence. On December 7,

FIGURE 3.1 Herblock' cartoon illustrates the excitement generated on Capitol Hill by the release of the pumpkin papers.

"Here They Come Now!"

Washington Post, 1948 © Herb Block Foundation

Sumner Welles, former undersecretary of state from 1937 to 1943, testified that the Chambers documents were critical to American security. He explained how they were particularly valuable for the Kremlin in its effort to break the American diplomatic codes.[9] HUAC tried to establish that its investigation transcended political in-fighting with the White House. Nevertheless, the hearings continued to reflect the friction between the committee and the Truman Justice Department and State Department as officials appeared before the committee to defend the administration.[10]

Despite the continued contentious political climate, the classified documents made it clear that now serious issues affecting American security had to be addressed. In contrast to earlier editorials that tended to focus on politics, editorials in the *New York Herald Tribune,* a publication noted for its anti-administration stance, and the *Washington Post,* more sympathetic to the administration, argued that politics had to be subordinated to what the *Herald Tribune* called "complete, careful and orderly investigation for itself, regardless of either party politics or interagency jealousies."

"THE CHAMBERS DOCUMENTS"

The discovery that Mr. Whittaker Chambers has long had in his possession a considerable file of top-secret documents which were abstracted from the State Department a decade ago is as sensational as it is serious. It is so sensational, in fact, and is from day to day being embroidered by so many fresh sensations, allegations, personal and political imputations that there is grave danger that the public will overlook the real serious aspects of this disclosure.

In all the alarm over Soviet espionage this is the first clear and concrete evidence to indicate that the Soviet Union was able to gain access to really important secret material. Even the Canadian espionage investigation never, so far as the published record goes, proved so definite, dangerous, and treasonable an invasion of the highest levels of governmental confidence. In face of the discovery of these documents all the other issues—the issue of whether it is Mr. Hiss or Mr. Chambers who committed perjury, of whether the Department of Justice was lax or the Un-American Activities Committee was merely dragging a "red herring," of the party political maneuvering which has consistently confused this subject—become insignificant, except to those personally involved. From a public point of view the one thing that now matters is a complete account of how these documents could have been removed

Source: New York Herald Tribune, December 7, 1948.

from the State Department, the nature and extent of the "apparatus" that removed them, the degree of security that now exists against this kind of infiltration of the government of the United States.

From the public point of view that is all that matters. Unfortunately, several of the protagonists in this drama seem to have forgotten the public interest; some seem not even to realize that the election is over. The Department of Justice, which now appears in a somewhat invidious light, since it never made this discovery itself, has snatched the witnesses and the evidence out of the hands of the Un-American Activities Committee and thus suppressed the committee's intended public hearing. The State Department has arrived very late upon the scene, apparently more interested in hushing up the evidence than in discovering what leaks may exist in its security. The committee's investigator was himself scarcely well advised in taking the papers to Mr. Sumner Welles before he laid them before the State Department, while Mr. Rankin has not added greatly to clarity or justice by his large pronouncements. The whole case is far too serious for maneuvers of this kind; it is so serious that it demands complete, careful and orderly investigation for itself, regardless of either party politics or interagency jealousies.

"PUMPKIN MYSTERY"

It seems pretty clear from the hearings yesterday that the House Un-American Activities Committee has got hold of something real this time—some genuine documentary evidence. This kind of material has been so scarce in the committee's past investigations that its members do not seem to know quite what to do with it. At any rate, they, and their chief of staff, have been behaving peculiarly. The moral justification for Mr. Nixon's disclosure of selected parts of Mr. Chambers' deposition made in a pretrial hearing on the Hiss libel suit is especially puzzling. But it is not the only enigma in this affair—which Mr. Mundt has prejudged by calling it the "Hiss-Chambers espionage case."

One of the first questions facing the committee, once it gained possession of the libel-suit documents and the pumpkin-shell microfilms, was whether their content could be publicly revealed without security risk. In seeking a preliminary answer to this question, Mr. Stripling went first, on Sunday evening, to visit Mr. Sumner Welles. Mr. Welles was also the committee's first outside witness on the matter in yesterday's open hearing. He was, to be sure, Undersecretary of State when the documents were pilfered some 10 years ago. But that does not, it seems to us, make him a qualified witness as to whether they are still confidential. It seems obvious that only the current officers of the State Department could answer those questions. Why didn't the committee initially call upon Mr. Peurifoy, who testified as a fairly qualified witness about the possible breaking of American codes?

As a matter of fact, the State Department itself might have shown more alacrity in finding out about the material taken from its files. From Friday morning, when existence of the microfilms and their nature was revealed in the press, until about Monday noon the department seems to have done nothing. Then, apparently despairing of an invitation from the committee, two departmental security officers visited the Hill to take a look at the documents. Knowing the committee's penchant for publicity, the State Department should have been immediately concerned to prevent any damage that might have been done by public exposure of the material. The delay seems to us as peculiar as the tactics of the Committee on Un-American Activities itself.

Still a "Red Herring" to Truman

At a news conference on December 9, President Truman found himself on the defensive. Yet despite the fact that the American public was taking the HUAC investigation more seriously, he continued to view things in political terms, as the following comments from his news conference illustrate. As reporters pushed for answers by citing specifics, he found himself hard-pressed to satisfactorily defend his administration's conduct.

PRESIDENT TRUMAN'S NEWS CONFERENCE, DECEMBER 9, 1948

THE PRESIDENT: I have no announcements to make this morning. If you have any questions you think I can answer, I will be glad try to answer them.

Q: Mr. President, there's lots being made up on the Hill over some reported secret papers of the State Department stolen. These papers are now

Source: Public Papers of the Presidents of the United States, Harry S. Truman, 1948, 959–60.

figuring quite voluminously in the Communist investigation. Do you know of any reason why those papers, dating back to the late thirties should not be made public now?

THE PRESIDENT: That matter is in the hands of the Attorney General and the courts. I have no comment to make on that.

Q: Mr. President, there does seem to be indisputable evidence, despite all the bizarre aspects of the case, that highly secret and confidential documents were stolen from the State Department files—taken out long enough to be microfilmed and then put back in the State Department files. Do you think, sir, that all our arms of Government should be used to find out if possible who stole those documents?

THE PRESIDENT: Why certainly. The Attorney General will do that. It is in his hands.

Q: Mr. President, last night at the night hearing, Acting Chairman Mundt accused the administration of being a "do-nothing" administration. Would you care—

THE PRESIDENT: That's a "me too" proposition.

Q: A what proposition?

THE PRESIDENT: A "me too" proposition.

Q: Mr. President, have you given any instructions to the Department of Justice on this case?

THE PRESIDENT: The Department of Justice has had standing instructions on the whole thing, ever since it started.

Q: What were those instructions, sir?

THE PRESIDENT: It's what the Attorney General's duties are, to enforce the law.

Q: I thought, sir, you meant they had instructions from you?

THE PRESIDENT: No. Of course the Attorney General discussed the matter with me at various times, and he has of course had instructions to enforce the law.

Q: Mr. President, do you still feel that this—as you did during the late summer, that this congressional investigation has the aspects of a "red herring"?

THE PRESIDENT: That's what the people thought.

Q: Do you think so now, sir?

THE PRESIDENT: I do.

Q: After these revelations that the documents were stolen?

THE PRESIDENT: I certainly do. If they were in dead earnest, they would have taken this matter to the Attorney General and let him go ahead with the prosecution. They aren't prosecuting anybody, they are just making headlines.

Q: Mr. President, the committee members said they have repeatedly taken action with the Attorney General in all of its aspects.

THE PRESIDENT: That's not what the Attorney General said.

Q: Mr. President, are you at all interested in this charge of Mr. Nixon's that the Department of Justice proposes to indict only Chambers—or first Chambers, and thus destroy his usefulness?

THE PRESIDENT: The Department of Justice will follow the law. It's in the hands of the Department of Justice and the courts, and that's where it will be so far as I am concerned. I have no intention of getting into a controversy with this dead committee. [*Laughter*]

Q: My question may be useless, after that, but there is a charge that there's politics being played at this hearing, and the inference is that the administration is playing the politics. You said nothing about that. May I ask you if you will say something about it?

THE PRESIDENT: I think the evidence speaks for itself on that—in that line.

Q: Mr. President, may I ask one thing? You call it a dead committee. It's a standing committee of the House. Do you think it will be, or should be abolished?

THE PRESIDENT: I think the Congress itself will take care of that when it meets after the first of January, so you had better ask the Speaker of the House what he intends to do about it.

Q: Mr. President, does it disturb you at all, sir, that although the FBI had the Chambers story for 9 years, it took this dead committee to come up with the documents?

THE PRESIDENT: Did the FBI have it for 9 years, do you know? Are you making that as a statement of fact? I want to know if you know that? I don't know—I say I don't know that that is a fact. I don't think you should enter into a controversy unless you know it is a fact.

Q: Did you say—you said that it is not a fact, Mr. President?

THE PRESIDENT: I do not. I don't think you do, either.

Q: Mr. President, the testimony has been that although—not the FBI necessarily, but other high officers, including Mr. Berle in the Democratic administration, had heard the whole story?

THE PRESIDENT: I know nothing about it.

No "Red Herring" to American People

The president's continued insistence that the whole affair was a "red herring" was no longer convincing. Undoubtedly HUAC was out for headlines, but now there was concrete evidence. Editorials excoriated Truman for his unwavering stance and urged that in the national interest the administration get to the bottom of this affair.

"RED BUT NOT HERRING"

President Truman's reiteration of his "red herring" charge against the Whittaker Chambers expose of a Communist conspiracy that reached into the State Department for confidential documents coincides with reports that Mr. Chambers is to be indicted in New York for perjury. It is possible, of course, that there is no connection between the two. It is possible also that Representative Nixon's fears that the Department of Justice is planning to act against the key witness in the scandal of the stolen documents before the expose has been completed has no foundation. Yet the President's attitude suggests a desire to suppress the whole business, and the indictment of Chambers at this time would certainly be a step in that direction.

If this is the Administration's policy, it is, in our opinion, incredibly short-sighted. Even during Mr. Truman's campaign for reelection we felt that he ventured onto spongy ground by calling the Chambers story a red herring. At that time, however, the magazine editor's charges that Communists had had access to confidential documents were unproved. His testimony had been sharply contradicted and made the basis for a slander suit. Mr. Truman then based his case on the assertion that the Committee on Un-American Activities had gotten nothing from Mr. Chambers that had not been previously known to the FBI and disclosed to the grand jury in New York. Now the situation has completely changed with the seizure of microfilms picturing secret documents obviously stolen from the State Department and delivered to an avowed Communist. For the President to cling to his "red herring" statement in the face of this scandal is certainly no service to either public understanding of the issue or to the national interest.

No exception can be taken to the President's statement that the Committee on Un-American Activities is out for the headlines. The facts indicate, however, that this time the committee has evidence which inevitably makes headlines. It appears to have proved beyond any reasonable doubt that Communists had a pipe line into the State Department. The public will not be satisfied until the details of that traitorous business have been fully laid bare. Yet the attitude of the President and the Department of Justice creates suspicion that they are more interested in concealing than in exposing the conspiracy.

That suspicion would be in large measure confirmed if the department should indict Mr. Chambers for perjury before the expose is complete. We hold no brief for this former Communist who has seen the error of his ways. But the undisputed fact is that he has brought to light the only substantial evidence the Government has of treachery in high official circles. His further cooperation is obviously needed. We should think that the Administration would be straining its resources to bring to book the traitorous former officials who permitted this encroachment upon our security before giving thought to what shall be done with the repentant Communist who has exposed their perfidy.

"A BETRAYAL OF TRUST"

In making his press conference remarks on the espionage case yesterday, President Truman cannot have foreseen the untenable position into which he is moving. He stood by his former characterization of the Congressional investigation as mere headline hunting, dragging out political "red herrings," yet he granted the deadly seriousness of the disclosures that have now come from its work. He admitted that they are so serious as to claim the best efforts of the government in running them down; yet he still left the task of doing so to his Attorney General and the Department of Justice—as if unaware of how deeply they are compromised in the public mind in regard to this matter. They are compromised by their own failure to bring the facts to light, by the political implications in their battle with the Congressional investigation and by the only too obvious indications they are now giving, in their sudden activity before the special grand jury, that they are more interested in hampering the Congressional committee and discrediting its chief witness than they are in getting at the truth of a plain and gross violation of the public trust.

It is now incontrovertible that during 1937 and 1938 some one stole quantities of the most highly secret papers from files of the American State Department and passed them, without detection or even suspicion, into unauthorized hands where they might have been used to the most serious injury of the United States. That is a now established fact toward which the President cannot possibly afford to take

Source: New York Herald Tribune, December 10, 1948.

an equivocal attitude. Who did this? How could it have come about? How long or how far did the infiltration extend, and is a repetition possible? What does it imply as to present policy or legislation in regard to Communist or other subversive conspiracy? These are questions crying aloud for answer; and when later yesterday afternoon a former confidential officer of the State Department spent a long hearing refusing to answer questions on the plea of self-incrimination, it left a sense of shock that makes the basic facts involved no less insistent.

Whatever his faults, Mr. Whittaker Chambers is at least one witness who has not hidden behind the self-incrimination plea (though it would seem that he might justifiably have done so), and it would be grimly ironic if the really critical facts behind all this business should be lost to view in a legal assault on the one man who has produced concrete evidence of a flagrant dereliction of public duty. But it is not Mr. Chambers or Mr. Hiss who is important; it is not the embarrassment of the Department of Justice or the undoubted failings of the Congressional committee or even the pique of President Truman. What is important is the infiltration and theft in the highest department of the government. This must be cleared up, and it cannot be done by a squabble among the agencies now involved. So far from destroying its standing committee. Congress should strengthen it with the ablest membership and ablest counsel available. But that will not be enough unless the President realizes the importance of actively intervening with the Justice Department to insure that these new disclosures, which are no longer "red herrings" by any stretch, are investigated to the end, regardless of consequences.

Nixon Appears Before the Grand Jury

As HUAC and the Truman administration sparred in the political arena, the New York grand jury examined the new evidence between December 6 and 13. Both Chambers and Hiss testified and were grilled for details. Hiss's wife, Priscilla, accused by Chambers of typing many of the documents, appeared to deny his accusations. But perhaps the most significant witness was Nixon, who brought the original microfilmed evidence with him.

For a congressman to appear before this body certainly had to impress the jurors. Nixon described his involvement in the investigation, his effort to get to the truth, and his growing conviction that Chambers was telling the truth. He refused to turn the microfilm evidence over to the grand jury, but described how HUAC had developed it and determined its authenticity. (At one point, HUAC had been told that one of the rolls of film had been manufactured in 1947, which would have undermined the authenticity of the material. But later, that 1947 date was determined to be incorrect.) Nixon's appearance added weight to the charges against Hiss. The way he carefully guarded the microfilm emphasized the national security value of the materials.

NIXON'S APPEARANCE BEFORE FEDERAL GRAND JURY, DECEMBER 13, 1948

I realized that you ladies and gentlemen are faced with probably the conundrum of the age for a grand jury, with conflicting testimony, with individuals who have concealed testimony and then have come forth with testimony later, and with the same conundrum with which our committee was faced, one individual saying that he knows a group of other individuals, and the other individuals not only denying the charges that individual made, but saying, "We have never seen that individual before."

That was the problem, I might say, with which our committee was concerned, and faced with, immediately after the testimony of Whittaker Chambers on August 3rd. Mr. Hiss came down on August 5th and said, "I have never seen this man before in my life. I do not know why he would say I was a Communist if I have never been a Communist."

I might say that it was at that time that every member of the Un-American Activities Committee who heard Mr. Hiss that day, with the exception of myself, felt that there was no question whatever but that what Mr. Hiss was telling the truth. But I felt it was essential to proceed and find out whether or not these two individuals knew each other, on the issue of whether one was a Communist or another was a Communist that couldn't be determined, but whether one man knew another, that can be determined, because if one man knew another, that can be determined, and that's the way we solved the problem, because Mr. Hiss after a good deal of persuasion and faced with certain facts changed his story, and changed it considerably, as most of you are aware.

In bringing that out I was interested only in getting at the truth. If I had found as a result of that Mr. Chambers had lied when he said he

Source: Records of U.S. Attorneys and Marshals: Transcripts of Grand Jury Testimony in the Alger Hiss Case, Record Group 118, Harry S. Truman Presidential Library, Box 3, 4162–66, 4178–81, 4190–91.

knew Mr. Hiss, I would be here before this grand jury, I would have gone to the Department of Justice, and I would have insisted that Mr. Chambers be prosecuted for telling that lie, and I think he should pay for whatever he has done, which is wrong.

But in the case of this film I want to say that when I returned from my trip to Panama, which was interrupted as a result of this investigation, that I returned on Monday, and—I am sorry, I returned on Sunday night—on Sunday night I examined the documents made from the films but not the films themselves because they were locked in the safe. We keep them under lock and key.

The following day I came down and examined the films and in examining them I told Mr. Stripling, the investigator that I wanted to have the major film, the film that had the most confidential documents on, at least that one, immediately checked as to the date of manufacture, because Mr. Chambers' story from what I learned was that the films were ten years old, and we knew of course that you can determine dates of film.

So in printing this one—I might say it doesn't injure a film after it's been developed to expose it to light—when you take a film of this sort and expose it to the light you can see, I think any of you can see written on the film with the word Kodak, Kodak Safety Film—do you see that?—and over here is a code which reads "Eastman-14," right on the top of the film you will see that. On the basis of that you can determine the age of the film by contacting the manufacturer. We called Mr. Lewis in Washington, who is the Washington representative of the Eastman-Kodak Company, to our office. We had him examine this roll of film, which was the film that was involved. He examined it, took down the code and said, "I will find out for you immediately what the situation is and give you a report."

He called Rochester, N.Y., and as soon as he received the report from Rochester he came into my office—he called in, I have two rooms—he called in the room, in the outside room, he came into my office on Monday afternoon, and said, "Mr. Nixon, the film is, according to the reports that we have from Rochester, the film that you speak of with this code name is 1947."

JUROR: 1937.

THE WITNESS: 1947. I said, "Well, that's very interesting. Under the circumstances it seems quite apparent that somebody is trying to concoct a most monstrous conspiracy here. That these documents must have been taken out much later and put on the film in 1947."

Then at that time I immediately called in the investigators. I indicated that we had an entirely new line to follow and that it was our duty and responsibility to bring these facts out if that were the case.

We were just prepared at that time—I had instructed them to call the newspapers to my office so that I could tell them of this new discovery—I was just prepared to tell them when Mr. Lewis called on the phone within 30 minutes after he called the first time—he was extremely embarrassed—he said that Rochester had called him back and said they were in error, that the film was 1937, that 1947 was incorrect.

I got on the phone with Mr. Lewis, and said, "Mr. Lewis, I want to be absolutely sure of this. Are you sure?" He said, "There is no question about it whatever." I said, "Now, what I want you to do is call Rochester again, go over it again, and be sure this is 1937 and not 1947." And he said, "I will do so." I said, "I want you to do that because I intend to call you as a witness tomorrow, on Tuesday, to testify to this fact under oath, as to the date of this film." He did so. Of course it was 1937. It was an error of ten years in the date and, incidentally, there was an error simply in the transmission of things, not an error because of the type of film. He made it absolutely clear.

We called him before the committee on Tuesday. I put him under oath before the committee, asked him what the date of the film was, and he testified in public session that the film was manufactured in 1937.

• • •

Q: Let me ask you this, Congressman: When these films were turned up and the Committee got them, why weren't they then taken to the FBI laboratories?

A: For development?

Q: Yes, for processing and rehabilitation and development.

A: I would say that, Mr. Campbell, the reasons would be quite obvious: I mean I would be glad to go into them if you want to press me.

Q: In other words, you chose the Veterans Administration rather than the FBI?

A: Yes. I think it's quite clear, I thought I made myself quite clear that the Department of Justice has issued instructions to the FBI not to cooperate with the Committee on Un-American Activities. We are aware of that. I mean, if you want to raise that issue—I mean, I was hoping that we wouldn't have to get into the controversies between Justice and the Committee.

Q: No, I'm not raising the issue; I'm merely saying that in criminal prosecutions the FBI is the investigating agency and anybody and everyone, the police department, the state police departments, city police, county sheriffs, the minute they get any evidence such as this, the first hour that they can possibly do it they immediately and speedily deliver it to the FBI for proper identification and processing.

A: Well, if you want to tell me now that from this day forth the Committee on Un-American Activities can use the FBI for the purpose of carrying on its investigations, you can be sure we will do that in the future.

Q: Well, I can't do that, of course.

A: I know you can't.

Q: But I think you have missed the point.

A: I haven't missed it.

Q: The United States Attorneys in the field do not use the Veterans Administration's processes to investigate crimes like committed here. The Courts and the United States Attorneys use the FBI. In other words, you could have taken this to the FBI laboratory. There is no question about that in your mind, is there?

A: Well, all that I can say is that I didn't think there was much question about this in your mind or in anybody else's, that we have been given to understand that when the Committee had work of that sort to do it would have to do it through some other facilities; and that's what we have done. We submitted it to the Veterans Administration because they have a technical laboratory which, I understand, is a very good one for this purpose. If you have any question about the work that was done in that laboratory or if it can be done better otherwise now, we have certainly no reason to keep it from the FBI: because all that, frankly, we are interested in is the truth in this matter, as I'm sure you are.

Q: That's exactly what we are trying to get at here, and have for 18 months.

BY THE JURY:

Q: It seems to me that there is some particular reason why you submitted it to the Veterans Bureau rather than the FBI. Now, what reason is that?

A: Well, the Committee, as I have indicated—strike that. And I will say this as briefly as I can. The Department of Justice is, of course, over the FBI; that is, the FBI is a part of the Department of Justice. And the Department of Justice, for reasons that may be very diligent, I might say, has not been particularly taken with the work of the Committee on Un-American Activities. Consequently, the Committee on Un-American Activities has not been able, frankly, to avail itself of FBI investigators and FBI laboratories to carry on our investigations, due apparently to the fact that the Department of Justice has so instructed the FBI. We took it, in other words, to the Veterans Administration because we had to have the work done and we knew that they would do it for us. We didn't want to get into that argument with the Department of Justice again as to whether we had any jurisdiction to have this work done. As I say, I for one think it's, frankly, a very unfortunate thing that the Department of Justice feels as it does concerning the Committee and therefore has seen fit to inform the FBI that that should be its attitude toward the Committee. But I can assure you that if the Committee had felt that we could get this work done through the Department of Justice, we would certainly have done so.

• • •

But our investigations, I might say, prior to the time of the discovery of the documents, brought out some very interesting information in that field which would be of help to you on that particular issue. And I would say, in that regard, that it particularly would be helpful to you in cross-examining Mr. Hiss. I might say that you are dealing here with two witnesses—speaking now of Mr. Hiss and Mr. Chambers and leaving out Mr. Wadleigh, Mr. Pigman and the others who have been named—you are dealing here with two witnesses who are most difficult to deal with. And I am sure that the representatives of the Department of Justice have been doing what they can to bring the facts out before the Grand Jury and you also have done so in your questioning. But we found, ourselves, in dealing with Mr. Hiss particularly, that Mr. Hiss is a very persuasive witness. When he first came down before the Committee and made his now famous statement that he didn't know Mr. Chambers, he convinced ninety per cent of the press and virtually all of the members of the Committee. The only way that Mr. Hiss can be cross-examined is by obtaining basic information and then confronting him with that information and then cross-examining him relentlessly and I mean relentlessly, until the truth comes out.

The Grand Jury Indicts Hiss

On the last day of the grand jury's tenure, it indicted Alger Hiss on two counts of perjury—that he had lied to the grand jury in denying that he had turned documents over to Chambers in early 1938 and that he had lied in denying that he had met with Chambers at this time. The statute of limitations on espionage had run out, otherwise the jury may have indicted him for espionage. But the perjury indictment itself was tantamount to a charge of espionage.

The *New York Herald Tribune* in a December 17 editorial expressed the prevailing sense of public relief that at last the important security questions would be answered. "The trial of Mr. Hiss," the newspaper declared, "should at last bring out those facts, freed of all political and personal overtones which heavily confused this case, by the orderly processes of a court of law."

"THE HISS INDICTMENT"

The indictment of Mr. Alger Hiss on two counts of perjury in the closing hours of the special grand jury seems to have come as a surprise to many and as a shock to some. The espionage investigations and their related controversies have generated on both sides a curious intensity

Source: New York Herald Tribune, December 17, 1948.

of emotion and violence of partisanship. In a situation in which it has been obvious for months that one of two men must be perjuring himself concerning matters of serious importance to the security of the nation and to our whole policy on infiltration and espionage, there has been a vast deal of impassioned attack or defense but only a minimum interest in the main issue—the facts of what actually happened. The trial of Mr. Hiss should at last bring out those facts freed of all the political and personal overtones which heavily confused this case, by the orderly processes of a court of law.

The indictment, of course, permits of no presumption as to the guilt or innocence of the accused. It implies only what it says on its face—that the grand jury, with the government's evidence before it, had reason to think that it is Mr. Hiss and not Mr. Chambers who has been lying. The weight and validity of the evidence remains to be tested. But the indictment does completely dispose of President Truman's contention, still repeated yesterday, that disclosures of the Un-American Activities Committee are mere "red herrings"; it shows that the Department of Justice is taking seriously a serious matter, and it is valuable as compelling the suspension of all prejudices and prejudgments until the courts have had an opportunity to decide.

Notes

1. Allen Weinstein, *Perjury: The Hiss-Chambers Case* (New York: Random House, 1997), 141–42.
2. Stenographic Transcript in the Case of Alger Hiss v. Whittaker Chambers, U.S. District Court for the District of Maryland, Baltimore, Maryland, November 4, 1948, 208.
3. Ibid., November 5, 1948, 211–13.
4. Allen Weinstein, in his study of the Hiss-Chambers affair, noted that some of Chambers's details were faulty. The "Messerschmidt" Chambers referred to in his testimony was actually Assistant Secretary of State George S. Messersmith. The document to which Chambers was referring, one he would later produce, was a report from a diplomat named Wiley stationed in Vienna, who had conversations with an Austrian Foreign Ministry official named Schmidt. Weinstein, *Perjury*, 150.
5. Ibid., 154.
6. Ibid., 150–52.
7. Whittaker Chambers, *Witness* (New York: Random House, 1952), 736.
8. Weinstein, *Perjury*, 163–67.

9. "Spy Papers Disclosed U.S. Code To Russians in 1937, Inquiry Finds; Jury Here Gets 'Real Evidence,' " *New York Herald Tribune,* December 8, 1948.

10. "Nixon Says Chambers Indictment Now Would Destroy Spy Inquiry; Truman's Intervention Is Sought," ibid., December 9, 1948.

4
The Perjury Trials

Technically, Alger Hiss was charged with two counts of perjury.
But to the American people, he was standing trial for espionage.
That such a prominent government official was charged added gravity to public concerns that the United States was losing ground to its
Soviet rival. The same newspapers that followed the daily developments in the Hiss case courtroom also chronicled disturbing
developments both abroad and at home, adding to the seriousness
of the Chambers accusations. Between the time of Hiss's arraignment in December 1948 and his ultimate conviction in January of
1950, the United States made a major military commitment to the
defense of Europe by signing the North Atlantic Treaty in April 1949.
That fall, Truman announced that the Soviet Union had successfully
tested a nuclear weapon, ending the U.S. monopoly and increasing
the public feeling of vulnerability. In Asia, the Chinese Communists
succeeded in their revolution against the nationalist government of
Chiang Kai-shek.

Revelations of other espionage activity added to public apprehension. In the same federal courthouse where Hiss stood trial,
Eugene Dennis and ten other Communist Party officials were being
tried for violating the 1940 Smith Act. Their trial began on January 17
and ended on October 21 with convictions. In Washington, D.C.,
Judith Coplon, a Justice Department clerk, and a Soviet consular officer, Valentin Gubitchev, faced charges of espionage. On June 30,
1949, they were convicted. The trials fed off each other adding to
public anxiety.

Hiss's conviction would verify not only that Communist espionage had penetrated the State Department, but also that it had infiltrated the higher levels of government. Espionage was no longer simply a partisan political charge, but it was now a reality.

CHRONOLOGY: THE PERJURY TRIALS

1948
December 16: After the grand jury had indicted Hiss for perjury on December 15, he pled not guilty at an arraignment hearing.

1949
May 31: Hiss's first trial opened in New York, Judge Samuel H. Kaufman presiding.
July 8: The first trial ended in a deadlock, the jury voting 8 to 4 to convict.
November 17: Hiss's second trial began in the courtroom of Judge Henry W. Goddard.

1950
January 21: The second trial ended with Hiss's conviction on both perjury counts.
January 25: Judge Goddard sentenced Hiss to five years in prison and released him on $10,000 bail pending appeal.
December 7: The United States Court of Appeals for the Second District rejected Hiss's appeal.

1951
March 22: Hiss began serving his five-year prison term.

Opening Statements, First Trial

On May 31, the trial began in the courtroom of Judge Samuel H. Kaufman. Jury selection proceeded swiftly, and on June 1 the prosecution and defense made their opening statements. Both attorneys laid out their intended strategy clearly.

In a business-like fashion, U.S. Attorney Thomas F. Murphy presented the case against Hiss. Likening the jury's task to parents faced with the possibility that their child had lied about playing hooky from school, he maintained that he would prove Chambers truthful and Hiss a liar. The facts—especially the documents typed on a Woodstock typewriter once owned by the Hisses and the five notes in Hiss's handwriting—to him were incontrovertible evidence. The typewriter was a particularly integral part of the prosecution's case. Murphy conceded that he did not have the actual typewriter, but he did have samples of correspondence that the Hisses had typed on the machine and experts who would verify that the stolen documents were typed on that same Woodstock. Murphy's presentation took barely half an hour.

THOMAS F. MURPHY, OPENING STATEMENT FOR GOVERNMENT

So there we have the substance of the crime, namely, that he lied when he was under oath in the grand jury in this building when he said—now I am talking about two separate things—one, that he did not give these documents to Chambers; two, that he did not even see him or converse with him since January 1, 1937.

That, ladies and gentlemen of the jury, is the indictment, or a summary of it. Of course you can see that the ultimate issue you have to decide is whether or not this man lied deliberately concerning those two subject matters.

How are we going to prove that? We are going to prove that the man lied in exactly the same way that you would prove that some friend or business associate or child of yours lied. Lying, as we know, is a sort of mental process. It goes on underneath the bone and hair, and you just have to prove it by other means. Anyway you cannot look in and see what is going on, so you have to prove it by other means.

It is not like taking a photograph. We are not going to give you photographs of the man lying. We are going to prove it the same way as you would prove it in your family life or business.

Let us suppose a child of yours came home and said he or she was in school on Tuesday, and you had some slight doubts about it, but you decide to investigate. So you went to the school and you found that the child was marked absent the whole day in question. That would make you begin to doubt, at least, that the child was telling the truth. But then if you pressed it a little further and you found your brother saw the child in a movie on that day, I daresay you would come to the conclusion, rather rightly, that the child was lying.

That is what we are going to do here. We are going to put Mr. Chambers on the stand and he is going to tell you in the most explicit fashion that I know how, how over a period of time from 1937 and part of 1938 this defendant, violating his sworn duty, handed over

Source: Stenographers Minutes, United States of America v. Alger Hiss, United States District Court, Southern District of New York, June 1, 1949, 15–23.

secret and confidential documents to him, Chambers, a Communist, when obviously he did not have any right to them at all.

He handed them over in wholesale fashion; not one or two or three, a dozen, or two dozen, three dozen, four dozen. We are going to show you 65 typewritten sheets which are either copies or paraphrases of original State Department documents, 47 in number of them dated in the first three months of 1938.

So it is not just a little thing that happened one afternoon or two afternoons, but we are going to show you it happened, as the indictment charges, in a wholesale fashion. The documents were all secret. In fact, one of them is secret to such an extent that we are going to have the Judge not to permit you to see it. We are going to show you all of the others.

How are we going to prove that Chambers was telling the truth? Because we have the documents, and we are going to have the State Department here and we are going to show you by them the documents and let you compare them and have the State Department men tell you that they are the identical documents on file in the State Department, highly confidential, and should not be seen by anybody except people in the State Department or in the Government.

They are typewritten. Mr. Chambers says that they were typewritten pursuant to an arrangement had between him and the defendant and the defendant's wife. He says the defendant's wife, pursuant to that arrangement, was to type them when he, Mr. Hiss, brought them home from the State Department, so that he, Mr. Hiss, could bring them back to the State Department in the morning.

As I said, 65 of those documents are on white paper, typewritten. You can see immediately that the question of a typewriter, ownership of the typewriter, became important.

Those documents were introduced in evidence by Mr. Chambers when he was being examined as an adverse party before trial in Baltimore. As a result of the hearing that was taken by the Committee on Un-American Activities of the House of Representatives, Mr. Chambers said something over the radio that Mr. Hiss decided was a lawsuit or at least grounds for a lawsuit, so he instituted a suit in the Federal Court in Baltimore for libel.

In connection with that lawsuit and under the practice in the Federal Courts, his attorneys in Baltimore, that is Hiss's attorneys, examined Mr. Chambers and Mrs. Chambers as adverse parties and a witness before trial. They examined him at length. As a matter of fact, here are the examinations (exhibiting volumes). They come to 1300-and-some-odd pages.

The examinations started in November and ended in March of this year. The libel was alleged to have occurred in 1948.

Getting back to the typewriter, some F.B.I. agents asked Mr. Hiss did he have a typewriter. "Yes," he remembered he had a typewriter.

"Do you remember what kind it was?" "Yes," he thought it was an office standard upright typewriter. He could not remember the name but thought perhaps it was an Underwood, but he remembered that his wife got the typewriter from her father, Mr. Fansler, who was an insurance agent in Philadelphia when he retired. And he remembered that he had that typewriter in their different houses and he fixes the end of 1938 as about the last time he saw it. His recollection was that his wife disposed of it by giving it away or selling it to a second-hand typewriter dealer in or near their house in Georgetown down in Washington. He had not seen it since. That was his then recollection. That was his recollection on December 4, 1948, and he said the document had been introduced in this lawsuit down in Baltimore on November 17th.

The F.B.I. then conducted a search of the City of Washington looking for the typewriter, or a specimen from the typewriter. To use the parlance of the district attorney's office, they shook down the City of Washington to a fare-thee-well. Approximately 25 or 30 agents scoured the City but could not find it.

But we were able to find specimens of the typewriter; that is, typewritten papers, papers, letters that were obviously written on that typewriter at or about that time or shortly before.

One was a letter, I forget now whether Mr. or Mrs. Hiss wrote it, to the school where their little boy was going. Another was a letter to an insurance company. Another was a speech that Mrs. Hiss prepared in connection with some of her college alumni activities.

Anyway, finally Mr. Hiss came forward and says, here is a specimen he thinks comes from that typewriter. Anyway, we were armed with quite a few of them, and we gave them to the F.B.I. and their experts, working independently of the other investigation, and he will testify here on the stand, have come forward and they are saying two things; one that 64 out of the 65 typewritten documents were undoubtedly typed on a Woodstock typewriter, pica type, 10 letters to the inch. The 65th one the agent said was not typed on that type of typewriter.

Now if we prove to you, as Mr. Chambers will, that he got the documents from Hiss, and we prove that they were typed on a typewriter in his possession or control, and that the documents themselves came from the State Department, and some of them right from his office, I daresay that you will be convinced that Hiss lied in the grand jury.

Now in addition to the typewritten documents, we have four handwritten documents, and Chambers will tell you he received them from Hiss. These were documents that Chambers will describe on small pieces of paper that Hiss copied or made notations on in the State Department when he did not have an opportunity of extracting the document and bringing it home. He will tell you about the modus operandi, the practice Chambers and Hiss adopted with regard to the documents.

There will be testimony by Chambers that in 1937 Chambers and a man by the name of Colonel Bykov and Hiss, pursuant to an arrangement made here in New York City, decided that Hiss, commencing from that time should expect documents from the State Department relating generally to Germany and give them to Chambers, and Chambers, in turn, was to photograph them or have someone photograph them and the developed microfilm would be delivered by Chambers to Colonel Bykov.

Chambers will testify that that procedure was adopted and carried into effect for a period of many, many weeks, and that it was decided that they were not getting enough material because under that plan Chambers would only come to Hiss's home perhaps every ten days or two weeks, and he would take that night only the documents that Hiss had brought home that night.

Since the documents had to be returned each morning, you can see that in the whole period of ten days or two weeks, quite a few documents were not going back to Bykov, and so they decided to speed up the process, and it was agreed that from that point on not only would he continue to bring home these official State Department documents, but while they were home and while Chambers wasn't there Mrs. Hiss would copy them or paraphrase them, and then when Chambers appeared on the 10th or 14th day or so he would take out with him the original documents that had been brought home that day and the copied documents that had been prepared in the prior ten days or two weeks. So we have only the typewritten documents, photographs of original documents, and the handwritten notes relating to documents that Hiss could not bring out.

Now, as to the handwritings, Mr. Hiss says that three out of the four look like his, that one he is not sure of, or he says he doesn't think it is his, or he only thinks it is, but as to dissipate these statements or admissions we are going to prove to you I think conclusively that the four are in his handwriting. We have a standard or a document that was used when he became a lawyer in the City of New York, and when he filled out a long, involved questionnaire that all lawyers had to fill out in 1933

I think it was, and we are going to use that, the experts are, and we are going to show that as to these documents there is no doubt about them, and based upon my knowledge and experience these four documents are undoubtedly in Hiss's handwriting, and we are going to point out why perhaps Hiss was a little doubtful about this fourth one, which is a very, very short telegram, as you will notice when it is introduced, and perhaps why he wasn't so sure, but in any event we will corroborate Chambers' testimony by the typewriting and by the handwriting.

Lloyd P. Stryker, Hiss's lead attorney, focused on questions of character—who the jury should believe, Alger Hiss with "no blotch or blemish on him," or Whittaker Chambers, whose "atheism, destruction of religion, lies, stealing, all were part and parcel of the bad life that he led for twelve years." In a telling revelation at the end of his presentation, he announced that his defense team had succeeded where FBI agents had failed. They had found the Woodstock typewriter so important to the case. He said that he was willing to allow the prosecution to examine the machine. Exploiting the fact that it was the Hiss team that produced the typewriter, Stryker raised the rhetorical question whether this was the action of a guilty man.

LLOYD P. STRYKER, OPENING STATEMENT FOR DEFENDANT

Now, as Mr. Murphy very well said, there are no photographs of handing the documents to Chambers. That whole story rests on Chambers. And Mr. Murphy has also told you that if you do not believe Chambers the Government has no case. So, narrowing it down then to what we are here about and accepting Mr. Murphy's statement as correct, what you here are going to determine is whether or not you believe Chambers. I think that is a fair statement of the case, and I am supported in it by Mr. Murphy's fair statement of the issue.

Now, perhaps, if we once get that simple thought in our minds we will begin to approach this case without confusion, without heat or emotion, or anything else, except the dispassionate judgment of twelve honorable ladies and gentlemen drawn from our community to sit here in this court of justice and to perform perhaps next to service in battle the most important function of a citizen.

Now, Mr. Murphy said to you, and here again I am with him, that if you have this kind of a problem, let us say, if someone made a

Source: Stenographers Minutes, United States of America v. Alger Hiss, United States District Court, Southern District of New York, June 1, 1949, 27–30, 38–42, 51–53.

charge about, as I heard it, your child being in a movie when the child said he was not, then you approach that in a commonsense way to determine that issue. I agree with that entirely, that that is just what you do, and that is just what I think, if I may say so, you should do.

Now, suppose a dearly beloved child was charged with some delinquency or other, what would be the first line of approach? I say this not at all as argument but as an explanation of the evidence that we will lay before you, because we want to lay before you as well as we can such evidence as will honestly enable you to arrive at a true verdict. So you would want to know, wouldn't you, who was the person that made this charge against your child? What kind of a person is he? Is he an honest man? Had he been a God-fearing, truth-loving and truth-telling man? How did he live? What had he done? You would want to know that, wouldn't you, about the accuser, to follow Mr. Murphy's illustration, before you would judge that child? Also, as close and as dear as the child might be you would want to understand the child. Had the child been a truth-telling, good child? Had the child been the kind of child who from your experience you had found that you could take its word? So you would consider two things obviously: in other words, the accuser and the accused.

I really do not know of any other way to approach this case. We can't put ourselves back in the year 1938, and I would like to have you remember that year and the months of February and March, 1938.

So we have, or you will have, the testimony of a man by the name of Chambers who I gather from the prosecution's opening and from the charge in the indictment, will say that he received the documents.

I propose, ladies and gentlemen, to help you every way I can as much as though I were your servant, and if you will treat me in that light I will try to be a good servant to you. I propose to lay before you in the most straightforward way I can all the evidence in our possession that will enable you to form a judgment as to the accuser and the accused, because remember if you don't believe Chambers, on Mr. Murphy's own statement, that is the end of their case no matter what else they may try to establish.

Now, then, with that end in view, and without malice and hatred for anyone, I will try to give you the best possible accurate and truthful picture of who and what the accuser is, and who and what the accused is, because from what we have said I think, and I see that you are interested in that regard, that you can have an even better basis for reaching your determination.

• • •

I will take Alger Hiss by the hand, and I will lead him before you from the date of his birth down to this hour even, though I would go the valley of the shadow of death I will fear no evil, because there is no blot or blemish on him.

So much, ladies and gentlemen, for the accused.

Now who is the accuser? He is a man who now styles himself as J. Whittaker Chambers. He began changing his names early. I think the name given him was J. Vivian Chambers. He was born in the United States on the 1st of April, 1901.

Now who and what is this man, this accuser of ours? Who is he? What is he?

My heart is full of many things, but I am very conscious of my limitations in this opening address and I shall, and I will admit it is difficult for me, try to be restrained and confine myself to the facts that I promise to prove.

Chambers began using an alias even before he joined the Communist Party. I think his first alias was Adams, wasn't it? Adams. Even then he was a furtive, secretive, deceptive, man.

In 1924, when he was then grown, 23, and at an age when Alger Hiss was giving the best example I can think of of being a fine citizen, this man Chambers chose to become a member of the Communist Party. It was not a hasty choice. It was a considered choice. He chose to enter into that, and I will prove to you what that Communist Party was from Chambers' own admissions. The only point of it is, of course, to help you along the line that Mr. Murphy so kindly suggested: let us see who these people are.

I am going to open and lift up the iron curtain a little and let you have a look. This thing that he joined, what was it? Well, his own admission was it was a conspiracy to overthrow the United States Government by any means. It was an ally of international communism. It was a conspiracy.

Mind you, ladies and gentlemen, I am staying very closely within the limitations of an opening, and I am promising to prove this to you. It was a conspiracy for the overthrow of his country. It was an organization that believed that wrong was right; that anything that would aid and abet the overthrow of this dear land of ours was a thing that the conspirators were for.

He belonged to that organization that it believed it right to commit any crime, and here I see you will be interested, especially lying—lying. That is one of the main tenets of this group of conspirators with which this man Chambers, alias Adams, alias Crosley, alias Cantwell, alias a great many other things, chose to connect himself.

Now, did he do that for a year or two and then stop for six months? Oh, me, not at all. He was a member of this low-down, nefarious, filthy conspiracy until at least the end of 1936, twelve long years. Twelve long years our accuser was a voluntary conspirator against the land that I love and you love. He got his bread from the band of criminals with whom he confederated and conspired. Every crust of bread that went down his throat for these twelve years of his criminal life were given to him by his Communist confederates.

Now, how many crimes he committed during that period I don't know, but I do know one, and that, of course, is that he cheated his government on income taxes and filed no returns for the money that he was being paid for the prostitution of his soul.

One of the tenets of this conspiracy in which he was an active member for twelve years was the defiance of God, atheism. Now, the interesting part about this thing, ladies and gentlemen, and I am sure it will be of interest to you as it develops, is that these particular criminal propensities, inclinations, and activities of our accuser come up very naturally. It was not hard for him because he had been a confirmed liar before he joined the band that believes in lying, as he had been a thief. His conspirators believe in larceny and thievery. He had been a blasphemer against a person who many of us believe to be the Son of God, and he had written a filthy, despicable play about Jesus Christ when he was in Columbia, and was dismissed, and how did he get back? By lying. How will I prove that? I will prove it in his hand-writing.

So, atheism, destruction of religion, lies, stealing, all of these things were part and parcel of the bad life that he led for twelve long years. Now, gentlemen, ladies and gentlemen, that is part of our accuser.

• • •

. . . When Chambers produced these papers that he said he got from Alger Hiss, and let me say at once that there are four hand-written notes, and three we are certain are in our hand-writing, no doubt about it, and we think the fourth is, too. However, what did he do? He could have made a quiet little settlement, you know, of the civil suit and let these papers alone, but he did not. Did Chambers bring them to the attention of the authorities? He did not. Who did? Alger Hiss.

Is that the conduct of a guilty man? When he was asked something about a typewriter, this typewriter in the grand jury, he bent heaven and earth through my good friend here, Ed McLean, a stalwart lawyer whom you will hear in this case, as he will take a part in it, who is not only a believer in Alger Hiss, but happened to be a classmate, also on the Harvard Law Review, although probably he would not like to say that he was, and he says, "Have you the typewriter that we want? See if you can find it. I will suppress nothing."

And here are these FBI fellows, and let us see, what did Mr. Murphy say they did, that they turned Washington upside down? I don't think it was that, but it was something like that, wasn't it, Mr. Murphy?

MR. MURPHY: Pretty close.

MR. STRYKER: Or close to it.

THE COURT: Shook it down.

MR. MURPHY: Shook it down.

MR. STRYKER: They did what?

THE COURT: Shook it down.

MR. STRYKER: Well, we have not the opportunities for shaking anything down that Mr. Chambers had, but we happened to have a stalwart, honest man, who was Ed McLean, and who was no FBI man at all, just a lawyer, and he went down to Washington time and again. He inspected garrets, and he poked around in cellars, getting himself covered with dirt in search for this thing wherever he thought he could find it, and at last he found it and produced it from the then owner, a truckman who had gotten it through a long series of colored servants that they had. We have the typewriter in our possession, and I think now that we will consent under such reasonable provisions as his Honor may prescribe, to let these FBI guys who could not find it come down and look at it all they want.

Now, I ask you again, is that the conduct of a guilty man?

The Prosecution Presents Its Case

Sitting in the courtroom as the trial began, James Reston, reporting for the *New York Times,* observed a different Alger Hiss than the "lonely and distressed man" who had appeared before HUAC. Hiss "sat quietly against the back rail of the court, dressed in a tan suit, looking somewhat younger than his 44 years." One reason for his new calm, according to Reston, was Stryker, his defense lawyer, "almost a Napoleonic figure: short, quick, composed, imperious." Stryker had marshaled the facts of the case and was ready to do battle.[1] His acumen was needed as the prosecution called its star witness, Whittaker Chambers.

For more than six days, Chambers repeated the testimony he had given HUAC and the grand jury. The *New York Times* described how, despite rigorous cross-examination by Stryker, Chambers maintained his composure and refused to diverge from his original testimony. But Stryker did succeed in planting seeds of doubt. He caught Chambers in many contradictions. And he badgered Chambers about his previous lies, some of them made under oath.

He also laid the groundwork for a later challenge to Chambers's mental stability. (A psychiatrist, Dr. Carl Binger, was in the courtroom at the request of the defense to evaluate the mental stability of Chambers. The jury was unaware of who he was, and the judge ultimately refused to allow Binger to testify for the defense. But he would later play a significant role in the second trial.) Stryker also raised the possibility that Chambers had received the documents in question, not from Hiss, but from Henry Julian Wadleigh, an economist working on trade matters in the State Department, whom Chambers had previously identified as another source for State Department materials.[2]

After Chambers had told his story, the prosecution introduced a plethora of evidence supporting his account. Chambers had insisted that Hiss had loaned him $400 in 1937 to purchase an automobile. The prosecution produced records showing that Priscilla Hiss, Alger's wife, had withdrawn $400 from their savings account during that identical time period. The prosecution presented records that supported Chambers's recollection that he had given Hiss an oriental rug in gratitude for his services to the party. Experts verified that various letters typed by the Hisses were typed on the same machine as sixty-four of the transcribed State Department documents Chambers had surrendered.

Then Murphy called Chambers's wife to the stand. Esther Chambers was an important witness. If she could demonstrate familiarity with the Hisses and prove that the two couples had had contact after January 1, 1937, the prosecution's case would be much stronger. For two days, Mrs. Chambers in a soft voice described her relationship with the Hisses in great detail. She said that they were known by the Hisses as "Carl" and "Liza," with no surname. Under cross-examination, the defense caught her in some contradictions. But for the most part she reinforced her husband's testimony. At one point, during particularly aggressive questioning, she adamantly defended her husband, calling him a "decent man, a great man." In the end, for the most part she proved to be a successful prosecution witness.[3]

When Esther Chambers finished her testimony, government prosecutors introduced the Baltimore documents and the pumpkin papers into evidence. Systematically prosecution lawyers correlated the stolen materials with cables and reports in State Department files. Expert witnesses explained the document routing and handling procedures used in the State Department. The defense rebutted by emphasizing the number of people besides Hiss who handled these materials and again suggested that someone else may have been Chambers's source, such as Henry Julian Wadleigh, whose name had already surfaced in the defense's cross-examination of Chambers. In previous appearances before HUAC and the grand jury, Wadleigh had refused to answer questions about alleged espionage activity. But in what was a surprise to the defense, on the thirteenth

PHOTO **4.1**   Whittaker and Esther Chambers at the trial. Esther was an important prosecution witness in support of her husband.

day of the trial Wadleigh took the stand and admitted that he had given documents to Chambers. However, he denied being the source for the material Chambers had surrendered. Caught off guard by this surprising turn of events, Stryker was unable to shake Wadleigh's recollections.

"HELP TO REDS IS ADMITTED BY WADLEIGH"

Henry Julian Wadleigh admitted in United States District Court yesterday that for almost two years while employed by the State Department he gave government documents to Communists every week for transmission to Russia.

Mr. Wadleigh said he did this from March, 1936, until a time some weeks before March 9, 1938. He said he was not a member of the Communist party then or at any time, but that in those days he was "willing to collaborate with the Communists."

Mr. Wadleigh was then employed in the trade agreements section of the State Department. He said he gave the Communists some of the documents which passed over his desk in the ordinary course of business, and he thought would be interesting or useful to them.

He said he usually gave his documents in the evening to "a man who has been identified to me recently as David Carpenter." Sometimes, he

Source: New York Herald Tribune, June 17, 1949.

said, he gave the documents to Whittaker Chambers, whom he then knew as "Carl Carlson." He did not remember how often he had given them to Mr. Chambers. On all occasions, he said, the documents were returned to him the next morning, and he returned them to the State Department.

FIRST TO ADMIT CHARGES

Of all those accused of giving government documents to Communists since the House Un-American Activities Committee began its spy investigation last year Mr. Wadleigh is the first to admit that he had done so. Of all those accused by Whittaker Chambers or Elizabeth Bentley of criminal or Communist activities of any sort he is the first to admit publicly that the accusation was justified.

Mr. Wadleigh's admissions were part of his testimony in the perjury trial of Alger Hiss. Mr. Hiss was indicted when he denied similar accusations made against him by Mr. Chambers. The statute of limitations protects Mr. Wadleigh from any indictment for espionage or violations of government security regulations on the basis of his testimony yesterday. Of the others accused by Mr. Chambers and Miss Bentley two are dead, some have denied the charges and some have refused to testify on constitutional grounds.

Mr. Wadleigh refused to testify before the House Committee last December on the ground that he might incriminate himself. At that time he told reporters his lawyer had advised him that the statute of limitations contained loopholes through which he might be prosecuted.

SENT INFORMATION FOR RUSSIA

Yesterday Mr. Wadleigh was not asked and did not say whether he had ever seen Mr. Hiss give documents to Mr. Chambers or any other Communist. He was not asked if he had ever seen Mr. Hiss and Mr. Chambers together, or whether he knew anything about their relationship with each other, or had any knowledge that would substantiate Mr. Chambers's charge that Mr. Hiss also provided documents for the alleged spy ring.

Mr. Wadleigh admitted that his purpose in giving documents to Communists was "to supply material which they could pass on to Russia." He was not asked for any details of what Mr. Carpenter and Mr. Chambers did after receiving the documents he testified he gave them. He was not asked if he knew anything about Colonel Bykov, whom Mr. Chambers had previously described as the Soviet agent for whom he worked. Mr. Chambers has indicated that he gave Colonel

Bykov microfilm photographs of documents obtained from both Mr. Hiss and Mr. Wadleigh.

Mr. Wadleigh did testify that he did not make any of the typed copies of government documents which Mr. Hiss is accused of making, nor supply any of the microfilmed documents which Mr. Hiss is accused of supplying. He said that he did not recall ever having seen the microfilmed documents before, and that they were not the sort of documents that would have passed over his desk. He said he had never taken documents from any one else's desk to give to Communists. Of the eight documents which were shown to him, he testified that he would have considered one of them a "rich find" if it had crossed his desk while he was collaborating with the Communists.

IDENTIFICATION ACCEPTED

Mr. Wadleigh's identification of Mr. Chambers as "Carl Carlson" was accepted without objection, although Mr. Chambers was not present to be physically identified and has never said he used the name "Carlson." Mr. Chambers previously testified that when acting as a spy courier he used the name "Carl" without a surname.

Mr. Wadleigh was not asked for any description or further identification of the man he described as "David Carpenter." A David Carpenter appeared as a witness before the grand jury last Dec. 8 and was identified by his attorney as a copy reader and book reviewer for "The Daily Worker." Mr. Carpenter's name had not previously been mentioned in public in connection with the Communist spy investigation.

Mr. Chambers mentioned David Carpenter once early in this trial. After naming two persons who allegedly photographed the government documents on microfilm, he added: "I cannot recall clearly, but it is possible that David Carpenter did on one or two occasions."

Mr. Wadleigh said he was born in Greenfield, Mass., was taken to Europe at the age of three, acquired a Master of Arts degree from Oxford University and a Bachelor of Science in Economics degree from the University of London, and returned to the United States in 1929 at the age of twenty-five.

WITNESS CALM ON STAND

A lanky, bony man with a thin face, large glasses and hair that stood up straight, he looked much younger than forty-five. He appeared composed, sometimes betraying nervousness for a moment by drumming his fingers on the arm of his chair. Sometimes, looking at the floor and searching for the exact words to define his motives, he seemed embarrassed.

On cross-examination he refused to be drawn into a discussion of his moral scruples or conscience during his period as a Communist sympathizer. He spoke in a cultured voice, with a faintly English accent. Defense Attorney Lloyd Paul Stryker labeled it an "Oxford accent" and teased him about it.

Mr. Wadleigh said he stopped passing documents to Communists on instructions from "Mr. Carpenter or Mr. Chambers," some weeks before going to Turkey on a State Department mission on March 9, 1938. Later, after the Nazi-Soviet pact of August, 1939, his attitude toward Communist espionage changed, he said.

"I had very serious misgivings and was not willing to take the risks and incur the other difficulties," he said. "After all, there was something quite distasteful about the procedure involved in this work, and I was not prepared to incur these things after the Nazi-Soviet pact."

The Defense Presents Its Case

Confronted with Wadleigh's admission and faced with a complex web of circumstantial evidence pointing to Hiss's guilt, the defense responded by attempting to implant doubts in the minds of the jurors. June 22 proved a particularly noteworthy day in this effort. The day began with a series of witnesses attesting to Hiss's stellar character, most notably two Supreme Court justices, Felix Frankfurter and Stanley Reed. Then the defense called Claudie Catlett and her sons Raymond and Perry to the stand.

Catlett, the Hiss's maid from 1935 to 1938, described details of the different residences where the Hisses had lived. More importantly, she remembered seeing Chambers at these residences only once. She knew him as Mr. "Crosby." This was important, since Chambers had said that he had gone regularly to the Hiss apartment to retrieve documents. The prosecution stressed the contradictions in her testimony, but under pressure of cross-examination, she did not change her story.

Her son Raymond also provided valuable testimony after the defense entered the Woodstock typewriter into evidence. He testified that the Hisses had given the typewriter to his family some time in 1936 or 1937. This date conflicted not only with Chambers's, but also with Hiss's, recollections. Many of the documents Chambers had surrendered were dated 1938. Hiss had said that the Woodstock had been in his possession as late as 1938. If the 1936 or 1937 date could be proven, it would raise questions about the sixty-four documents typed on that typewriter.

"WITNESSES ASSERT HISS DID NOT HAVE 'SPY' TYPEWRITER"

Two witnesses at the perjury trial of Alger Hiss testified yesterday that the old Woodstock typewriter on which Mr. Hiss is accused of copying government documents for a Communist spy ring was in their possession—not Mr. Hiss's—at the time.

They were Mrs. Claudia Catlett, known as Clytie, who worked in the Hiss home as a full-time maid from August or September, 1935, until September, 1938, and her son, Raymond Sylvester Catlett, who worked as handyman for the Hisses during the same period.

Mrs. Catlett, who said she was at the Hiss home daily until 8 or 9 P.M., with Thursday and Sunday afternoons off, said she had seen Mr. Chambers there only once, in 1935, and that he used the name "Crosby." Her son said he had never seen Mr. Chambers anywhere at any time. Mrs. Catlett indignantly denied that defense lawyers had suggested the name "Crosby" to her, and said she first recalled it when Assistant United States Attorney Thomas F. Murphy asked her about that name and a long list of others.

WITNESSES' STORY UNSHAKEN

Mr. Murphy launched an intensive cross-examination of both witnesses, whose testimony could destroy the main foundations of the government's case if it is substantiated to the jury's satisfaction. Both witnesses revealed an uncertain recollection of dates, names, and other details, but they both refused to be shaken in the main facts of their story.

The typewriter itself was introduced in evidence, and part of the story was told of how it was recovered and whose hands it had passed through in the last twelve years. Later the defense said at least two more witnesses would be called to testify about the typewriter today.

This critical development in the trial followed the appearance of two justices of the United States Supreme Court—Felix Frankfurter and Stanley Reed—and one judge of the United States Court of Appeals as character witnesses for Mr. Hiss. All three were cross-examined by Mr. Murphy, who at one stage accused Justice Frankfurter of "fencing" with him.

Source: New York Herald Tribune, June 23, 1949.

JUSTICES PRAISE HISS

Justice Frankfurter said Mr. Hiss's reputation for "loyalty, integrity and veracity" was "excellent." He added that he had never heard it questioned. Justice Reed said Mr. Hiss's reputation was "good so far as I know," and that he had never heard it questioned. Judge Calvert Magruder, of the United States Court of Appeals, First Circuit, Boston, said Mr. Hiss's reputation was "excellent." Gerard Swope jr., counsel for the International General Electric Company, who had shared an office with Mr. Hiss when they were both young lawyers, called it "unequivocally excellent." A deposition was read from Governor Adlai Stevenson of Illinois, who said Mr. Hiss's reputation was "good."

After the character witnesses had gone the defense began introducing the main line of testimony with which it hopes to obtain Mr. Hiss's acquittal. Mr. Hiss is accused of perjury on two counts—that he lied when he denied giving confidential government documents and copies of such documents to Whittaker Chambers in or about February and March, 1938, and that he lied when he denied seeing Mr. Chambers after Jan. 1, 1937. The second count alleges that Mr. Hiss's statement was false in that he did see Mr. Chambers in or about February and March, 1938.

Mr. Chambers has testified that he went to Mr. Hiss's home regularly once every ten days or two weeks between 5 and 7 P.M. to receive government documents and copies of documents from Mr. Hiss not only in February and March, 1938, but over a period extending back to early 1937, and that at that time he used the name "Carl" without surname. Mrs. Esther Chambers has described social visits to support his story of intimate friendship dating back to 1934. Before the trial began Mr. Hiss testified that he knew Mr. Chambers only in 1934 and 1935, and by the name of George Crosley.

PAPERS IN EVIDENCE

Mr. Chambers has testified that the copies and excerpts from government documents which he says Mr. Hiss gave him were typed on an old Woodstock typewriter by either Mr. or Mrs. Hiss. These papers were introduced in evidence and compared with known samples of the work of the Woodstock. The samples bore various dates, the latest of which was May 25, 1937.

A documents expert from the Federal Bureau of Identification demonstrated that ten characteristics of the known samples appeared also on the alleged spy papers, and on that basis testified that both were typed on the same machine. The defense did not cross-examine him or dispute his testimony.

WOMAN ON STAND

Earlier in the trial, which is now in its fourth week. Mr. Murphy read a deposition from Mr. Hiss dated last Dec. 4. In it, Mr. Hiss denied typing the papers or giving them to Mr. Chambers, but said he had lost track of the Woodstock machine. He said he thought he had disposed of it to a secondhand dealer "some time subsequent to 1938." Mr. Murphy and Lloyd Paul Stryker, chief defense counsel, both said in their opening statements that they had searched for the typewriter. Mr. Murphy had not found it; Mr. Stryker said it had been found by his associate, Edward C. McLean.

A few minutes before noon yesterday Mrs. Catlett took the stand. Under direct examination by Mr. McLean she said she worked for Mrs. Hiss regularly from August or September of 1935 to September, 1938, doing general housework full time, with Thursday and Sunday afternoons off. Then she got sick, and afterward did an occasional day's work for Mrs. Hiss until 1941.

Clytie, as Mr. McLean called her throughout his interrogation, said she had been visited by F.B.I. agents seven or eight times since last winter, and that on Feb. 1 she was confronted with Mr. Chambers in an F.B.I. office in Washington and asked to identify him.

She said she recognized him right away as a man who had come to the Hiss home at 2905 P Street, Washington, soon after she started to work there in 1935. He had rung the bell at about 4 P.M., and he didn't stay long, but he had tea with Mrs. Hiss, she said. She said he was "poorly dressed and did not look like the people who usually called on the Hisses."

Mrs. Catlett said she had a good memory for faces but not names. "I could be away as long as thirty-five years and still recognize a face," she said. At the time of the first F.B.I. interview she did not recall the name Crosby, and under cross-examination later she became more and more confused about just when she did recall it. She conceded that it might have been Crosley or various other things. At one point she was sure it wasn't Carl, but the transcript of one of her interviews with the F.B.I. showed that at that time she was not so sure.

Mrs. Catlett was sure she had never seen Mr. Chambers after that one time at P Street. She was equally sure she always answered the doorbell, and was at the Hiss home, wherever it was, till 8 P.M. or sometimes 9 P.M. She said that Mr. Chambers did most of the talking at the F.B.I. office.

"He said, 'You remember me, you're the one that could mash pota-
toes,' " she testified. "Could you mash potatoes?" asked Mr. Murphy.
"Anybody could mash potatoes," she retorted. And later she added:
"But I never cooked no potatoes for him."

Mrs. Catlett said Mr. Chambers questioned her in the F.B.I. office
about the furniture and the arrangement of the rooms at 1245 Thirtieth
Street, where the Hiss family lived from July, 1936, to December, 1937,
after leaving P Street.

SAYS SHE GOT TYPEWRITER

Mrs. Catlett's recollection of the typewriter was vague, and it became
still more confused under cross-examination. She said that when the
F.B.I. first asked her she had forgotten all about it and said she didn't
know anything about any typewriter. Later it was found, she said, and
when her son showed it to her she remembered that the Hisses had
given it to the Catlett family once when the Hiss family was moving

She did not remember whether it was when they moved from
2905 P Street to 1245 Thirtieth Street in July, 1936, or when they
moved from Thirtieth Street to 3415 Volta Place in December, 1937.
But she was sure it was in connection with the Hisses moving out. She
said she was no longer working for the Hisses when they moved out
of Volta Place in October, 1943.

Mrs. Catlett was followed on the witness stand by her son, Raymond,
who is known as Mike. He said he was twenty-seven years old and had
been about fifteen when he got the typewriter. He said he worked for
the Hisses at all three of their residences, washing the car, washing win-
dows and floors, cleaning the yard, and doing other cleaning jobs. He
said he never saw Mr. Chambers at all anywhere at any time.

Mr. Catlett said he and his brother, Perry Murphy Catlett, got the
typewriter together when the Hisses moved out of one of their houses.
He also could not remember which house it was, or whether it was
Mr. or Mrs. Hiss that said the boys could have the typewriter.

But he was certain that the typewriter had remained in a little
room called "the den" in the Catlett home at 2728 P Street for three
or four years after they got it. He said it was never taken out of the den
during that time. He said he sometimes typed his name out on it with
one finger, but otherwise made no use of it. Eventually it passed into
the hands of his brother's wife, Ursula, and to his sister Bernetta, and
to other people.

At the beginning of cross-examination Mr. Murphy asked the witness if he could call him Mike, as Mr. McLean had done.

"My name is Raymond Sylvester Catlett," the witness replied coldly. As Mr. Murphy tried to pin him down on dates and details of his conduct in relation to the typewriter the witness became more and more resentful.

He complained that Mr. Murphy was getting him "all crossed up," was deliberately trying to confuse him, and was making it look as if he had done something wrong.

"They told me about people like you," he said at one point. "Who told you?" Mr. Murphy demanded. "When I was growing up, they warned me about your kind of fellow—" the rest was lost in inaudible expostulation.

Judge Samuel H. Kaufman tried to persuade the witness that he had nothing to fear and the court was only trying to get at the facts. Mr. Murphy was able to get little more out of him. Before Mr. Murphy finished the cross-examination the court adjourned until 10:30 A.M. today.

If the further examination of the typewriter evidence is concluded today Mr. Hiss may take the stand late this afternoon. Otherwise he is expected to begin testifying tomorrow. The defense attorneys said he will not be their last witness.

Following the testimony about the typewriter that potentially weakened the prosecution's case, Alger Hiss took the stand. He proved an impressive witness as he restated much of the same information he had given to the HUAC and the grand jury. He confidently detailed his relationship with Chambers. Even under Murphy's aggressive cross-examination, reporters covering the trial noted that he remained calm, cleared up many discrepancies that the prosecution resurrected from his past testimony, and even seemed to be "enjoying" the whole affair. He was "fabulously precise" in most of his testimony, one account noted, except when the issue of when he and his wife gave the Woodstock typewriter to the Catletts was discussed.[4]

When Priscilla Hiss was called to the stand following her husband, she corroborated his story, just as she had done in previous appearances before the grand jury and HUAC. Murphy tried to undermine her credibility by presenting board of elections records documenting that she had registered as a Socialist in 1932, an affiliation that she had previously denied. He also questioned the $400 she had withdrawn from a savings account in 1937, which she insisted was used to furnish a new apartment, but which coincided with Chambers's account that Hiss had loaned him money to purchase a car. She steadfastly denied typing the State Department documents and even provided new details about the events surrounding the gift of the typewriter to the Catletts in December 1937.[5]

PHOTO 4.2   Alger and Priscilla Hiss arrive at the courthouse. Priscilla backed her husband's account of their relationship with the Chambers and denied that she typed the State Department documents.

© Bettmann/CORBIS

The Case Goes to the Jury

On July 6, Robert Stryker began a four-hour summation for the defense that extended into the next day. He forcefully denigrated the prosecution's evidence and decried State Department security policy. He emphasized that someone other than Hiss could have removed the notes in Hiss's handwriting from a wastebasket. He intimated that Henry Julian Wadleigh was the source of the Chambers material. Then he contrasted Chambers, a man of "abnormal" background and a liar, to Hiss, "a pillar of righteousness." Prosecutor Thomas Murphy followed with a three-hour summation likening Hiss to traitors like Judas Iscariot and Benedict Arnold.

Then Judge Kaufman read the charge to the jury. He stressed that federal law required that there must be two witnesses to an act of perjury, or one witness and corroborating evidence. Since Whittaker Chambers was the sole prosecution witness to the alleged acts, the jury had to evaluate Chambers's veracity as well as determine the strength of the evidence. Here the *New York Herald Tribune* describes the final two days before the jury began deliberating.

"HISS'S COUNSEL SUMS UP; CALLS CHAMBERS LIAR"

Alger Hiss's defense against the perjury indictment on which he has been on trial since May 31 was summed up in United States District Court yesterday by Lloyd Paul Stryker, Mr. Hiss's flamboyant trial attorney. Mr. Stryker said the charges against Mr. Hiss were "preposterous." He said that Whittaker Chambers, author of the charges, was a "psycopathic sadist" and "a liar by habit, by training . . . and by preference." He accused Mr. Chambers of concocting the story to further his own personal ambition.

Mr. Stryker reminded the jury over and over again, in shouts and whispers and with the emphasis on a different part of the sentence each time he used it, that: "If you don't believe Chambers the government has no case." He read from the record to show that Assistant United States Attorney Thomas F. Murphy had used this sentence himself when he opened the case for the prosecution.

• • •

Mr. Stryker argued in his summation that "to believe Chambers's story you have to believe that Alger Hiss was far below normal intelligence, and there is no one in this case that has suggested that."

He said it was a "preposterous" idea that if Mr. Hiss was, as Mr. Chambers contends, a conspirator stealing government documents for the use of a Communist spy ring, he would have incriminated himself by giving Mr. Chambers papers in his own handwriting and documents carrying his own initials. Mr. Stryker said it was "absurd" to suggest that a genuine spy would publicly associate with a fellow-conspirator the way Mr. Chambers and his wife, Mrs. Esther Shemitz Chambers, said Mr. Hiss associated with them.

"It is as though Benedict Arnold had gone around with Andre all over the place," Mr. Stryker said, referring to the treason plot made by Major General Arnold and Major John Andre, a British officer, in 1780.

• • •

Source: New York Herald Tribune, July 7, 1949.

CITES WADLEIGH TESTIMONY

Mr. Stryker contrasted Mr. Chambers's story about Mr. Hiss with the testimony of Henry Julian Wadleigh, a former State Department employee in a less important post, who said he gave government documents to Mr. Chambers in 1938 but never gave him any handwritten papers, and who had never even been heard of by Mrs. Chambers.

Mr. Stryker contended that Mr. Chambers's ambition first made him want to be a Communist commissar, and that later he gave up that idea and thought he could go further by accusing some one else of being a Communist.

He said Mr. Chambers thought during the Presidential election campaign of 1948 that he could curry favor with the opponents of President Truman and the Roosevelt tradition by naming Mr. Hiss as a man who had gone to Yalta with the late President Roosevelt and was at the same time a former Communist.

Mr. Stryker's theory was that Mr. Chambers "chose what he thought was the stronger side" in the election campaign, relying on the Gallup Poll, and expected to become "quite a prominent man in the successful party" after the election as a result of his "very considerable contribution."

ATTRIBUTES MOTIVES TO CHAMBERS

Then, according to Mr. Stryker, when Mr. Hiss sued for libel Mr. Chambers produced the typed copies and paraphrases of government documents because he was hard put to defend himself. Mr. Stryker said he did not know how they had come into Mr. Chambers's possession; he suggested that he might have got them from Mr. Wadleigh or any of his other "fellow conspirators." Mr. Stryker made much of the fact that it was Mr. Hiss who first asked for the documents to be produced and insisted on handing them over to the Justice Department after Mr. Chambers had hesitated "in turmoil" for three days; and that Mr. Chambers did not reveal all his documents at once, but kept some of them hidden in his pumpkin. • • •

CALLS STORY "FANTASTIC"

Mr. Stryker was most scathing about this part of Mr. Chambers's story when he came to it in his summation. He called it "fantastic," and criticized the Federal Bureau of Investigation for producing a prosecution witness who suggested that the Hisses might not have been at Chestertown at all that summer, even though the F.B.I. and Mr. Murphy had themselves seen records showing that they were there at least during that period, if not on the night in question.

Mr. Stryker was in his most melodramatic form in the first hour of his summation before lunch. He blackened Mr. Chambers's character with as many disreputable details of the testimony as he could recall in the time available, pointed to the American flag behind the witness stand and accused Mr. Chambers of dishonoring it, and shouted that neither "wild horses" nor "the pressures of Russian torture" could make him believe Mr. Chambers's story.

Mr. Stryker denounced the House Un-American Activities Committee for giving credence to Mr. Chambers when he made his original accusations against Mr. Hiss last August.

Mr. Stryker conceded that the committee did not know at the time that Mr. Chambers, as he has later testified, went to them "intending to commit perjury and did commit perjury." Had the committee known that, and nevertheless deliberately "foisted" Mr. Chambers on the credibility of the public, it would have been "one of the most diabolical acts in American history," Mr. Stryker said. He hastened to add that any good lawyer could have proved Mr. Chambers a perjurer had he been allowed to cross-examine him before the committee last Aug. 3.

He compared the committee to a milk distributor that "filled several bottles from the gutter . . . to send out as Grade A certified milk."

"You might say the distributor didn't know," he said, "but you would say they shouldn't have certified it. That's what the committee did."

"ONLY ONE WITNESS"

Two other refrains ran through Mr. Stryker's summation. He emphasized that the indictment against Mr. Hiss alleges that Mr. Hiss "furnished, delivered and transmitted" restricted government documents to Mr. Chambers, and that in order to convict Mr. Hiss the jurors must satisfy themselves on this point "beyond a reasonable doubt." Mr. Stryker added:

"There is only one witness in the whole world who says that Alger Hiss furnished, transmitted and delivered those papers—and that is Whittaker Chambers." At this point Mr. Stryker quoted for the first time Mr. Murphy's statement that: "If you don't believe Chambers, then we (the government) have no case."

In the afternoon Mr. Stryker was more restrained. He went over more details of the testimony, offered his own explanation of some of the unanswered questions, and asked some questions of his own. Most of the time he kept his voice down and avoided sensational metaphors and hyperboles.

The most important piece of evidence he touched on was the typewriter. He reminded the jury that an F.B.I. documents expert had testified that the incriminating documents were typed on an old Woodstock machine once owned by Mr. and Mrs. Hiss. Mr. Stryker pointed out that the expert had only examined letters written on the machine, and compared them with the documents in question. He asserted that the expert had not examined the machine itself, although the defense had already offered it to the court for the F.B.I.'s inspection, and had not examined the question of whether the comparison papers were typed by the same person, as distinct from the question of what machine was used.

For these reasons, Mr. Stryker said, he was not personally convinced by the prosecution's typewriter expert. He added that he did not really care whether the Woodstock machine was used for the spy papers or not, because he believed the testimony of other witnesses who said the Woodstock was not in Mr. Hiss's possession in 1938 when the spy papers were typed. He added that there was uncontradicted evidence before the court that the Hisses had acquired another typewriter in the fall of 1937 and documents typed on it by Mr. Hiss's stepson, Timothy Hobson, had been introduced in evidence. He stressed the fact that although the F.B.I. had admittedly combed the country for papers written by the Hess family on the old Woodstock, they had found none dated later than May 25, 1937.

Mr. Stryker then threw in a few questions of his own. If Mr. Hiss had typed the sixty-four documents he was accused of typing, why did he not also type out the four documents that were in handwritten form, he asked. And who was responsible for the handwritten notations which appear on some of the typewritten documents, and which the prosecution has not contended were in the handwriting of either Mr. Hiss or Mr. Chambers?

His final point was that the initials "A. H." which appear on some of the documents were put there by Mr. Hiss to indicate that he was finished with them, and thus show that it was not he but some "other thief or rogue conspiring with Mr. Chambers who got them after they left Mr. Hiss's possession."

"It wouldn't be enough to travel all around Washington with his conspirator Chambers, and give him handwritten documents," Mr. Stryker wound up sarcastically. "But to make perfectly sure— everything was there except an affidavit—we give him documents with the initials A. H., so he could establish our guilt beyond a peradventure of a doubt. I tell you the story is preposterous."

"HISS JURY IS LOCKED UP AFTER FOREMAN REPORTS 'NO IMMEDIATE VERDICT' "

A jury of ten men and two women deliberated for six hours and ten minutes yesterday without reaching a verdict in the perjury trial of Alger Hiss, former State Department official and secretary general of the San Francisco Conference where the United Nations Charter was adopted.

The jury will resume deliberations at 10 A.M. today.

The jurors began their deliberations at 4:20 P.M. Twenty minutes later they asked and received permission to inspect the indictment, the bill of particulars and the most controversial of the tangible items of evidence in the case.

• • •

On the final day, the jury heard the last words of all three of the principal figures in the court—Lloyd Paul Stryker, who wound up a four-and-a-half-hour summation of the case for the defense in the opening hour of yesterday's session; Assistant United States Attorney Thomas F. Murphy, who used not quite three hours to sum up for the prosecution, and Judge Samuel H. Kaufman, who charged the jury in a little less than an hour.

Mr. Stryker asked the jurors to search their consciences, and assured them he had complete confidence they would find the defendant not guilty. Mr. Murphy called Mr. Hiss a "traitor," compared him to Benedict Arnold, Judas Iscariot, and the Devil himself, and said: "A brilliant man like this . . . betrays his trust . . . inside of that smiling face that heart is black and cancerous . . . he is a traitor."

Mr. Murphy said he was asking the jury "as a representative of the United States government to come back and put the lie in that man's face."

JUDGE EXPLAINS INDICTMENT

Judge Kaufman, explaining the indictment against Mr. Hiss, said that in substance he was accused of furnishing, transmitting and delivering secret government documents and copies of such documents to Whittaker Chambers in February and March, 1938, and of committing perjury when he denied that he had done so.

Judge Kaufman emphasized that the burden of the proof was on the government to show that Mr. Hiss had actually "furnished,

Source: New York Herald Tribune, July 8, 1949.

transmitted and delivered" the documents to Mr. Chambers, and that the government relied solely on the testimony of Mr. Chambers himself plus corroborative evidence, some of which was circumstantial.

Judge Kaufman instructed the jury to choose one of the following alternatives:

If the jury did not believe Mr. Chambers's testimony "beyond a reasonable doubt" they must acquit Mr. Hiss.

If the jury believed Mr. Chambers but did not find "independent corroboration," they must acquit Mr. Hiss.

If the jury believed Mr. Hiss's testimony they must acquit him.

If the jury believed "beyond a reasonable doubt" Mr. Chambers's story that Mr. Hiss furnished, transmitted and delivered the incriminating documents to him, and that testimony had been corroborated, Judge Kaufman said "you may find the defendant guilty" on both counts.

Count one alleged that Mr. Hiss swore falsely when he denied giving the documents to Mr. Chambers, and count two alleged that he swore falsely in denying that he had seen Mr. Chambers since Jan. 1, 1937. Judge Kaufman explained that the language of the indictment and the bill of particulars accompanying it make it clear that both counts refer to the same alleged meetings between Mr. Hiss and Mr. Chambers.

"If you find the defendant not guilty on the first count you must find him not guilty on the second count," Judge Kaufman said. "If you find him guilty on the first count you may find him guilty on the second count."

• • •

"THREE SOLID WITNESSES"

Mr. Murphy opened his summation by saying that the typewriter, the documents which he said were typed on it, and the original State Department documents of which they were copies, were the government's "three solid witnesses."

He said there were certain "undisputed, uncontradicted facts" in the case—that the typed documents were copies of State Department originals, that the documents were in Mr. Chambers's possession before the trial, and that they were all dated in the first three months of 1938. He also said it was an "uncontradicted fact" that sixty-four of the documents were typed on "the Hiss typewriter."

Mr. Murphy criticized the suggestion—made by Mr. Stryker—that the apparent uncertainty of the Catlett boys' recollection was the result of unfair tactics on the part of the Federal Bureau of Investigation. Mr. Murphy made this declaration to the jury:

"I'm going to make a firm offer to you now. If any juror thinks—not all twelve of you or even six—but if any one juror thinks that the F.B.I. at any time in this case with respect to the Catlett boys or anybody else—if any juror thinks that the F.B.I. was unfair in any wise—acquit this man! Acquit him!" Mr. Murphy, whose voice can be louder that Mr. Stryker's when he cares to use it, fairly shouted. "That's how confident I am that you won't be taken in by this side-swipe at the F.B.I."

Mr. Murphy, referring back to the repeated derogatory references Mr. Stryker had made to the F.B.I. and Mr. Stryker's cross-examination of one of the F.B.I. agents who had questioned the Catlett boys, prefaced his offer with this statement:

"It's the open season on the F.B.I. It's the smart thing to do. It's the liberal approach. . . . It's probably getting popular but . . . I don't think it will be successful."

BEGINS AFTER LUNCHEON

Mr. Murphy began his summation at 12:20 P.M., after calling a luncheon recess when Mr. Stryker finished at 11 A.M. He said he wanted to have time to prepare his answer to what Mr. Stryker had just said, and to be able to speak for his three hours without interruption.

He ran fairly quickly over the question of Mr. Chambers's character. Of Mr. Hiss, the prosecutor said it was the defendant's special skill to "combine truth with half-truth—a little bit to color it, a little bit more to deceive, and then if he is placed in a corner he can rely on the truthful part."

Mr. Murphy asked what motive Mr. Chambers could have had for accusing Mr. Hiss falsely, and derided Mr. Stryker's suggestion that Mr. Chambers was driven by political ambition. He said Mr. and Mrs. Chambers must have been "psychic" to know so much about the homes and habits of the Hiss family if they had not actually been intimate friends as Mrs. Chambers said they were.

As to Mr. Chambers's testimony that he left the Communist party in 1938, and his previous testimony that he left in 1937—a point which Judge Kaufman mentioned in his charge as an important question affecting Mr. Chambers's credibility—Mr. Murphy said: "So he was wrong by a year the first time. What significance has that?"

Toward the end of his summation Mr. Murphy, evidently smarting under the taunts that Mr. Stryker had earlier tossed his way, declared:

"I am a paid advocate. I'm paid by the government—not much, but I'm paid—and I'll stand up here and fight all the time for my client—and that client is the government, your government and mine!"

The Jury Fails to Reach a Verdict

The *New York Herald Tribune* closely followed the tense final day as the jury struggled for fourteen hours to reach a verdict. After consulting with the judge three times and being sent back to deliberate further, they remained dead-locked, eight to four to convict. Judge Kaufman finally dismissed the jury. Jurors later attributed the deadlock to two factors—first, that the jury foreman, who was sympathetic to Hiss and had made statements in support of Hiss previously, influenced three of the other jurors; and second, that the prosecution had not firmly established that Priscilla Hiss had typed the documents on the Woodstock typewriter.[6] According to the *Herald Tribune,* the jury's division accurately reflected the split among observers throughout the trial.

Hiss's travails did not end here, however. The U.S. attorney announced that the case would be retried as soon as possible.

"HISS JURY GIVES UP, DISCHARGED; 8 FOR CONVICTION; RETRIAL SLATED"

The perjury trial of Alger Hiss ended at 9 o'clock last night in United States District Court with a hung jury. Jurors said the vote was eight for conviction, four for acquittal.

The jurors said that when the jury first got the case four members were undecided, but within half an hour they had joined with those who wanted to convict. For the rest of the deliberations lasting 28 hours 40 minutes nobody's opinion changed in the slightest, the jurors said.

Not until the jury insisted for the third time that they could not reach a verdict did Judge Samuel H. Kaufman discharge them. Then, at 9 P.M. he asked them if they thought it would do any good for them to keep the case over night, go back to the Knickerbocker Hotel, 120 West Forty-fifth Street, where they passed Thursday night, and start again today.

NO CHANCE TO AGREE

The foreman Hubert Edgar James, answered: "I think I can reflect the opinion of the jury, your honor, in saying 'no.' " He leaned heavily on the word "no."

Source: New York Herald Tribune, July 9, 1949.

The judge said: "Then I have no alternative but to discharge the jury. I am certain you have given this case your best attention and earnest consideration."

The jurors seemed to sigh almost audibly with relief. As they left the courthouse—they looked as if they could not hurry fast enough— they didn't even want to talk about the case. Their gestures indicated complete frustration and exhaustion. Their actual deliberations had consumed 14 hours 10 minutes.

It was Edward McLean, one of the defense counsel, who rushed up and got the count—eight to four—from one of the jurors.

HISS LOOKS BEATEN

Mr. Hiss looked like a beaten man when he heard the decision. One of his lawyers leaned toward him to ask a question, and Mr. Hiss only nodded, silently. Later someone asked him if he would make a statement. He smiled with an effort, but said nothing. He stayed in the well of the court with his wife, Priscilla Hiss, and waited for the crowd to leave. Robert Von Mehren, one of the younger members of the defense team of attorneys, gently urged Mrs. Hiss toward the door. She went quietly, seeming wistful and demure as she had throughout the trial.

The trial began on May 31 and consumed twenty-three court days of testimony plus one day to pick the jury at the beginning and two days for summations and the judge's charge at the end.

United States Attorney John F. X. McGohey said he would move to put the case on the calendar for re-trial at once, and that Assistant United States Attorney Thomas F. Murphy would again be the prosecuting attorney. Mr. Hiss, it was believed, would be represented by the same team of lawyers—Mr. McLean, Mr. Von Mehren, Lloyd Paul Stryker, chief trial attorney, Harold Shapero, and Harold Rosenwald.

In Washington, The United Press said, Attorney General Tom C. Clark announced the Justice Department will "vigorously prosecute" the case again "as quickly as the docket of the court will permit."

Mr. McGohey said the retrial would begin as soon as a judge is available, which may not be until the fall. The conspiracy trial of Judith Coplon and Valentin Gubitchev, scheduled for next week, has been put off until October for lack of a judge to try it in the meantime.

• • •

The jury's verdict roughly paralleled the mixture of opinions among the press and spectators.

Of these at least it could be said that many came to the trial six weeks ago with their minds made up on one side or the other, and that nothing in the trial had changed their opinions at all.

Of the relatively few among the press and spectators who came to the trial with no fixed opinion, a quick check yesterday showed that the trial had swayed some in one direction and some in the other, and left some as baffled and uncertain as when it started.

• • •

HISSES APPEAR CONFIDENT

It was a hard day for everyone connected with the trial, but it appeared to be hardest for the jury. Mr. and Mrs. Hiss maintained their appearance of cool confidence, sometimes chatting and smiling with their friends in the corridor and courtroom, sometimes resting in the seclusion of the counsel room.

Attorneys, spectators, newspaper men and court officials came and went or lingered, some nervous and impatient, some bored, some finding jokes to amuse themselves, each reacting according to his individual personality and degree of personal involvement in the case.

Downstairs in the main floor pressroom newsreel cameramen and radio and television technicians played cards and fiddled with their equipment. Upstairs on the thirteenth floor pressroom, adjoining the courtroom, reporters flashed periodic bulletins over the telephone, and argued the case with each other.

Judge Kaufman came to the courtroom when the jury sent word to him, or when he wanted to tell them something himself. The rest of the time he was away on other business. Mr. McGohey, free from his duties at the trial of eleven Communist leaders when it adjourned for the weekend at 1 P.M., visited Judge Kaufman's courtroom during the afternoon.

JURORS' FACES SCRUTINIZED

The jury had to work. No one knew what arguments were going on in the room assigned to them for their deliberations, behind doors closed and guarded by deputy United States marshals. Everyone searched their faces, each time the jury appeared in the court room, looking for some sign of what was in each juror's mind. Mr. Hiss seemed to probe them with his deep-set eyes looking for answers he could not find.

The jurors' faces were inscrutable, as they have been all through the trial; but with each successive appearance some of them seemed to have lines of determination set more firmly in their faces. Others appeared each time more puzzled, more harassed, more wearied by the argument.

• • •

TIMETABLE OF JURORS

Five times before their discharge the jurors filed into the courtroom. This was the timetable:

At 11:39 they sent out a note asking the judge to restate that part of his charge relating to corroborative and circumstantial evidence. Judge Kaufman read the note first to the attorneys for both sides, obtained their agreement on which parts of his charge should be read, and called in the jury at 11:50.

It was apparent that the jury then deadlocked over the questions raised by the documents which Mr. Hiss denied having given to Mr. Chambers and the typewriter which he denied having typed them on.

The judge instructed the jury, in the same language he had used on Thursday, that in order to convict the defendant they must find that the evidence corroborates "that portion of Mr. Chambers's testimony which relates to the furnishing, delivering and transmission of documents to Chambers," and that the evidence of the documents, being circumstantial, "must be not merely consistent with the guilt of defendant; it must be inconsistent with any reasonable hypothesis of innocence and susceptible of no reasonable hypothesis other than that of guilt."

REPORT DISAGREEMENT

At 3:15 P.M. the jury sent out another note and ten minutes later filed into the courtroom to hear it read and answered. The note, signed by Mr. James, said they were unable to arrive at a verdict.

The jury retired to deliberate some more and went out at 1 P.M. in the marshal's custody for lunch at Caruso's Restaurant on the opposite side of Foley Square from the courthouse. They returned at 2 P.M.

Judge Kaufman answered it by reading to the jury another passage from his instructions of Thursday evening—reminding them that "it is the duty of everyone to go into the jury room with a disposition to listen patiently to his colleagues and with a disposition to be convinced."

He asked the jury to go back for further deliberation, and make one further attempt to reach a verdict. He said that if they still felt they could not agree after further discussion, he would, "take you at your word" and discharge the jury.

Mr. James, prompted by another juror, asked if the jury might have a copy of judge's instructions to take back to the jury room. The judge said that was impossible.

At 4:20, exactly twenty-four hours after the jury received the case on Thursday, Judge Kaufman called them back into the courtroom.

He said he had searched the authorities and found that it was possible for him to give the jury a copy of his instructions after all. Mr. James replied that at this point "I do not think it would materially help us."

At 4:55 the jury for the second time sent word that they could not reach a verdict. Judge Kaufman asked the attorneys for suggestions. Mr. Murphy said he would like to have the jury discharged but did not want to make a formal motion to that effect for fear that questions of double jeopardy might be raised to prevent a re-trial. Mr. Stryker said he would leave it up to the judge.

URGES ONE MORE EFFORT

Judge Kaufman summoned the jury into his presence. He reminded them that the trial had lasted six weeks at great expense to the government and the defendant, and that it might have to be tried all over again if the jury did not reach a verdict. He said he was going to ask the jury to make one more effort to reach a verdict, bearing in mind the passage he had previously quoted from his instructions to them. He asked the jury if they believed it possible to make another effort.

Mr. James said he believed it was possible to make another effort, emphasizing the word "effort." The judge immediately asked the jury to retire again and "see if you cannot get something out of the effort we have all made in the last six weeks."

Some of the other jurors glared angrily at the foreman. Judge Kaufman repeated what he had said the first time—that if they found after further discussion that they could not reach a verdict, he would take them at their word and discharge them.

The jury's fifth appearance in court was at 6:41 P.M., when they were summoned by Judge Kaufman for a progress report.

Reaction to the Hung Jury

Reaction to these developments was swift. Richard Nixon led the way in demanding new HUAC hearings. But with the Democrats now in control of the committee, renewed hearings were not a foregone conclusion.[7] Nixon castigated Judge Kaufman's handling of the trial and called for his impeachment. He pointed out that the judge had refused to allow the testimony of important witnesses like Hede Massing, the only person other than Chambers who would attest to Hiss's active involvement in the Communist Party. Nixon also pointed out that early in the proceedings the foreman of the jury had expressed to his wife sympathy for Hiss, but that Judge Kaufman had refused to remove him.

"HOUSE GROUP SPLIT ON HISS TRIAL INQUIRY"

WASHINGTON, July 9.—Reopening of the Congressional investigation into the Hiss-Chambers case and inquiry into the conduct of Judge Samuel H. Kaufman was urged today as a result of the hung jury in the perjury trial of Alger Hiss, and promptly encountered sharp criticism.

Four members—three Republicans and a Democrat—of the House Committee on Un-American Activities, which originally "broke" the sensational case, were in favor of reinstating their inquiry, although they differed as to whether it should be done in open or secret session.

Their chairman, however, was against it. Representative John S. Wood, Democrat, of Georgia, said he believed reopening the committee investigation would be "unjustifiable interference" with the Department of Justice and said he opposed it. The committee meets Tuesday. He had no comment on Judge Kaufman's conduct of the case, and suggestions that his committee investigate the matter. But speaking solely of procedure, he said:

"If the judge's conduct was improper this committee could investigate it. But the matter should be turned over to the Judiciary Committee for impeachment."

• • •

The Congressmen asking the investigation want, among other things, to summon Mrs. Hede Massing, former wife of Communist leader, Gerhart Eisler, who fled the United States in May.

The government tried to put her on as a witness in the Hiss trial but Judge Kaufman refused to permit it. The Representatives disagree, however as to whether Mrs. Massing should testify in public or secret session. Mr. Nixon wants it on the record. Mr. Case wants it kept secret until after the new Hiss trial.

Judge Kaufman's "prejudice for the defense and against the prosecution was so obvious and apparent that the jury's 8-to-4 vote for conviction frankly came as a surprise to me," said Mr. Nixon.

"When the full facts of the conduct of this trial are laid before the nation I believe the people will be shocked," Mr. Nixon said. "It is my intention shared by a number of my colleagues that the full facts shall be presented in due time."

• • •

Source: New York Herald Tribune, July 10, 1949.

Mr. Nixon amplified his comments on the case in a broadcast interview this evening with Bert Andrews, chief Washington correspondent of the New York Herald Tribune over station WMAL, the American Broadcasting Company. Mr. Nixon declared then that "the entire Truman administration was extremely anxious that nothing bad happen to Mr. Hiss" because it would prove Communist infiltration of the Federal government.

"A new trial should be held just as soon as possible," he said. "The issues in this case are so important that the country wants a decision. It is true that Mr. Hiss is technically accused merely of perjury. . ., but the real truth is that if he is guilty of the perjury charges he is also guilty of having been a traitor to his country. Therefore it is of the utmost importance that his guilt or innocence be completely established and not left in doubt because of technicalities."

In response to a question from Mr. Andrews as to what he meant by "technicalities," Mr. Nixon said:

"For one thing, there was the judge's refusal to let two important witnesses testify. One was Hede Massing. Another was William Rosen, who received the 1929 automobile which Mr. Hiss insisted he gave to Mr. Chambers. Perhaps the judge has good technical grounds for barring these witnesses. But I think the average American wanted all technicalities waived in this case. I think those two witnesses should have been permitted to testify about their knowledge, if any, of Mr. Hiss. For all anyone knows their testimony might have made a great difference in the minds of the jurors."

"Is there any way of getting their testimony on the record?" asked Mr. Andrews.

"There certainly is" replied Mr. Nixon. Referring to Mrs. Massing he said, "It is my intention to ask the House Committee on Un-American Activities to call her as a witness and to find out just what she would have said had she been allowed to testify in court. In that way the American people will at least have the knowledge of what she would have sworn to. And they will be able to form their own opinion as to what effect her testimony might have had on the jury."

Mr. Nixon said he saw little point in summoning Mr. Rosen, who refused to answer committee questions last year on the ground that his replies might incriminate him, but said he believed Mr. Rosen should have been allowed to testify at the trial—"if merely to let the jury decide what reasons he had for refusing to answer."

The California Congressman, to whom Mr. Andrews gave credit for keeping the Hiss-Chambers case open before the House committee last year, declared that Assistant District Attorney Thomas F. Murphy, the prosecutor in the Hiss trial, "did a great job against great odds in trying to bring out the whole truth."

Mr. Nixon branded as "ridiculous" and "nonsensical" defense charges that Whittaker Chambers's charges against Mr. Hiss were brought out to aid the Republican campaign last year, noting that they were not made until after the election.

"Then you don't think politics entered into the case at all?" asked Mr. Andrews.

"I didn't say that," Mr. Nixon said. "I certainly do think politics entered into it. I think the entire Truman administration was extremely anxious that nothing bad happen to Mr. Hiss. Members of the Administration feared that an adverse verdict would prove that there was a great deal of foundation to all the reports of Communist infiltration into the government during the New Deal days. The fact that there was a great deal to them was shown vividly by the testimony of Julian Wadleigh. He admitted that he did give documents to Mr. Chambers. I think the value of his testimony was to take the charges out of the realm of fantasy and to convince the jurors that some Americans—for whatever motive—did choose to betray their country and betray it knowingly."

Reverting to his criticism of Judge Kaufman, Mr. Nixon said:

"This was a case of utmost importance to the American people. The issue was rightly defined as depending on the jury's opinion of the credibility of the two main figures—and on the corroboration or lack of corroboration offered. Judge Kaufman allowed Mr. Stryker (Lloyd Paul Stryker, defense counsel) to question Mr. Chambers at great length on the suicide of his brother—as if that had anything to do with the case on trial. He refused to let Prosecutor Murphy ask Mr. Hiss a single question about any similar episode in his family. I think the average layman wished that the judge had let the truth—the whole truth and nothing but the truth—come out so that the jury could have had every single solitary fact before it."

A little later, Mr. Nixon said:

"You have read the reports that the jury foreman told his wife, very early in the trial, that he felt sympathetic to Mr. Hiss. I have no way of knowing whether that is true or not, but when the matter was called to the attention of the judge early in the trial, I think he should have taken steps to learn whether there was any truth to it. And he should not have allowed the juror to continue sitting if there was any possible chance the report was true."

CHAPTER 4

Opening Statements, Second Trial

The criticism of Judge Kaufman's conduct had its effect. The second trial began on November 17 in a different courtroom, that of Judge Henry W. Goddard. Again, Thomas F. Murphy led the prosecution team. But Alger Hiss had a new lead defense attorney, Claude B. Cross. Less flamboyant and dynamic than Stryker, Cross relied more on his solid command of the facts than theatrics to make his case.

Again, it took only one day to seat the jury of eight women and four men. Then on the morning of November 18, the attorneys made their opening arguments. The facts of the case remained the same. It was how the evidence was presented to the jury that would be important. In his opening arguments, Murphy, rather than focusing on the credibility of his chief witness, Whittaker Chambers, stressed that the evidence in and of itself would show Hiss to be a liar.

THOMAS F. MURPHY, OPENING STATEMENT FOR GOVERNMENT

What is the issue? In simple terms as can be said the issue is, did this defendant lie? Now the lie is, as we know, the words coming out of a person's mouth, contrary to what he in conscience knows to be the opposite. You can see how difficult it is to prove a lie, and I am going to ask you ladies and gentlemen to reflect and see whether you don't prove it the way you do in ordinary business and home matters. How do you prove a person [5] lies? Obviously we cannot have a motion picture of it and you have to do it by circumstantial evidence, as the lawyers call it.

I am going to ask you to think of the way jurors come to conclusions in other cases. Let us suppose now we have a case of a man shooting another but not killing him—assault with a gun. What does the proof usually amount to? Somebody goes on the stand and says they saw this man with a pistol; they heard the noise and they saw the victim fall.

Then they put another man on the stand and he says he examined the bullet that was found in the victim's body and he examined other

Source: In the United States Court of Appeals for the Second Circuit, United States Against Alger Hiss, On Appeal From the District Court of the United States for the Southern District of New York, Transcript of Record, Vol. 1, 164–65, 170, 174–77.

bullets that had come out of that same gun and the markings on both bullets are the same. Then you are asked to come to the conclusion that the defendant shot or assaulted that man. You are asked to draw an inference from those facts. Nobody could see the bullet go of course. It travelled too fast, but some man, a ballistic expert, told you that the markings on that bullet are identical with the markings on other bullets from that same gun, and you have the testimony of the man who heard the shot, the report from the gun. Now I dare say there would not be any doubt about that if that was all the testimony in the case, that that was an assault. Now in lying you have almost the same type of proof.

[6] Another example: let us suppose a man is charged with having received stolen goods. You have to prove that he knowingly received the goods knowing they were stolen.

Well, a man testifies that he sent the goods via truck to someone else; and the truck driver says, yes, he had the goods on his truck, and he parked the car at a certain place, and came back and the goods were gone. Nobody saw anyone take them, but they were gone. And subsequently they are found in the possession of the defendant.

A man testifies that when he first asked the defendant where he got them, he said—well, he just did not say; he did not know.

Another man testifies he was the one who sold him the goods but he did not steal them, but he sold them to him, sold them to him for cash, and there is no bill.

He told him that they were hot, and that is why they were cheap.

I dare say you would come to the conclusion if there was not other proof that that man was guilty of receiving stolen goods.

And how did you arrive at that conclusion? Nobody in the case proved that the goods were stolen [7] by a particular man. You just had to come to that conclusion by the other facts. They started out for the consignee and they did not arrive there. The truck driver says they were gone when he made a delivery, and we find them in somebody else's possession.

So, you see, we do not always have direct proof, and that is why, ladies and gentlemen, I say to you in this case you are going to be asked as intelligent American citizens to exercise your reasoning powers, to look at this case and the facts with complete cold abstraction. Be as analytical about it as you would if you were buying a piece of property. Your emotions are one thing, but when you are spending your own money you like to get right in there and see and weigh and measure so that you make no mistakes.

• • •

The defense will make great capital out of the fact that Chambers lied; that he lied on innumerable occasions; that he lied before the House Committee, talking now of the Committee of Congress, but we will use that phrase "the House Committee" where he was under oath; that he lied when he was called by the grand jury in October 1948; that [21] he lied when he saw Mr. Berle, Adolf Berle, who was Assistant Secretary of State, in 1939; that he lied about what? What did he lie about? They won't say that he lied when he said that Hiss was a Communist. There is no dispute that in all of these occasions, the House Committee, Mr. Berle, and the grand jury, that he told them that Hiss was a Communist and he was a Communist and a Party functionary. The gist of the capital they will make about the lie is that he did not tell the whole truth when he testified about those things.

What did he leave out? What did he hide? What did he lie about? He lied when he said he had no evidence of any espionage. The grand jury asked him in October, "Do you have any evidence of espionage?" And he said, "No, I do not."

The House Committee on a number of occasions asked, "Do you have any evidence of espionage?" "No, I do not."

He did not tell Mr. Berle that he had evidence of espionage, but by the repetition of that you will be asked to discredit Mr. Chambers. In other words, what he did over a period of many days of testifying was not to tell the whole truth with regard to the same subject matters.

But there came a time when he did. When did he [22] do that? The first time was in connection with a lawsuit that was instituted in Baltimore by Mr. Hiss against Mr. Chambers, and that will be referred to as the "Baltimore lawsuit."

That arose in this fashion: at one of these executive sessions that I told you about, where the members of the House Committee were interrogating both Mr. Chambers and Mr. Hiss, Mr. Hiss asked Mr. Chambers whether he would, he dared him, call him a Communist outside the halls of Congress.

In other words, when you say something before a House Committee, whether it is false or true, you have a certain immunity and you cannot be sued for anything you say. If you say it in a courtroom under oath and call somebody a thief, you have a certain immunity from being sued, but when he said to him, "Say that outside, that I am a Communist, where you won't have this immunity," Chambers says "Fine."

He said it outside. He said it over a radio national hook-up. So Hiss sued him for libel, this man who was then president of the Carnegie Endowment For Peace, who was formerly for 10 or

11 years assistant to the Assistant Secretary of State, sued Chambers for libel for calling him a Communist, and he valued his damages at $50,000.

[23] Two days later he amended his complaint because Chambers reiterated it, and increased his demand for damages to $75,000, and Chambers, represented by attorneys, put an answer in that lawsuit.

He admitted that he said that, and pleaded what as a defense to that lawsuit, to that charge? He pleaded the truth. It is a perfect defense in a libel suit to plead truth. Truth is a perfect defense. If the charge is true it is not libel.

Now, what happened in that lawsuit? Both Chambers and Mrs. Chambers were examined as adverse parties and witnesses. In other words, under the law either side is entitled to examine the other before trial and the testimony is under oath, taken down by a stenographer.

These examinations commenced on November 4, 1948. You will see the date was prior to the grand jury inquiry that we are concerned with, and during the course of those examinations Chambers was asked by Mr. Hiss's lawyer, "Do you have any papers, anything typewritten or hand-written that you could offer this plaintiff, Mr. Hiss?" And a week later, and Mr. Chambers will describe how he got the papers, he produced the papers which are in this lawsuit and put them on the desk, and there was the immutable evidence of espionage.

[24] There was the evidence that this charge was true.

"These are the papers I received from Mr. Hiss; they were typed in his house, handed to me in his house, and they are copies, exact copies," in most instances, of secret State Department documents.

That was on November 17, a year ago yesterday.

Now, the libel or the charge of libel was either in August or September 1948, and examined Chambers commencing in November and continuing through the intervening months up until March of this year. In other words, they were examining him after the indictment was handed down here, and we have the transcript here, some 1300 pages. Chambers was asked almost everything from the day he was born until that day; and every answer was straightforward, to the point; he did not refuse to answer any question. He told them everything of his personal life.

And his wife too was examined—where they lived; what names they used while they were in the Party; how often they saw the Hisses; where they saw them; how old the baby was; how old the second baby was; what they are doing now—everything they told.

So you are going to be confronted here with that testimony of Mr. Chambers in that lawsuit. They are going to say, as I said, that he lied in the [25] grand jury in October when he did not tell them about espionage; down in the House Committee when he did not tell them about espionage.

"Why did you lie, Mr. Chambers?" the grand jury asked him, as you would too. "Why didn't you tell us about Hiss before?"

They asked him that in Baltimore too, "Why didn't you tell us?" and he told them why. He said he was fortunate in being given the time as a former Communist to see the light of day. He had hoped—still hopes—that all Communists will be given that time to see the error of their ways. He at least was fortunate; he saw it and he quit, broke with them.

He was very friendly with Mr. Hiss, very, very, friendly, on an intellectual basis. They were both brilliant men, and he said he just could not bring himself, just could not bring himself to harm him in that sense. He had a duty to break up the Communist conspiracy, and that is why he named Hiss. He named others, not only Hiss; he named others, many others, but he just could not with these former friends go that far. But when that lawsuit was started then he saw the Communist Party at work, he says, and that is what made him say, "Well, all the cards are down now; they are all down; there it is. If you don't [26] believe me, those are the papers." And that is why he lied.

But when the chips were down in December in the grand jury, when the grand jury, a body like yourself—twice as many—called him and called Mr. Hiss, first one, then the other, first one, then the other—where was the truth here? Where was the truth? Did you or didn't you?

And they, indicted Hiss.

When Cross rose to speak, he, like his predecessor Stryker in the first trial, contrasted the characters of Hiss and Chambers, but he placed more emphasis on the possibility that someone other than Hiss may have been the source of the Chambers documents. He proposed that Chambers had two sources within the State Department—Henry Julian Wadleigh, who had admitted in the first trial that he had provided documents to Chambers, albeit not the documents offered into evidence, and a mystery person in the Far Eastern Division. He based his argument on the one document that had been typed on a typewriter other than the Woodstock. Furthermore, while admitting that the other documents had been typed on the Woodstock, he noted that only Chambers claimed that Priscilla Hiss had typed the materials. He implied a conspiracy to frame Hiss. He argued that anyone could have typed them at anytime after the spring of 1938.

CLAUDE B. CROSS, OPENING STATEMENT FOR DEFENDANT

Now, let me say one word about the difference between the so-called Baltimore exhibits—that was the term used at the first trial; what term will be used here will be for his Honor to say. The Baltimore exhibits consist of 47 exhibits. Four of them are little pieces of paper that are all in Alger Hiss's handwriting; not the slightest question about that. They are the memoranda that Mr. Hiss made on notations of all the papers that came across his desk that he would discuss at lunch or report to his boss. Sometimes he had thrown them in the wastebasket and sometimes they would be left in the file. How they were obtained we will never know, except that we will show you the purpose of those papers. Those are the first four exhibits, 1 to 4. Exhibits 5 through 47 are typewritten documents.

Now, you are going to hear a lot about documents, I am sorry—not in my opening but in the evidence—but [54] in order to really find out and determine the only issue in the case, whether Alger Hiss ever turned over papers to Chambers, we have got to refer to documents, and where those documents start from, and where they went, and who had access to them.

The evidence will be that all of those documents, typewritten documents, 5 through 47, except Exhibit 10, were typed on a Woodstock typewriter that once belonged to Hiss.

The evidence of the Hisses, of the colored maid and her two sons, Claudia Catlett, Raymond Catlett and Perry Catlett—sometimes referred to as Mike and Pat—they will testify here that that typewriter, Woodstock typewriter was given to them when the Hisses moved from the 30th Street house, which was December 29, 1937, to the Volta Place home in Washington, December 1937.

The Hisses will testify to that; the Catletts will; and it is for you to say whether you believe that from about December 1937 that Woodstock typewriter was in the possession of the Hisses.

Now, why did I mention Exhibit 10? Exhibit 10 is on Government bond. It has the Government watermark in it, and it was not typed on the Woodstock. It is an MID dispatch that comes from the

Source: In the United States Court of Appeals for the Second Circuit, United States Against Alger Hiss, On Appeal From the District Court of the United States for the Southern District of New York, Transcript of Record, Vol. 1, 194–96, 201.

War Department, and the [55] only office in the State Department where that paper went, as will be shown from documentary evidence, the only office in the State Department was the Far Eastern Division of the State Department. Nothing to do with Mr. Sayre's office, and nowhere about Mr. Hiss's office. And yet on November 17, 1948, one year ago yesterday, Whittaker Chambers turns up with some papers, and by some oversight, or something, there is a document written on Government bond paper, typed on Government bond paper that went only to the Far Eastern Division of the State Department, not Mr. Sayre's office, not Mr. Hiss's office. And that is the only office in the whole State Department where that document went.

As to that you will consider whether or not there was not a pipeline to Whittaker Chambers out of the Far Eastern Division, and I am going to tell you why that is important a little bit later.

Mr. Murphy did not mention Mr. Chambers' reports to Hiss, and how he was torn by turmoil.

From March 1936 until at least March 1938 there was a thief in the State Department—a department called Trade Agreements—headed by Mr. Hawkins, who was stealing papers for two years and turning them over to Whittaker Chambers and his confederates. Whittaker Chambers admits that, and that man is Julian Wadleigh, [56] who appeared at the first trial and admitted that. If he appears again, watch him, and see what his answers are when he is asked, "Did you deliver any of these papers to Hiss?"

We say that there was a pipeline out of the Far Eastern Division, as shown by Exhibit 10 and various other documents.

• • •

Now, as to the typewriter, we say that the Hisses did not type those documents, some of which never [64] came to Alger Hiss. If the Hisses did not, who did?

As to whether it was on the Woodstock typewriter, the Government produced a witness at the first trial who said in his opinion it was done on the Woodstock typewriter—of course, we had it until December 1937—and there is no cross-examination of that witness. I tell you, in frankness, that we have consulted some experts and they say that in their opinion it was typed on the Woodstock typewriter. That is an opinion. What the fact is as to who actually typed it only the person who typed it knows. And it is our contention that either Whittaker Chambers or his confederate typed those Baltimore documents other than Exhibit 10.

Defense Casts Doubt on Hiss as Source of Documents

The second trial unfolded much the same way as the first. The prosecution presented expert witnesses linking the typed documents to the Woodstock typewriter and verifying that Hiss's handwriting matched the four handwritten notes. Other witnesses corroborated the mass of circumstantial evidence. Once again Whittaker and Esther Chambers were the chief prosecution witnesses. As in the other trial, the defense countered with an array of prominent character witnesses. Alger and Priscilla Hiss repeated their earlier testimony. The Catletts returned to testify about Chambers's visits to the Hiss apartments and to explain the disposition of the Woodstock typewriter. Both the prosecution and the defense caught witnesses in contradictions and inconsistencies. They constantly pointed out the deviation from testimony in the first trial.

Similarities aside, there were some noteworthy new developments in the second trial that contributed to a different outcome. One came during the defense's response to the prosecution's evidence linking the classified documents to Hiss. After suggesting that some of them never crossed Hiss's desk and challenging the assumption that Priscilla Hiss had typed the copied materials, Cross exploited Henry Julian Wadleigh's admission during the first trial that he had been one of Chambers's sources. This *New York Herald Tribune* article depicts how, on December 8, Cross broached the possibility that Wadleigh could have provided the materials, not Hiss. In the first trial, Stryker had been caught off guard by Wadleigh's unexpected admission that he indeed had been one source of State Department materials. In the second trial, Cross was ready to go on the attack.

"WADLEIGH CAN'T IDENTIFY PAPERS IN HISS TRIAL"

Henry Julian Wadleigh, former State Department economist, testified yesterday that although he turned over more than 400 government documents to a Communist spy ring between 1936 and 1938, he did not recognize any of the fifty-four sets of papers in evidence at the

Source: New York Herald Tribune, December 9, 1949.

perjury trial of Alger Hiss. He said it was conceivable he might have handled a few of them, but he was certain he did not handle most of them, and he did not remember any of them.

• • •

Mr. Wadleigh received a more exhaustive examination yesterday than he had in the first trial, because in the mean while the defense had sought to show that he and an alleged confederate in the Far Eastern division of the State Department were responsible for giving Whittaker Chambers all the documents which Mr. Chambers says he got from Mr. Hiss.

Mr. Hiss was indicted for perjury when he denied this charge.

Mr. Wadleigh inspected each of the forty-seven handwritten and typewritten exhibits and seven sets of microfilm photographs produced by Mr. Chambers. He said he had definitely never seen any of the handwritten or typewritten papers before and had definitely not given them either to Mr. Chambers or any other member of the spy ring.

He added that eight of the typewritten papers were copies of summaries of documents which might have reached his desk in the State Department. He said it was conceivable he might have given the original document to Mr. Chambers in these cases, but he did not remember doing so.

He also said that five of the seven microfilm exhibits were photographs of documents which he might conceivably have given to Mr. Chambers. The other two related to the Far East, and he said he certainly did not give Mr. Chambers "any significant quantity" of such documents, though he might have given him some.

DENIES TYPING DOCUMENTS

Mr. Wadleigh reiterated that he never personally typed any copies nor summaries of State Department documents, nor gave any such typed copies or summaries to Mr. Chambers or any one else. He added that he went to Turkey on March 11, 1938, before the dates on some of the documents.

The rest of Mr. Wadleigh's story tallied generally with what Mr. Chambers had previously said about him except for a few details. Mr. Chambers had testified that Mr. Wadleigh gave him documents in batches of from ten to twenty-five at a time; Mr. Wadleigh said the average was four or five, but sometimes there were half a dozen or more. Mr. Wadleigh stuck to his story that the "boss" of the spy ring, variously known as Sasha, Peter and Colonel Bykov, had lost his right arm and spoke English well with a Russian accent. Mr. Chambers, the only other person who has ever described this individual, said he had both his arms and spoke only Russian and bad German.

Mr. Wadleigh admitted that he had knowingly committed espionage in violation of the law, but he refused to permit his action to be described as "stealing" the documents. Claude B. Cross, chief defense counsel, repeatedly used this word in questions, and each time Mr. Wadleigh began his answer by saying: "With the same reservation about the use of the word 'stealing.' ". . .

This and other verbal quibbles between witness and attorney prompted the first laughter in the courtroom since the trial began.

Judge Allows Hede Massing to Testify

In a second new development, the prosecution scored points with the testimony of Hede Massing, a former member of the Communist underground and wife of Gerhart Eisler, a leading Communist who had fled the country. Until now, Chambers was the only witness the jury heard from who offered firsthand testimony that Hiss was a member of a Communist apparatus. In the first trial, Judge Kaufman had refused to allow Massing to testify. Judge Goddard, however, decided to permit Massing's testimony. The jury had a second eyewitness to Hiss's alleged Communist Party activities.

"EISLER'S EX-WIFE SAYS SHE MET HISS WHEN HE WORKED FOR REDS"

Mrs. Hede Massing, forty-nine-year-old former Viennese actress, testified yesterday that she once met Alger Hiss in 1935, when she was "working for the Communist party." She implied that Mr. Hiss was also working for the Communists at the same time, but objections from defense counsel prevented her from saying so.

It was the first time Mrs. Massing has given public testimony, though her name has been mentioned in Communist spy investigations for more than a year. She is the former wife of Gerhart Eisler, who fled to Germany after being branded the No. 1 Communist agent in this country.

She testified yesterday that she became "affiliated" with the Communist party as a sympathizing non-member in 1919, and began "working" for it in 1933, six years after becoming a naturalized citizen of the United States. She did not specify the nature of this "work."

Source: New York Herald Tribune, December 10, 1949.

Mrs. Massing was not asked when she stopped working for the Communist party, though it appeared from her testimony that she must have done so. Claude B. Cross, chief defense counsel, promised to produce another witness who would testify that Mrs. Massing had boasted before the trial began that her evidence would "convict Mr. Hiss," and that she was writing a book about the case with the help of Eugene Lyons, anti-Communist author and former newspaper correspondent in Moscow.

Mrs. Massing admitted that she was often at parties in Mr. Lyons's apartment and might have said there that she was planning to write a book after the trial. She pointed out Mr. Lyons in the spectators' section of the courtroom, and said she had seen many other persons at his apartment who were also among the spectators, but were not pointed out. She balked only at the name of Henricus Rabinovicius, who was not otherwise identified.

Mrs. Massing's identification of Mr. Hiss was positive, although she said she had never seen him after the one meeting in 1935, until they met at the grand jury investigation in December, 1943. She said that Mr. Hiss then told her he did not recognize her or recall meeting her before, and that she told him all about herself in an effort to remind him of the circumstances.

SAYS HE WAS FRIENDLY

"He was very friendly and polite, and he thanked me for being so helpful," she said. She told Assistant United States Attorney Thomas F. Murphy that she had put on weight and begun wearing glasses since 1935, but her appearance had not otherwise changed.

She said she had met Mr. Hiss in 1935 at the home of Noel H. Field, who has been described by Whittaker Chambers as another member of the Communist apparatus which he has accused Mr. Hiss of working for.

She described the conversation as follows:

"I said to Mr. Hiss, 'I understand that you are trying to get Noel Field away from my organization into yours,' and he said, 'So you are this famous girl that is trying to get Noel Field away from me,' and I said 'yes.' He said, 'Well, we will see who is going to win.' At this point I said, 'You realize that you are competing with a woman,' at which either he or I said—I forget which of us said it, but it was either he or I—'Whoever is going to win, we are working for the same boss.' This sentence I remember very distinctly because it was very important."

Mrs. Massing said she could not remember who else was present besides Mr. and Mrs. Field.

Mrs. Massing said she had been married to her present husband, Paul Massing, for eighteen years. She added that she was divorced from her second husband, Julian Gumpers, in 1932 in Berlin, and divorced her first husband, Mr. Eisler, in 1924 in Germany. She said she was "legally married" to Mr. Eisler for three years, and that she was not now living with her husband. She spelled out "Hede" and "Gumpers," for the court stenographer, and added that her first name originally was "Hedwig."

Defense Questions Chambers's Mental Stability

If Massing's appearance strengthened the prosecution's case, another decision by Judge Goddard was potentially helpful for the defense. In the first trial, Hiss's defense team had planned to undermine Chambers's credibility by questioning his mental state. They had asked psychiatrist Carl Binger to sit in the gallery as Chambers testified with the intention of calling him as an expert witness. But when the defense was ready to call Binger to the stand, Judge Kaufman refused to allow him to testify. When the defense called Binger during the second trial, however, Judge Goddard, over strong prosecution objections, allowed his testimony. The judge acknowledged that permitting Dr. Binger to testify to the mental condition of a witness was unprecedented in federal cases. Nevertheless, he ruled the doctor's testimony relevant to the matter at hand.

After listening to a litany of Chambers's background and unorthodox conduct read by Cross that went on for more than an hour, Binger presented his diagnosis that Chambers suffered from a mental disease called "psychopathic personality," a condition characterized by persistent lying and acts of deception, among other symptoms. Binger's diagnosis led to an aggressive three-hour cross-examination by the prosecution. But the defense then bolstered Binger's conclusions by calling a Harvard psychologist, Dr. Henry A. Murray, to corroborate Binger's conclusions. The *New York Herald Tribune* account of Doctor Binger's first day of testimony follows.

"HISS TRIAL TOLD CHAMBERS HAS MENTAL AILMENT"

A practicing psychiatrist testified yesterday that Whittaker Chambers, key prosecution witness in the trial of Alger Hiss, was suffering from a mental disease known as psychopathic personality. It was the first time psychiatric testimony had ever been used in a Federal Court to impeach the credibility of a witness.

Source: New York Herald Tribune, January 6, 1950.

Dr. Carl A. L. Binger, a faculty member at the Cornell University Medical College and the first of two witnesses to be called for this purpose by the defense, said the outstanding features of the disease were "behavior of an amoral or asocial and delinquent nature." He said that among its symptoms were "chronic, persistent and repetitive lying; stealing, acts of deception and misrepresentation, alcoholism, drug addiction, abnormal sexuality, vagabondage, panhandling, inability to form stable attachments and a tendency to make false accusations."

He said that "pathological lying and pathological accusations" were frequently found in psychopathic personalities, and that they differed from "what is commonly recognized by laymen" as lying.

Dr. Binger's testimony was admitted over government objections at the second trial of Mr. Hiss, who was accused by Whittaker Chambers of giving secret State Department documents to Mr. Chambers in 1938 for transmission to a Communist spy ring. Mr. Hiss was indicted for perjury when he denied this accusation.

BARRED AT EARLIER TRIAL

At the first trial, which ended in a hung jury last July 8, Dr. Binger took the witness stand but was not allowed to give his opinion of Mr. Chambers's mental condition.

On that occasion Lloyd Paul Stryker, then trial counsel for Mr. Hiss, read a forty-five-minute hypothetical question summing up the questionable incidents in the career of Mr. Chambers which had appeared in the testimony. Judge Samuel H. Kaufman then ruled that the record was sufficiently clear for the jury to decide on the credibility of all witnesses, and Dr. Binger left the stand without answering the question.

Yesterday Thomas F. Murphy, Assistant United States Attorney, renewed the government's objections before Dr. Binger took the stand.

"This is the first time in the history of Anglo-Saxon jurisprudence that the testimony of a psychiatrist is being admitted to impeach the credibility of a mere witness when there has not been a scintilla of proof that the witness has had any treatment by a psychiatrist or a physician except for his teeth," Mr. Murphy said.

OBJECTION OVERRULED

Judge Henry, W. Goddard overruled the objection. He said that such testimony had been admitted in a number of state courts although it had not been introduced before in a Federal Court. He said he would endeavor to tell the jury how much weight they might give to "this opinion testimony" and added that it is the jury's opinion that counts above that of anyone else.

In a memorandum filed with the court, Judge Goddard wrote that "evidence concerning the credibility of the witness is undoubtedly relevant and material and under the circumstances in this case, and in view of the foundation which has been laid, I think it should be received.

"It is apparent that the outcome of this trial is dependent to a great extent upon the testimony of one man—Whittaker Chambers," the judge wrote. "Mr. Chambers's credibility is one of the major issues upon which the jury must pass . . . the opinion of the jury is decisive.

"The existence of insanity or mental derangement is admissible for the purpose of discrediting a witness." The judge added that the reason psychiatric testimony had not previously appeared in Federal courts was the newness of the science, and that its use was sanctioned by precedent in state courts and authoritative books on evidence.

QUALIFICATIONS STATED

Defense attorney Claude B. Cross began by asking Dr. Binger to state his qualifications. These included the degree of Doctor of Medicine from Harvard Medical School, study of psychiatry in Heidelberg and Zurich, medical practice in the Rockefeller Institute and the United States Marine Corps during World War I, psychiatric training and practice at the Cornell and Vanderbilt Clinics and the New York Hospital of Cornell University Medical Center, associate professorship of clinical psychiatry at Cornell and service as psychiatric consultant to the Selective Service System during World War II and to the Veterans Administration at present.

He added that he had listened to the testimony of Whittaker Chambers in court on June 2, 3, 6, 7 and 8 of the first trial and Nov. 28 of the second trial, and studied poems and articles he had written and books he had translated.

Mr. Cross then asked him a hypothetical question that required sixty-five minutes to read. It was more comprehensive than that asked by Mr. Stryker and included new evidence which had appeared at the second trial.

HYPOTHETICAL QUESTION

The question began: "Assume that the following facts are true" . . . and recited the numerous false names Mr. Chambers used during his life, the many occasions on which he has admitted telling lies, the theft of books from the New York Public Library and the Columbia University Library, the record of the Public Library investigator stating that library books were found in his locker although he denied in his testimony at this trial that the investigators had found such books there. Also the suicide of his brother, and Mr. Chambers's statement that he found out after his brother's death that he loved him, and that this "set the seal on my being a Communist"; the different stories Mr. Chambers has told about how he broke from the Communist party and lived for a year in hiding with a gun always within reach, his association with a prostitute and other unmarried women, and virtually every other item of testimony referring to Mr. Chambers.

At the end, Mr. Cross asked Dr. Binger if, assuming these facts to be true and considering his observations of Mr. Chambers on the witness stand and his studies of Mr. Chambers's literary works, he could give an opinion "within the bounds of reasonable certainty" as to his mental condition.

"I think Mr. Chambers is suffering from a condition known as psychopathic personality—a disorder of character," Dr. Binger said. Under further questioning he elaborated his answer, adding these details among others:

"Amoral conduct is behavior that does not take into account the ordinary accepted conventions of morality; asocial conduct has no regard for the good of society and the individual and is therefore frequently destructive of both."

Psychopathic personality, Dr. Binger said, has been recognized as a distinct mental disease by the Mental Hygiene Department of the State of New York for at least fifteen years. He added that the sufferer is "quite aware of what he is doing but does not know why he does it. . ."

"These unfortunate people have a conviction of the truth and validity of their own imaginations and fantasy without respect to outer reality—they play a role; it may be a hero one moment and a gangster the next. They act as if a situation were true when in fact it is true only in their imagination. They will claim friendships where none exist and will make accusations that have no basis in fact."

Defense and Prosecution Sum Up

The second trial neared an end on January 19 and 20 as the opposing attorneys made their closing arguments. On January 19, Cross spent nearly five hours challenging Chambers's truthfulness. The *New York Herald Tribune* described how he concocted a web of hypotheticals pointing to individuals other than Hiss as the source of the documents. Cross again insisted that Henry Julian Wadleigh and an unknown individual in the State Department Far Eastern Division were Chambers's sources. In an effort to undermine the

Woodstock evidence, he stressed the Catlett testimony that the typewriter was no longer in the possession of the Hisses in 1938. He proposed that it was "not a question of what typewriter was used, but who did the typing." He also had an explanation for why Chambers had a file of information pointing to Hiss. Chambers was not only a Communist seeking to protect himself, but also a pathological liar as suggested by Doctors Binger and Murray.

"HISS'S DEFENSE SUMS UP; JURY TO GET CASE TODAY"

Defense counsel in the second Alger Hiss perjury trial summed up the case yesterday with the contention that the documents which Mr. Hiss is accused of giving to Mr. Chambers in 1938 were actually given to him by other persons, "confederates" of Mr. Chambers.

Thomas F. Murphy, Assistant United States Attorney, will sum up for the prosecution at 10 A.M. today, after which Judge Goddard will deliver his charge and give the case to the jury, which has been sitting since Nov. 17. In the first trial, which lasted six weeks until last July 8, the jury disagreed after deliberating almost twenty-nine hours.

Claude B. Cross, defense lawyer, in a five-hour address to the jury yesterday, said some of the documents came from Henry Julian Wadleigh, former employee of the Trade Agreements section of the State Department, who has admitted giving documents to Mr. Chambers. He said other documents were provided by an unnamed person in the Far Eastern Division of the State Department. He referred to the name of "Mr. Lovell," previously described as a Communist by Mr. Chambers, as a possibility, but added that he was not making any accusation against Mr. Lovell.

Mr. Cross contended that the typewritten papers in the case could not have come from Mr. Hiss because in many cases he did not have access to the documents on which they were based.

Mr. Cross accepted the government's contention that these papers were typed on a Woodstock typewriter once owned by Mr. Hiss, but asserted that even the testimony of George Roulhac, produced by the government as a rebuttal witness, showed that the typewriter passed out of Mr. Hiss's possession at about the time of the last date on the papers, while the testimony of Raymond and Perry Catlett, defense witnesses, indicated that Mr. Hiss gave them the machine at an earlier

Source: New York Herald Tribune, January 20, 1950.

date. Mr. Cross suggested that the memory of the Catlett brothers might be more accurate than that of Mr. Roulhac.

"It is not a question of what typewriter was used, but who did the typing," Mr. Cross said. "If some of these documents never came to him they could not have been typed by Alger Hiss. . . . How did Chambers know about it? How did he get it? He didn't do it himself, you can bet your life on that. He acts through confederates. Anyone, who through confederates, can steal top secret documents from the State Department would not have much trouble locating a big office typewriter."

He suggested that Mr. Chambers's confederate might have found out that the typewriter was in the Catlett home by posing as a typewriter repair man and talking to Mrs. Clytie Catlett, mother of the Catlett brothers, who still worked as a maid in the Hiss household. The Catletts kept the machine in a room easily accessible from the outside, and in a house filled with "people coming and going," Mr. Cross said.

Mr. Cross contended that Mr. Chambers fabricated the typewritten papers in May or June of 1938 just before he gave them to Nathan Levine, his wife's nephew, for safekeeping.

Mr. Cross also cited testimony which he said indicated that Mr. Chambers had "prepared a file" of material relating to Francis B. Sayre, then Assistant Secretary of State, and Charles Darlington, then assistant chief of the Trade Agreements section, to be used "as a cover" in case "any finger of suspicion ever pointed toward Julian Wadleigh as a thief of papers from the Trade Agreements section."

HANDWRITTEN MEMOS

The defense attorney argued that Mr. Chambers prepared a similar "file" on Mr. Hiss, and lumped it with the papers he got from Mr. Wadleigh and the "confederate in the Far Eastern Division" to support his accusation against Mr. Hiss.

Mr. Cross contended that the four handwritten memoranda were prepared by Mr. Hiss for his own use and never intended to be spy papers. He said that Mr. Chambers himself did not call them spy papers when he first produced them in Baltimore, but described them as "specimens of Mr. Hiss's handwriting."

Mr. Cross said Mr. Chambers made his false accusation against Mr. Hiss from "dishonest bad, untrue motives." "If it had been made from honest motives Mr. Chambers need not have backed it up by so many lies," he said. He did not analyze the motives in detail but suggested that they were made up of Mr. Chambers's effort to protect himself during his career as a Communist spy courier, his effort to defend himself against the libel suit brought by Mr. Hiss when

Mr. Chambers first called Mr. Hiss a Communist, and the tendency toward pathological lying described by Dr. Henry A. Murray, psychologist, and Dr. Carl A.L. Binger psychiatrist, who testified that Mr. Chambers was suffering from a psychopathic personality.

The next day, Murphy devoted nearly three hours to making the case against Hiss. To him, the evidence spoke for itself. The documents Hiss transmitted—and to him there was little doubt that Hiss was the source—damaged U.S. security. He suggested that the psychiatric testimony, questioning Chambers's mental stability, was a case of "unconscious bias." He ridiculed Hiss's story about his relationship with Chambers and argued that the defense presented no credible motive for Chambers to want to "frame" Hiss. When Murphy concluded, Judge Goddard read his charge to the jury before it began deliberating.

The *New York Herald Tribune* account of events in the courtroom included a description of prosecutor Murphy's scathing summation attacking Hiss.

"HISS JURY GETS CASE; LOCKED UP FOR NIGHT"

The jury debating the fate of Alger Hiss for the second time was locked up, without reaching a verdict, at 10:45 o'clock last night. The jury had received the case, after a trial lasting thirty-nine days, at 3:10 P.M. yesterday.

• • •

Mr. Murphy in his summation asserted that all the facts alleged in Mr. Chambers' testimony had been corroborated. He ridiculed the arguments of Claude B. Cross, defense counsel and said that the defense had failed to offer any credible motive for Mr. Chambers to have "framed" his accusation against Mr. Hiss.

MURPHY ASSAILS HISS

As he had done in the first trial Mr. Murphy compared Mr. Hiss to the devil, called him a traitor and dismissed the nineteen character witnesses as so many purveyors of gossip. He did not, however, repeat his first trial effort to compare Mr. Hiss to Judas Iscariot.

Mr. Murphy answered the defense contention that Mr. Chambers by himself or through a confederate had typed the Woodstock papers by saying it was "poppycock." He told the jury that if they thought

Source: New York Herald Tribune, January 21, 1950.

any evidence had been manufactured or any false testimony suborned by the Federal Bureau of Investigation they should acquit Mr. Hiss.

Mr. Murphy said he thought "unconscious bias" influenced the two defense experts who testified that Mr. Chambers was a pathological liar—Dr. Carl A. L. Binger, psychiatrist, and Dr. Henry A. Murray, psychologist. He said that their opinions were "without factual foundation" and that "there was no suspicion of anything wrong with Mr. Chambers at all."

"If I thought there was a real serious question of the mental condition of Mr. Chambers the government could afford competent advice," he said. "But I didn't call any. I don't think that question arose. I think perhaps there was another purpose behind the doctors' testimony. Each testified without fee. Perhaps they were unconsciously biased—perhaps they had a cause, too; they wanted to help a friend."

PROOFS OF ASSOCIATION

Mr. Murphy contended that Mr. Chambers's story of borrowing $400 from Mr. Hiss in 1937, the rug which he gave Mr. Hiss, and the knowledge displayed of the interior of the houses Mr. Hiss lived in were all proofs of close association and close friendship between the two men. He said they were also proofs that Mr. Hiss saw Mr. Chambers after Jan. 1, 1937, as alleged in the second count.

Mr. Murphy reasoned that "if they were close friends, they were in agreement on their basic philosophy, and they were both Communists—then it is probable that each Communist helped the other, and Mr. Hiss helped Mr. Chambers by giving him the documents.

The Guilty Verdict

On January 21, 1950, the jury, after nine hours and thirteen minutes of deliberation, returned a guilty verdict. Defense tactics suggesting other sources than Hiss for the State Department documents proved unconvincing to the jurors. And the testimony of Hede Massing provided a second eyewitness to Hiss's involvement with the Communist Party, strengthening Chambers's allegations. The next morning, the *New York Herald Tribune* front-page article described the reaction in the courtroom. Hiss accepted the verdict "with the same stoic calm" he had shown throughout the two trials. His defense counsels announced their intention to appeal.

"HISS CONVICTED OF PERJURY ON BOTH COUNTS, TO BE SENTENCED WEDNESDAY, PLANS APPEAL"

Alger Hiss was found guilty yesterday of lying under oath when he denied that he had ever given secret State Department documents to Whittaker Chambers or any other unauthorized person, or that he had ever seen Mr. Chambers between Jan. 1, 1937, and Aug. 17, 1948.

A jury of eight women and four men in United States District Court in Foley Square convicted Mr. Hiss on both counts of the perjury indictment at 2:50 P.M. Judge Henry W. Goddard said he would pronounce sentence Wednesday at 10:30 A.M.

The verdict meant that Mr. Hiss was found guilty of giving government secrets to a Communist spy ring in 1938, when he was an executive in the State Department. Any possibility of prosecution for such acts, however, is ruled out by a three-year statute of limitations.

THE POSSIBLE PENALTY

Mr. Hiss is forty-five years old. He faces a maximum penalty of five years in prison and $2,000 fine on each of the two perjury counts.

Claude B. Cross, defense trial counsel, said he would make all motions on Wednesday. He is expected to move to set aside the verdict.

Later he told reporters, "You can be sure the case will be appealed."

Mr. Hiss was continued in the same bail—$5,000—that was posted when he was first arraigned.

Mr. Chambers, for whom the verdict was a personal victory in a public duel that began Aug. 3, 1948, commented at his farm in Westminster, Md.:

"I don't see how they could have returned any other verdict. I hope the American people realize what they owe to this jury, to Mr. Murphy (Thomas F. Murphy, Assistant United States Attorney, who prosecuted) and to the splendid work of the F.B.I.

"My work is now finished. I have told the F.B.I. all I know."

• • •

The verdict came at the end of the second trial of the indictment, which was brought Dec. 15, 1948. The convicting jury had the case 23 hours 40 minutes. Deducting time for sleep and meals, their actual deliberations consumed 9 hours 13 minutes. The verdict came on the

Source: New York Herald Tribune, January 22, 1950.

fortieth court day of the trial, which began Nov. 17. It was interrupted twice by the illness of two jurors, as well as by the Thanksgiving, Christmas and New Year's holidays.

The first trial ended in a deadlocked jury at the end of twenty-eight days. That jury had the case 28 hours 40 minutes, of which 17 hours 10 minutes were consumed in deliberations. One of the jurors who voted for conviction at the first trial, John S. Adrian, of 294 Bronxville Road, Yonkers, was in the courtroom yesterday to hear the verdict.

Mr. Hiss heard it with the same stoic calm which he has shown throughout the two trials. He sat in his usual seat, just inside the rail of the court, beside his wife, Priscilla.

Mr. Joseph Toner, clerk of the court, called the roll of the jury, Mrs. Hiss looked straight ahead as though seeing nothing. Mr. Hiss sat with his head high, chin up, expressionless face turned toward the jury, seeming to turn his eyes from each juror to the next as their names were read.

Mr. Hiss was seated with his right leg crossed over his left, his arms akimbo. On his left was Mrs. Hiss, with her hands clutching the black leather handbag in her lap.

Mr. Toner asked the foreman of the jury, Mrs. Ada Condell, of 835 Riverside Drive, whether she and the jury had reached a verdict.

"I have," she answered. Then the verdict of guilty was pronounced. Mr. Hiss showed no sign of emotion. Mrs. Hiss looked straight ahead as before. Newspaper men dashed for the door; voices were heard from spectators, but no words were distinguishable. Mr. Toner said "Quiet, please."

On motion from Mr. Cross the jury was polled, and Mr. Toner asked each juror if his verdict was the same as that of the forelady. Some said "Yes," some said "I do," and some said "It is."

Again Mr. Hiss's eyes rested on each juror in turn. Then, his arms still crossed, he touched his wife's folded hands with his own right hand. All in an instant he smiled, and she smiled back.

Nixon's Response to the Verdict

After the guilty verdict, *Washington Post* reporters sought Chambers's reaction. They tracked him down at his Maryland farm, busy tending his cattle. Chambers saw the Hiss conviction as only the beginning. He expressed gratification at the verdict and praised the role Nixon had played from the

FIGURE 4.1 The Truman administration had tried to control congressional probes, but with Hiss's conviction Congress became more determined to investigate other accusations of Communist subversion.

early stages of the investigation. He said he was willing to cooperate with the government in any effort to go after other members of the Communist apparatus.[8]

Nixon, who also saw the conviction as only a beginning, went on the offensive. Appearing on an American Broadcasting network news program moderated by Bert Andrews of the *New York Herald Tribune*—a confidante of Nixon's from the earlier HUAC investigation—he accused the Truman administration of trying to hinder the Hiss investigation. He claimed that there was a "definite, determined and deliberate effort on the part of certain public officials in two administrations to keep the public from knowing the facts." He promised to bring information before the House of Representatives that would prove his charges. Finally, he ridiculed Truman's description of the whole affair as a "red herring" and belittled statements Secretary of State Dean Acheson made in defense of his former colleague, Alger Hiss.

"NIXON CHARGES 'HIGH OFFICIALS' KEPT HISS 'CONSPIRACY' BURIED"

WASHINGTON, Jan. 21.—Representative Richard M. Nixon, Republican, of California, announced tonight that he has information that "high officials in two Administrations" deliberately kept information of the Alger Hiss "conspiracy" from the public.

This information, Mr. Nixon said, he will present to the House next week. Representative Nixon, a member of the House Committee on Un-American Activities, predicted that the conviction of Mr. Hiss is not the end of the case, that President Truman will "have further reason to regret his 'red herring' remark," and suggested that Secretary of State Dean Acheson, who indorsed Mr. Hiss as a friend, should be "sure that he is not giving his friendship to our enemies."

Mr. Nixon spoke on an American Broadcasting Company network interview with Bert Andrews, chief of the Washington Bureau of the New York Herald Tribune. He credited Mr. Andrews with having had a key role in the events which brought Mr. Hiss to the perjury trial which resulted in his conviction today.

Mr. Nixon's announcement that Mr. Hiss's conviction is not the end of the case came in the following exchange:

MR. ANDREWS: One of the things which will always rise to puzzle us is this: Why did it take the government so many years to get to the bottom of this case? Why, for example, weren't some of the earlier rumors, earlier tips, about Alger Hiss, investigated in real down to earth fashion?

MR. NIXON: I don't want to be mysterious . . . All I can tell you at this moment is that I believe President Truman will have further reason to regret his "red herring" remarks.

MR. ANDREWS: Do you mean by that, Congressman Nixon, that the verdict in the Hiss case is not the complete and final finish of the whole story?

MR. NIXON: It is not, Mr. Andrews. As Whittaker Chambers has stated, there has been too much of a tendency to make this a fight between two individuals. It is larger than that. I have information—which I intend to place before the House next week—which will show that this conspiracy would have come to light long since had there not been a definite, determined and deliberate effort on the part of certain high officials in two administrations to keep the public from knowing the facts.

Source: New York Herald Tribune, January 22, 1950.

Earlier, in response to a question from Mr. Andrews as to what he thought of President Truman's repeated assertions that the Alger Hiss and other Communist penetration investigations was merely a "red herring," Mr. Nixon said he would subscribe to the comment given this afternoon by Representative Harold H. Velde, Republican, of Illinois, a former F.B.I. agent, also a member of the Un-American Activities Committee.

Mr. Velde said: "I think the President's red herring is a cooked goose now. I hope he enjoys eating it."

"How about Secretary Acheson?" asked Mr. Andrews. "He said Alger Hiss was his friend and added that he did not give his friendship lightly."

"My advice to Secretary Acheson," replied Representative Nixon, "would be that he ought to be more careful about giving his friend-ship. He ought to be sure that he is not giving his friendship to our enemies."

Earlier in the broadcast, Mr. Nixon had said the Un-American Activities Committee in 1948 had been "just about to drop" the Hiss case when Mr. Andrews suggested that both Mr. Hiss and Mr. Cham-bers be subjected to a lie detector test, and co-operated with the committee in questioning Mr. Chambers.

Mr. Nixon told how he and Mr. Andrews visited Mr. Chambers at the latter's Westminster, Md., farm on Aug. 14, 1948, and questioned Mr. Chambers for nearly three hours.

"You did most of the questioning," Mr. Nixon told Mr. Andrews in the broadcast. "If you had a law degree, you could get almost as much recognition for being a tough cross examiner as Thomas Murphy, the government attorney in the case, acquired at both the first and second trials. And that is high praise."

Mr. Andrews opened his broadcast tonight with the statement that Mr. Hiss's conviction today "carries with it the implication that the jury believed Mr. Hiss guilty of a graver crime, for the perjury was alleged to have occurred because Mr. Hiss wanted to cover up the fact that he had delivered to Mr. Chambers secret State Department documents—this at a time when Mr. Hiss was a highly-placed State Department employee and when Mr. Chambers was an admitted agent for Soviet Russia."

Mr. Andrews said that he was going to be "highly immodest," and then declared: "If it had not been for Mr. Nixon—and for me—I doubt that Alger Hiss would have ever had to face trial."

Mr. Nixon agreed, and declared Mr. Andrews was more modest than himself in taking credit where credit was due.

Secretary of State Acheson Defends Hiss; Republicans Berate Him

On January 25, Judge Goddard sentenced Alger Hiss to five years in prison. Addressing the court, Hiss persisted in maintaining his innocence and predicted his ultimate exoneration. "I would like to thank your honor for the opportunity again to deny the charges that have been made against me," he told the court. "I am confident that in the future the full facts of how Whittaker Chambers was able to carry out forgery by typewriter will be disclosed."[9]

The following day, the *Washington Post* reported that many Democrats continued to support Hiss, even as Republicans drew other lessons from the Hiss affair. At a news conference on the day Hiss was sentenced, Secretary of State Dean Acheson, citing the twenty-fifth chapter of the Gospel of Saint Matthew, adamantly refused to turn his back on his friend and former colleague. In contrast, on Capitol Hill, Former Congressman, now Senator,

FIGURE 4.2 The Hiss case remained a contentious political issue, particularly when Secretary of State Dean Acheson refused to repudiate his friend and former colleague, Alger Hiss.

Permission granted by Tribune Media Services.

Karl Mundt demanded an investigation of Hiss's "impact and influence" on U.S. foreign policy. Invoking the memory of the Yalta Conference, he called for the Republican Party to take greater responsibility for foreign policy so that such agreements "will never be repeated." Senator Joseph McCarthy of Wisconsin, whose name would soon become synonymous with the investigation of Communists in government, was one of the many senators who supported Mundt's request.

"ACHESON WON'T TURN BACK ON HISS, HE SAYS; MUNDT CALLS FOR PROBE"

Secretary of State Acheson declared yesterday he did not "intend to turn my back on Alger Hiss" regardless of the outcome of the former State Department employe's appeal from a perjury conviction.

Asked at his news conference for comment on the Hiss case, Acheson replied without hesitation, speaking slowly, deliberately and with obvious emotion. He gave permission for direct quotation.

Hiss, convicted by a jury of eight women and four men in Federal Court in New York of lying when he denied passing State Department documents to Whittaker Chambers, confessed Communist courier, was sentenced yesterday to serve five years. Acheson earlier had told a congressional committee that Hiss was a friend of his and that "I do not give my friendship lightly."

WHATEVER THE OUTCOME OF APPEAL

When asked yesterday for comment, he said it would be "highly improper" for him to discuss the case while it was before the courts. Then he added that he thought the questioning reporter intended to "bring something other than that out of me," and went on:

"I should like to make it clear to you that whatever the outcome of any appeal which Mr. Hiss or his lawyers may make in this case, I do not intend to turn my back on Alger Hiss."

"I think every person who has known Alger Hiss or has served with him at any time has upon his conscience the very serious task of deciding what his attitude is and what his conduct should be. That must be done by each person in the light of his own standards and his own principles."

Source: Washington Post, January 26, 1950. Copyright © 1950, *The Washington Post*, reprinted by permission.

PRINCIPLES STATED LONG AGO

"For me, there is very little doubt about those standards or those principles. I think they were stated for us a very long time ago. They were stated on the Mount of Olives and if you are interested in seeing them, you will find them in the 25th Chapter of the Gospel according to St. Matthew, beginning at Verse 34."

This citation, a State Department spokesman later explained, extended from Verse 34 through Verse 40. These verses are:

> "34. Then shall the King say unto them on His right hand, come, ye blessed of My Father, inherit the Kingdom prepared for you from the foundation of the world;
>
> "35. For I was a hungered, and ye gave me meat; I was a stranger; and ye took me in;
>
> "36. Naked, and ye clothed me; I was sick, and ye visited me; I was in prison and ye came unto me.
>
> "37. Then shall the righteous answer Him, saying, Lord, when saw we Thee an hungered, and fed Thee or thirsty, and took Thee in? Or naked, and clothed Thee?
>
> "39. Or when saw we Thee sick, or in prison, and came unto Thee?
>
> "40. And the King shall answer and say unto them, verily I say unto you, inasmuch as ye have done it unto one of the least of these my brethren, ye have done it unto Me."

In other segments of the capital, the Hiss verdict and sentence evoked diametrically opposite sentiments. Senator Mundt (R., S.D.), for instance, demanded on the floor of the Senate yesterday that Congress investigate "the impact and influence" of Hiss on United States foreign policy.

REVISE LIMITATIONS STATUTE

Mundt, a member of the House Un-American Activities Committee before his election to the Senate in 1948, also demanded revision of the statute of limitations in the case of persons charged with crimes against the national security. He charged that it was unreasonable to permit Hiss or anyone else to "buy immunity" from prosecution for espionage through the lapse of "three short years." Mundt added:

"We must bear in mind that many employes of the State Department were brought into positions of responsibility and importance through their connection with Hiss and his misguided friends."

AVOID YALTA "MISTAKE"

The Republican Party, he declared, should assume "greater responsibility in the formation of foreign policy so that such agreements as were made at Yalta will never again be repeated." Hiss was an adviser to President Roosevelt during the Yalta conference.

Mundt was interrupted by Senator McCarthy (R., Wis.), who read Acheson's news conference statement, and said he wondered if Acheson intended to "turn his back on other Communists who were associated with Hiss." The Cabinet officer, he said, "possibly spoke from the affinity of a long and established friendship with Alger Hiss" and relationships developed from a law partnership with Hiss' brother.

Senator Capehart (R., Ind.), who previously had demanded that President Truman fire Acheson because of his association with Hiss, interrupted McCarthy to say he was "prouder than ever" that he had voted against Acheson's confirmation as Secretary of State.

Senator Hickenlooper (R., Ia.) told the Senate there would be "a mass revolt by the American people" if they were told to what extent the Administration had gone in concealing facts about the Hiss case.

Nixon Condemns Truman Administration on House Floor

Hiss's conviction gave impetus to the movement that would become known as McCarthyism. Genuine concerns about security breaches combined with political opportunism to keep the issue of espionage alive into the mid-1950s. On January 26, the day after Hiss was sentenced, Richard Nixon rose on the floor of the House of Representatives shortly before adjournment and asked to be recognized. He proceeded to read into the record the facts of the Hiss investigation as he saw them, emphasizing the preponderance of evidence that accumulated against Hiss and highlighting his own role in exposing Hiss's crimes. Nixon stressed three important themes—that the leak of documents was a serious breach of American security, that the affair went much deeper than Alger Hiss, and, perhaps most significantly, that the Truman administration on a "politics-as-usual" basis had failed to root out this conspiracy. The Hiss affair clearly contributed momentum to the political and ideological debate about communism that would permeate much of 1950s America. Part of Nixon's report published in the *Congressional Record* follows.

NIXON'S REMARKS BEFORE CONGRESS, JANUARY 26, 1950

Whether Mr. Hiss was to be found guilty of the technical crime of perjury with which he was charged was not primarily important as far as the security of the Nation is concerned. What is important is that we not allow the conflict between these two men to obscure the broader implications of the case. This is not a simple case of petty larceny where a common thief sold stolen documents to the highest bidder. This is a case involving far-reaching implications going to the very security of our country, and it is essential that each and every American citizen recognize those implications for what they are.

In the first place, the conspiracy which existed was amazingly effective. Chambers turned over to the Committee and the Justice Department hundreds of pages of confidential and secret documents from the State Department and other Government agencies. The theft of documents in this quantity would in itself be sufficient to cause us grave concern. But Chambers testified that on at least 70 different occasions the members of his espionage ring had obtained a similar amount of documents for transmittal to Soviet agents.

Some State Department apologists have attempted to belittle the gravity of the crime on the ground that the documents were not important. An indication of their importance is that today, 10 years after they were taken from the State Department, three of them have still not been made public because the State Department claims that to make them public would be injurious to the national security of this country.

Even more pertinent on the matter of the importance of the documents is the testimony of Mr. Peurifoy, Assistant Secretary of State in charge of Security, and Mr. Sumner Welles. Both testified that a foreign agent having in his possession even one of the many documents which Chambers turned over to the Government could have broken our secret code. This meant, in other words, that the foreign agents who obtained these documents from Chambers broke the American code and were reading all of our confidential communications with foreign governments during that critical period immediately preceding the Hitler-Stalin pact.

The second point we should not forget is that a great number of people other than Mr. Hiss were named by Chambers as being members of his espionage ring. A run-down of the various positions held by the members of the ring indicates the effectiveness with which the

Source: Congress, House 81st Cong., 2nd sess., *Congressional Record*, vol. 96, pt. 1, 1002–1006.

conspiracy was able to infiltrate into vital positions, both in Government and in industry. Mr. Chambers' contacts included: Four in the State Department; two in the Treasury Department; two in the Bureau of Standards; one in the Aberdeen Arsenal; a man who later became general counsel of the CIO; one in the Picatinny Arsenal; two in the Electric Boat Co.; one in the Remington Rand Co.; and one in the Illinois Steel Co.

It is significant that the individuals named, almost without exception, held positions of influence where they had access to confidential and secret information. The tragedy of the case is that the great majority of them were American citizens, were graduates of the best colleges and universities in this country, and had yet willingly become members of an organization dedicated to the overthrow of this Government.

· · ·

The third point we should bear in mind is that the conspiracy was so effective, so well-entrenched and so well-defended by apologists in high places that it was not discovered and apprehended until it was too late to prosecute those who were involved in it for the crimes they had committed. There were several occasions during the past 10 years on which, if vigorous action had been taken, the conspiracy could have been exposed and its effectiveness destroyed.

The tragedy of this case is summed up right in the charge itself, because what was this man charged with? With stealing documents? With passing them to a foreign agent? No. He was charged with perjury, for lying when he said that he did not turn over these documents. The reason is that neither Mr. Hiss nor Mr. Wadleigh nor any of the people who were engaged in this activity and who turned over documents, even if they were to admit it today, can be prosecuted under the laws of the land, because the 3-year statute of limitations has lapsed and it is too late to do anything about the crime they have committed.

· · ·

To complete this story of inexcusable inaction upon the part of administration officials to attack and destroy this conspiracy, let me review briefly the conduct of the President and the Department of Justice during the investigation of this case by the Committee on Un-American Activities. On August 5, the day Mr. Hiss first appeared before the committee and denied the charges which had been made against him, the President threw the great power and prestige of his office against the investigation by the committee and for Mr. Hiss by declaring that the hearings of the committee were simply a "red herring."

In other words the "red herring" statement was made in direct reference to the Alger Hiss case.

That same day, he issued a Presidential directive which ordered all administrative agencies of the Government to refuse to turn over any information relating to the loyalty of any Government employee to a congressional committee. This meant that the committee had to conduct its investigation with no assistance whatever from the administrative branch of the Government. Included in this order was, of course, the FBI, who, by reason of that fact, was unable to lend assistance to the committee.

The most flagrant action, however, was yet to come. As I have already stated, the day Mr. Chambers turned over documentary evidence in the handwriting of Mr. Hiss, together with typewritten documents which were later established to be written on his typewriter, the Justice Department was immediately notified and the material was on that day, November 17, turned over to Alexander Campbell, head of the Criminal Division of that Department. The various participants in the deposition were directed in the interests of national security to keep silent on the whole matter.

• • •

Why was it that administration officials persisted in their refusal to act through the years, even when substantial evidence of espionage activities was brought to their attention? A number of reasons have been suggested for this failure.

It has been said that the Soviet Union was an ally of the United States and that therefore we should take a charitable attitude toward those administration officials who failed to act when the evidence was presented to them. But Mr. Chambers first presented his information to Mr. Berle during the period of the Hitler-Stalin pact when it could not be said, under any stretch of the imagination, that the Soviet Union was an ally of this country. Nor can anyone possibly justify the obstructive policies followed by administration leaders even as late as 1948 when the Committee on Un-American activities was attempting to bring all the facts out into the open and when our announced national policy was to contain communism abroad if not at home.

On the other extreme, there are some who claim that administration officials failed to act because they were Communist or pro-Communist. I do not accept this charge as a fair one as applied at least to the great majority of those officials who could and should have acted on the evidence which was laid before them through the years.

The reason for their failure to act was not that they were disloyal, but this in my opinion makes that failure even more inexcusable.

What was happening was that administration leaders were treating the reports of Communist espionage on a "politics-as-usual" basis. It is customary practice for any administration, be it Republican or Democrat, to resist the disclosure of facts which might be embarrassing to that administration in an election. This is a statement of fact though, of course, I do not mean to justify that practice, regardless of the nature of the skeleton in the political closet.

Because they treated Communist infiltration into our American institutions like any ordinary petty political scandal, the administration officials responsible for this failure to act against the Communist conspiracy rendered the greatest possible disservice to the people of the Nation.

Notes

1. "Hiss Trial Here Contrasts with Washington Hearings," *New York Times,* June 7, 1949.
2. Ibid., June 3 and 7, 1949.
3. *Washington Post,* June 11 and 14, 1949.
4. *New York Herald Tribune,* June 28, 1949.
5. *New York Times,* June 29 and 30, 1949.
6. Allen Weinstein, *Perjury: The Hiss-Chambers Case* (New York: Random House, 1997), 417–18.
7. Ibid., *Perjury,* 373 and 387.
8. "Chambers Is 'Willing' to Help If U.S. Acts Against Others," *Washington Post,* January 22, 1950.
9. Quoted in "Hiss Sentenced to 5 Years for Perjury, Released on Bail," *Washington Post,* January 26, 1950.

5
The Debate Continues

The guilty verdict did not end the debate over Hiss's guilt or innocence. After his release from Lewisburg Prison in Pennsylvania on November 27, 1954, Hiss devoted the rest of his life to proving his innocence and clearing his name.[1] The Hiss case soon died as a political issue. But the ideological divide continued. Hiss's supporters and critics often divided along ideological lines. Conservatives determinedly maintained his guilt, citing the preponderance of circumstantial evidence presented at the trials. Liberal defenders, in contrast, questioned the evidence and challenged Chambers's veracity. They viewed Hiss as a victim of McCarthyism. They interpreted the whole affair as an attack on New Deal liberal principles, not just a personal tragedy for Alger Hiss. Nevertheless, for a long time, neither side could produce new evidence beyond all that had been brought out in the trials. And the debate was essentially confined to academic circles.

Nixon, Watergate, and New Evidence

This changed in the early 1970s when Richard Nixon's struggle with the Watergate scandal revived interest in the Hiss case. Nixon, who rose to national prominence on the heels of the Hiss case, now president of the United States, found himself embroiled in a scandal that ultimately led to his resignation from the presidency in 1974. The lies, deception, and misuse of government agencies to further Nixon's political ends during this episode once again raised questions of Nixon's credibility, providing reinforcement for those who still defended Hiss. To Hiss's supporters, the same deception and

FIGURE 5.1   The Hiss affair was an issue that would not die. Hiss's conviction validated Republican charges of Communist subversion and proved a liability for the Democratic Party during the elections of 1952. It continued to haunt Truman as he left office.

Reprinted with permission of THE *DALLAS MORNING NEWS*

illegality that characterized Nixon's conduct during Watergate was instrumental in the conviction of Alger Hiss more than two decades earlier.

In the aftermath of Watergate, Allen Weinstein, then a professor at Smith College, sparked anew the public debate when he published *Perjury: The Hiss-Chambers Case* in 1978.[2] Weinstein relied on extensive use of the Freedom of Information Act to obtain Federal Bureau of Investigation and Justice Department files on the case and conducted private interviews with a broad array of figures involved in the Hiss investigation and trials. He asserted that, when he began his project, he was convinced that Hiss had not engaged in espionage. He had lied about his relationship with Chambers, but Chambers for his part had lied about Hiss's ties to the Communists and espionage. In a 1972 article in *The American Scholar* summarizing his preliminary research, Weinstein admitted that, "although Hiss's *guilt* seems to me still unproved beyond a reasonable doubt, it would be equally difficult, in light of available evidence, to *prove* him innocent."[3] But when Weinstein concluded his project, new evidence led him to believe Hiss to be guilty.

Soon after the publication of *Perjury,* Hiss's long-time supporters attacked Weinstein's book. Most notably, Victor Navasky, editor of *The Nation,* wrote a scathing critique of Weinstein's work. He denigrated Weinstein's research. Much of the article was a detailed description of what Navasky characterized as false facts and the misuse of the more than eighty interviews. Many of the interviewers denied their comments when approached by Navasky. He accused Weinstein of being "an embattled partisan, hopelessly mired in the perspective of one side." An excerpt from Navasky's attack follows.

VICTOR NAVASKY, "ALLEN WEINSTEIN'S 'PERJURY': THE CASE NOT PROVED AGAINST ALGER HISS"

In interviews, advance publicity and his publisher's advertising and jacket copy for *Perjury: The Hiss-Chambers Case*, Allen Weinstein, the Smith College historian temporarily at the Hoover Institution in Stanford, Calif., has presented himself to the world as a young man who "set out to write the definitive, objective work in the belief that Hiss was innocent" and that Whittaker Chambers has "falsely accused him of Communist ties and espionage," but who concluded after five years of intensive research that Hiss had indeed been guilty.

As *Time*, to which an advance copy of the book "was made available" two months before publication, put it in a 3-page feature, "Weinstein turned up previously undisclosed evidence that inexorably led him to his unqualified verdict: 'The jurors made no mistake in finding Alger Hiss guilty as charged.' " It is, at first, difficult not to be swept along by the avalanche of people and documents which, according to the author, "confirm" or "corroborate" one or another aspect of Chambers' story.

The image Weinstein projects is of the truth-seeking scholar who traveled 125,000 miles, interviewed "over eighty people who had special knowledge of the case or its protagonists," carefully studied the transcripts of a score of Congressional hearings, two trials and various appeals, analyzed 80,000 documents made available under the Freedom of Information Act, and diligently plowed through archive after archive in this country and abroad, files at departments throughout the federal government, and the voluminous Hiss defense files, before

Source: Victor Navasky, "Allen Weinstein's 'Perjury': The Case Not Proved Against Alger Hiss." *The Nation* 226 (April 8, 1978): 393–94 and 401. Reprinted with permission from *The Nation*. For subscription information, call 1-800-333-8536. Portions of each week's *Nation* can be accessed at http://www.thenation.com.

painfully deciding that Alger Hiss indeed passed stolen State Department papers to Chambers as part of an underground Soviet espionage apparatus in the late 1930s.

• • •

The book is important because the case is important. Not merely Hiss, wrote Alistair Cooke in 1950, but a generation was on trial. Chambers himself called the case an epitomizing one. "It epitomized a basic conflict. And Alger Hiss and I were archetypes. That is of course what gave the peculiar intensity to the struggle." Arthur Schlesinger, Jr. (who believes Hiss guilty) complained of Chambers's writings—after Hiss was convicted of perjury at a second trial (the first ended in a hung jury)—that they divided the world into "messianic Christian anti-Communists" and "aesthetic Communists"; but for many others, if Hiss was guilty then the New Deal was corrupt, the State Department had been subverted, Yalta was a sellout, the U.N. was a Communist plot, the possibilities of peaceful coexistence with the Soviet Union were shattered, incipient cold-war repression became defensible. While Weinstein gives the Hiss case too much credit for inciting the cold-war hysteria (the Un-American Activities Committee hearings on Hollywood, preparation for the trial of Communist Party leaders under the Smith Act, the Truman Executive Order on loyalty, the Mundt-Nixon bill all predated Hiss), it undoubtedly facilitated and accelerated the meteoric rise of McCarthy and McCarthyism.

John Strachey, writing in 1962, put the case in its most cosmic context when he identified Chambers as part of the literature of reaction, "not only against Communism but against five hundred years of rationalism and empiricism; against in short, the enlightenment."

Weinstein takes it upon himself to update what he calls the "iconography" of the cold war with the iconography of Watergate. He quotes philosopher Richard Popkin, who argued that "Unravelling the Ellsberg burglary will unravel what was involved in Richard M. Nixon's whole career: fraud, fakery, framing of innocent victims . . . When we know more about how the Ellsberg case was plotted, we will know how the Hiss case itself was constructed . . . the Hiss case may turn out to be the American Dreyfus case."

Weinstein seems put out that many liberals and moderates began to view Hiss as a spiritual ancestor of the Ellsbergs, Berrigans, Spocks and Coffins—conspicuous for having fought government injustice and illegality during politically motivated trials. "As anti-war sentiment converged with popular outrage over Watergate," he writes, "Hiss found himself transformed from a symbol of deception into one of injured innocence. Watergate and more responsive media brought Hiss, in short, a renewed measure of public acceptance . . . Watergate helped create a new generation of believers in Hiss's innocence. The cultural verdict of the previous quarter century—indeed, the jury's verdict itself—was abruptly brought into question by Americans unfamiliar with the complex facts and history of the case."

Weinstein has aligned himself with those cold-war intellectuals who presumably sleep better at night secure in the knowledge that there *was* an internal Communist espionage menace (Hiss, the Rosenbergs, Remington, Sobell, Coplon, et al.) which might have justified the cold-war repression with which they collaborated and/or helped rationalize.

Here it should be noted that Weinstein himself seems not above enjoying a little iconographic con, so to speak, of his own. A review of his previous writings reveals no commitment to the innocence of Alger Hiss. If he did believe Hiss to be innocent, he never said so in print— certainly not in his major writings on the case in *The American Scholar* (1971), *Esquire* (1975), *The New York Times* (1976) and *The New York Review of Books* (1976). And even though he recently told the editor of *The Daily Hampshire Gazette* (Northampton, Mass.) in a front-page interview that in 1974 he wrote with R. Jackson Wilson a high school textbook *Freedom and Crisis: An American History,* "which concluded that Hiss was innocent," a close reading of the chapter on the case fails to reveal any such conclusion (although in fairness it should be pointed out that, as in his *American Scholar* article, he raises real questions about Chambers's reliability).

My own suspicion that Weinstein was not quite as scholarly as he appears to be commenced, I should confess, a few years ago when I was shown a copy of his letter to the Justice Department requesting access to materials on the Rosenberg case. He assured the U.S. Attorney General that, unlike some other writers whom he proceeded to name with quite reckless abandon, he believed the Rosenbergs guilty. I say "reckless," because I was one of the writers he named (although his reference to me was syntactically ambiguous) despite the fact that at the time I had written nothing about my views on the Rosenbergs' innocence or guilt. Anyway, my suspicion was sufficient to cause me, after rereading Weinstein's earlier articles on the Hiss case, to conduct an elementary source check with some of the people he interviewed for *Perjury* (to see if they were accurately quoted), and to examine some of the documents he cites (to see if they are cited in context). The preliminary results suggest that the hurry to any sort of judgment on the case, based on *Perjury* alone, may be somewhat premature.

In his *American Scholar* article ("The Hiss Case Revisited") Wein-stein concluded a rigorous, tough-minded and generally fair discussion of the pros and cons of the case by restating the uncertainties which he seemed to feel made contemporary assessments of innocence or guilt incautious. He wrote:

> Perhaps only a master novelist can bridge our present impasse, but the historian still must attempt to establish the facts where possible and where not, to expose the inconsistencies of partisan accounts. The time has come for a thoroughly researched reassessment of the Hiss case, but without the release of the grand jury records, the executive files of HUAC and the relevant records, the "complete" story of that controversial affair may never be known. Granting the episode's pivotal importance in the political life of recent America, however, historians must begin to confront the case itself to prevent either of its partisan versions from hardening into myth.

After reading and rereading *Perjury*, I couldn't agree more. What-ever his original motives and aspirations, Professor Weinstein is now an embattled partisan, hopelessly mired in the perspective of one side, his narrative obfuscatory, his interpretations improbable, his omissions strategic, his vocabulary manipulative, his standards double, his "corroborations" circular and suspect, his reporting astonishingly erratic (brilliantly enterprising where it serves, nonexistent where it complicates, and frequently unreliable). His conversion from scholar to partisan, along with a rhetoric and methodology that confuse his beliefs with his data, make it impossible for the nonspecialist to ren-der an honest verdict on the case. This condition, however, should not inhibit us from rendering a necessarily negative verdict on the schol-arship itself.

• • •

Perjury settles nothing about the Hiss case. It sets forth some new riddles, fails to solve them and ignores some old ones. Oddly, it doesn't really seem to take full advantage of the new Freedom of Information Act materials, thousands of which were still coming in as *Perjury* was coming out. It doesn't provide a serious motive or theory to account for Hiss's behavior since he was released from prison. Whatever new data Weinstein may have gathered are fatally tainted by his unprofessionalism, his apparent intolerance for ambiguity, espe-cially when it gets in the way of his thesis. It would be a tragedy if the immediate impact of this unfair book were to deprive Alger Hiss, now 73, of a fair hearing on his upcoming *coram nobis* petition to set aside the verdict of the trial (his first court challenge to his perjury convic-tion since 1952). One suspects, though, that the only permanent damage Weinstein has wrought may be to the reputations of himself and those who too eagerly endorse his findings. The target of *Perjury* is Alger Hiss and his claim of innocence, but its temporary victim is historical truth.

Pressed to defend his research, Weinstein responded in *The New Republic*. He argued that Navasky failed to deal with the book's "central arguments, evidence and conclusions." He also offered an alternative explanation for why some of those individuals he had interviewed now denied what Weinstein quoted them as saying. He accused Navasky of desperately trying to undermine his study. Here are portions of Weinstein's response.

ALLEN WEINSTEIN, " 'PERJURY,' TAKE THREE"

Victor Navasky, editor of *The Nation*, devotes a large part of that magazine's April 8 issue to an attack on *Perjury*, my book on the Hiss-Chambers case. Navasky alleges that I misquoted six people whom I interviewed, misstated basic facts, and distorted evidence—grave accusations against a scholar. Had he contacted me I would have invited Navasky to examine the material in my archive which proves that I have cited all six accurately. Three of the six interviewees who recanted their stories—Maxim Lieber, Karel Kaplan, and Sam Krieger—are on tape. One (Kaplan) published a magazine article reiterating the facts told earlier to me. In all six cases—these three plus Paul Willert, Ella Winter, and Alden Whitman—I have not only the notes of my interviews but also letters from them, defense file memos, FBI records, and other interviews that corroborate their statements.

Why would these people now say I misquoted them? Well, three of the six—Lieber, Krieger, and Whitman—have written me expressing disagreement with my conclusions about the Hiss-Chambers case. Lieber told *The Washington Post* on April 6: "I may have said things [to Weinstein] I wouldn't have said under different circumstances." Five of the six—Lieber, Krieger, Kaplan, Winter and Willert—deny having said things I never quote them as saying. Navasky apparently did not compare their letters of denial to their statements in my book.

Source: Allen Weinstein, " 'Perjury,' Take Three." *New Republic* 178 (April 29, 1978): 17–18 and 21. Reprinted by permission of *The New Republic*, © 1978, The New Republic, LLC.

Navasky dismisses the critics who have commented favorably on my book as "generalists" insufficiently versed in the case's complex facts and incapable of rendering an independent judgment on the evidence. Navasky suggests the following people as qualified to comment about the case, men whose "independent studies" best explain the evidence: John Lowenthal, a Rutgers law professor who (as identified in his *Nation* credit line) "has sometimes served as counsel for Hiss"; William A. Reuben, author of an early book arguing a frameup against Hiss and currently the latter's co-plaintiff in a lawsuit for FBI files; Fred Cook, whose book and articles have argued since 1957 that Hiss was framed; and Peter H. Irons, plaintiff in a lawsuit filed in association with Hiss's and who also has argued that Hiss was framed. I discuss the conspiracy theories favored by all four men in a lengthy appendix to *Perjury*.

The true measure of Navasky's desperation emerges from his entire eight-page collection of trivial allegations of error. They all concern matters that are completely peripheral, and they mostly attempt to impugn my evidence for statements that are—in any event—virtually beyond dispute (such as the fact that *Chambers*, let alone Hiss, was a member of the Communist underground). Even if I actually had committed every error and misrepresentation Navasky accuses me of, even if we chose to believe every detail of all six recantations, *Perjury*'s central arguments, evidence and conclusions would survive unscathed. Navasky has not dealt with them.

• • •

Two years ago, I wrote that "newer and perhaps more ingenious defenses of Hiss will soon follow." Thus far, I have been wrong. Navasky's complaint, which he calls an "investigation," is as old as the initial Hiss defense campaign in style, tone, content, and (in some cases) personnel. It is merely the latest variant of what the late Professor Herbert Packer called Hiss's "alternative pleading": "the kind of argument that lawyers make when they do not have a case: The defendant was not there; but if he was there, he did not do it; but if he did it, he was insane; but if he was not insane, he had provocation."

The remarkably disorganized character of Victor Navasky's "investigative" article is a reflection of his and his advisors' desperate culling of *Perjury* to rip out of context or to distort *anything*, no matter how trivial, in an attempt to undermine the whole study. But this accusatory smokescreen cannot conceal from the careful reader the total absence of real evidentiary "fire." Navasky's assertion that only his "independent" investigators, as distinguished from readers and other reviewers whom he disparages as "generalists," can be trusted to draw the proper conclusions about *Perjury* is a facile ploy: "Hiss's defenders are termed "independent" while disagreement with Hiss becomes *prima facie* evidence of ignorance. I can only suggest, modestly, that interested people read the book carefully and make up their own minds.

The End of the Cold War and More New Evidence

As interest in the Hiss affair revived, the end of the Cold War and the collapse of the Soviet system offered opportunities to delve more deeply into the accusations leveled against Hiss. New information sporadically trickled out of archival sources in the former Soviet bloc, and historians succeeded in securing the declassification of previously closed U.S. government documents. This material, while admittedly incomplete and fragmentary, offered new insights into the Hiss-Chambers affair.

At one point, it seemed that Soviet sources might vindicate Hiss. In 1992, Hiss and John Lowenthal, a long-time supporter who in 1980 had directed the documentary film "The Trials of Alger Hiss," asked General Dimitri A. Volkogonov, chairman of the Russian military intelligence archives, to conduct a search in the KGB files for Hiss material. In October 1992, Volkogonov announced that, after an examination of Soviet era archives, he had concluded that espionage charges against Hiss were "completely groundless." This was exactly what Hiss and his supporters wanted to hear. The following *New York Times* article describes how Hiss believed Volkogonov's findings had at long last exonerated him.

"AFTER 40 YEARS, A POSTSCRIPT ON HISS: RUSSIAN OFFICIAL CALLS HIM INNOCENT"

In the latest chapter of a case that catapulted Richard M. Nixon to national prominence and has divided Americans for more than 40 years, a high ranking Russian official says a review of newly opened archives clears Alger Hiss of accusations that he ever spied for the Soviet Union.

"Not a single document, and a great amount of materials has been studied, substantiates the allegation that Mr. A. Hiss collaborated with the intelligence services of the Soviet Union," the official, Gen. Dimitri A. Volkogonov, chairman of the Russian Government's military intelligence archives, declared. He called the espionage accusations against Mr. Hiss "completely groundless."

Scholars of Soviet affairs said they were struck by the categorical, almost passionate, nature of the Russian official's statement. They said that as a respected historian and close adviser to President Boris Yeltsin, General Volkogonov should be taken seriously on the matter. But they cautioned that given the labyrinthine nature of the Soviet bureaucracy and the sensitivity of military and foreign intelligence operations, General Volkogonov may have unknowingly overstated his findings.

"I don't doubt that he's given an honest report on what he saw, but there are a lot of things he might not have seen," said Richard Pipes, a Soviet scholar at Harvard University. "There are archives within archives within archives. To say there is no evidence in any of the archives is not very responsible on his part."

HISS ASKED FOR FILE REVIEW

General Volkogonov, the author of a biography of Stalin, delivered the statement this month in Moscow to John Lowenthal, a historian and filmmaker who has long studied the Hiss case. Mr. Hiss was a high-ranking State Department official who was convicted of perjury in 1950 for denying that he had been a Soviet spy. In May, he asked General Volkogonov to inspect all Soviet files pertaining to him, his case, and his accuser, Whittaker Chambers.

It was Mr. Chambers, a member of the Communist Party in the 1930's and later an editor at Time magazine, who charged both that Mr. Hiss belonged to the American Communist Party in the 1930's and that he had provided Mr. Chambers with classified State Department documents for transmission to the Soviet Union. Mr. Chambers called Mr. Hiss "the closest friend I ever had in the Communist Party."

Mr. Hiss has always denied the charges, and he exulted over the statement from Moscow.

"It's what I've been fighting for for 44 years," Mr. Hiss, now 87 years old, said in an interview this week. "It won't settle things for people I've regarded as prejudiced from the beginning, but I think this is a final verdict on the thing. I can't imagine a more authoritative source than the files of the old Soviet Union.

"Rationally, I realized time was running out, and that the correction of Chambers's charges might not come about in my lifetime. But inside I was sure somehow I would be vindicated."

Source: New York Times, October 29, 1992. Copyright © 1992 by New York Times Co. Reprinted by permission.

CALLED A COLD WAR VICTIM

General Volkogonov issued his opinion on Oct. 14. In a separate statement videotaped the next day, he elaborated on his findings. He said that as a State Department official in the 1940's, Mr. Hiss had "normal official working contacts" with Soviet officials and was "never a spy for the Soviet Union." Instead, he called him a victim of the cold war.

"The fact that he was convicted in the 50's was a result of either false information or judicial error," he continued. "You can tell Alger Hiss that the heavy weight should be lifted from his heart."

As for Mr. Chambers, the Russian official said that files confirmed his membership in the American Communist Party but not that he had any contact with Soviet intelligence.

Scholars of Soviet history, including Prof. Alexander Dallin of Stanford and Prof. Robert C. Tucker of Princeton, said it was beyond the powers of even the most highly placed Russian official to reach into every nook and cranny of Soviet intelligence. But Mr. Lowenthal insisted that Mr. Volkogonov's search was comprehensive—so much so that he was apparently willing to stake his reputation as a general, historian and politician on it.

"This man is a professional historian who has spent decades in the archives," Mr. Lowenthal said. "He would not lightly render an official opinion without being sure of his research. He was not born yesterday."

Allen Weinstein, who in his book "Perjury: The Hiss-Chambers Case," (Knopf, 1978), essentially sided with Mr. Chambers, said Mr. Volkonogov's statement "reopened the case."

"It means that every serious scholar has to take a fresh look," said Mr. Weinstein, president of the Center for Democracy in Washington. "But we can't take Volkogonov's word alone. We have to see all the documents on Soviet espionage."

• • •

In August, Mr. Hiss wrote to a number of Russian officials, including General Volkogonov, seeking his records. He told them that Mr. Lowenthal would seek appointments with them when he visited Moscow. Mr. Lowenthal met for 30 minutes with General Volkogonov in early September.

"RESPONDED AS HISTORIAN"

The Russian official pledged to search for the Hiss files and personally inspect them. He said he had also asked Yevgeny M. Primakov, director of the foreign intelligence service, to instruct his staff to find all materials on the Hiss case. "It was obvious that he knew the case's importance," Mr. Lowenthal said. "He responded as a historian and a compassionate human being to Mr. Hiss's plight as a possibly wronged victim of the times."

In mid-October Mr. Lowenthal returned to Moscow, where the Russian official handed him a one-page opinion, typed on Russian Federation letterhead.

Time has diminished the ranks, but not the ferocity, of partisans in the Hiss-Chambers case. Both men, like Clarence Thomas and Anita Hill four decades later, have those who lionize them or demonize them. Indeed, if the past is any guide, few minds are likely to be changed by the evidence.

William F. Buckley Jr., the conservative commentator, was unimpressed by the Russian announcement. "One declaration by a General cannot undo the typewriter and all the evidence that overwhelmed the Hiss defense and persuaded court after court after court after court that Hiss was guilty," he said in an interview.

Mr. Hiss said he expected such reactions, and that his detractors would accept documents from Soviet archives only if they were incriminating. "They're so committed to their point of view that it's psychologically impossible for them to be open-minded," he said.

Mr. Weinstein said the polarization is unlikely ever to end. "Given the role of Nixon and the passions the case aroused, the hardest thing that anyone can do is remain open to new evidence," he said. "There ought to be a statute of limitations on historical anger in this case, whether at Nixon or at Hiss."

Fate and time have changed the Alger Hiss of the grainy newsreels, who fenced cockily with Mr. Nixon, Representative Karl Mundt of South Dakota and other members of the House committee. His voice has grown shaky, his eyesight is so poor that he can read his wrist watch only with a magnifying glass, and he can identify birds only by their sound, though he is hard of hearing as well.

"What are known as 'the infirmities of old age' are not as unpleasant as the indignities of old age," he said.

A psychiatrist who wrote about Mr. Hiss described him as "neurotically objective." And, indeed Mr. Hiss appears to have wasted little time feeling either martyred or embittered or self-righteous. "I'm proud of my durability: let's leave it at that," he said.

He does not dwell on what life might have been for someone of his pedigree and polish. He said he held neither Mr. Chambers nor Mr. Nixon fully accountable for their deeds—the one because he was a "psychopath," the other because he was merely an "opportunistic politician." Mr. Nixon was said to be traveling and unavailable for comment.

Nor does Mr. Hiss consider it significant that what he sees as vindication comes from the Russians rather than the courts. "I learned through experience that courts can make mistakes," he said. "I still think we have the best judicial system in the world."

But less than two months later, Volkogonov retracted his declaration. He confirmed what Hiss's critics had argued when hearing the original announcement, that he could not make a blanket declaration that Hiss was innocent. He had only done a cursory check of the KGB archives. Numerous other archives both in the Soviet Union and Eastern Europe might very well hold incriminating material.

"RUSSIAN GENERAL RETREATS ON HISS"

MOSCOW, Dec. 16.—The Russian official who was reported to have cleared Alger Hiss of spying for the Soviet Union says that he was "not properly understood," and that he only meant to say he found no evidence of the charges in the K.G.B. documents to which he had access.

The official, Gen. Dimitry A. Volkogonov, a military historian who has been closely involved in studying various Soviet-era archives, said that at Mr. Hiss's request he had searched through K.G.B. files for the 1930's and 1940's and in them he found only one mention of Mr. Hiss, in a list of diplomats at the United Nations.

"I was not properly understood," he said in a recent interview. "The Ministry of Defense also has an intelligence service, which is totally different, and many documents have been destroyed. I only looked through what the K.G.B. had. All I said was that I saw no evidence."

On Oct. 14, answering a query from Mr. Hiss, General Volkogonov wrote: "Mr. A. Hiss had never and nowhere been recruited as an agent of the intelligence services of the U.S.S.R. Not a single document, and a great amount of materials have been studied, substantiates the allegation."

HISTORIANS' CAUTIONS CONFIRMED

That letter was taken by Mr. Hiss and his supporters as an exoneration.

In a celebrated case, a former Communist named Whittaker Chambers asserted that Mr. Hiss had spied for the Soviet Union as a

State Department official in the 1930's. Mr. Hiss was eventually convicted of perjury.

Now 88, Mr. Hiss has insisted ever since his conviction in 1950 that he had never spied for the Soviet Union and that he was the victim of an anti-Communist witchhunt.

General Volkogonov's acknowledgement that he was in no position to fully clear Mr. Hiss, and that perhaps no one ever can, confirmed the cautions of many American historians who had warned that a categorical vindication was dubious given the volume, complexity and incompleteness of available Soviet archives.

As the general said, even if he had scoured all the voluminous archives of the K.G.B., the Defense Ministry and the Communist Party, there were also untold files that were destroyed in the unheavals after Stalin's death.

"TAKEN ABACK"

General Volkogonov said he was "a bit taken aback" by the commotion his letter caused. He acknowledged that his motive in writing the letter was "primarily humanitarian," to relieve the anguish of a man approaching death.

"Hiss wrote that he was 88 and would like to die peacefully, that he wanted to prove that he was never a paid, contracted spy," General Volkogonov said. "What I saw gives no basis to claim a full clarification. There's no guarantee that it was not destroyed, that it was not in other channels.

"This was only my personal opinion as a historian," he said. "I never met him, and honestly I was a bit taken aback. His attorney, Lowenthal, pushed me hard to say things of which I was not fully convinced."

General Volkogonov evidently meant John Lowenthal, a historian and filmmaker who has long studied the Hiss case. It was Mr. Lowenthal who traveled to Moscow to meet with General Volkogonov and receive the letter.

"But I did spend two days swallowing dust," General Volkogonov said, referring to the old K.G.B. archives.

The Venona Files

Hiss's adversaries, who had been skeptical of Volkogonov's findings, soon uncovered new evidence of their own pointing to Hiss's guilt. During the 1940s, the U.S. Army Signal Intelligence Service, the precursor to the

National Security Agency, began to intercept encrypted diplomatic communications between Moscow and various Soviet missions in the United States. Beginning in 1943, the Service launched a program to decode these messages. Before this project ended in 1980, cryptographers succeeded in decoding several thousand of these communications in whole or in part. The cables painted a picture of Soviet espionage activity in the United States during and immediately after World War II. In 1995, the National Security Agency declassified these decrypted messages.[4]

For those interested in the Hiss case, two of the communications were particularly noteworthy. The first, a partially decoded message from New York to Moscow, dated September 28, 1943, referred to Hiss by name. (photo 5.1) The second, a March 30, 1945, message from Washington to Moscow described how an agent with cover name "Ales" had traveled to Moscow after the 1945 Yalta Conference and was awarded Soviet decorations in gratitude for his work. (photo 5.2) The decoded message identified Ales as "probably Alger HISS."

To Hiss's critics, these communications were irrefutable proof of his guilt. Yet his defenders were still unconvinced and challenged this new evidence. John Lowenthal took issue with the work of the Venona decoders. He criticized their method of determining cover names. Besides, he maintained, referring to Hiss by name in such correspondence went against a fundamental practice in the espionage community. Lowenthal summarized his conclusions in this way:

If the Soviet messages as presented by Venona are to be believed, their only reference to Hiss is by his real name, which virtually rules him out as a spy. The Venona team nevertheless employed false premises and flawed comparative logic to reach the desired conclusion that Alger Hiss was the spy Ales, a conclusion psychologically motivated and politically correct but factually wrong.[5]

The Debate Persists

Today, half a century after Alger Hiss went to prison for perjury, the question of his innocence or guilt remains a contentious issue. To many liberal intellectuals, Hiss has become an icon. To repudiate him would be to reject their principles and beliefs. Even presented with growing evidence validating Whittaker Chambers's charges, these "best people" persisted in their advocacy of Hiss's innocence. When a revised version of Weinstein's book appeared in 1997, incorporating the new evidence including the Venona messages,

Photo 5.1 Venona Document—September 28, 1943.

GRU

From: NEW YORK

To: MOSCOW

No: 1579

28 September 1943

To DIREKTOR.

1. Reference your No. 12527[a].

    (a) MATVEJ[i] is requesting a loan to pay off debts which he has incurred as a result of the assistance which he has been giving to his sick father for a long time.

        [33 groups unrecoverable]

    to TOM[ii], who was also [1 group unrecovered] in good time.

    (c) The names MATVEJ, FRANK, GUSTAV, SANDI and RICHARD are respectively[b] Milton SHWARTZ, Arthur MOOSEN, George GORCHOFF, Stephan RICH, Robinson[c] BOBROW.

2. The NEIGHBOR[SOSED][iii] has reported that [1 group unrecovered] from the State Department by the name of HISS[iv] (

        [121 groups unrecoverable]

No. 243   MOL'ER[v]

Notes: [a] Not available.
       [b] From here to the end of the sentence the names were spelled out in the Latin alphabet.
       [c] Sent as "Ribinson".

Comments:
       [i] MATVEJ: Identified as Milton SHWARTZ in paragraph 1(c).
      [ii] TOM: Probably Colonel Aleksej Ivanovich SORVIN of the Tank Department of the Soviet Government Purchasing Commission.
     [iii] NEIGHBOR: Member of another Soviet intelligence organization.
     [iv] HISS: Spelled out in the Latin alphabet. At this time Alger HISS was Assistant Political Adviser for the Far East, Department of State.
      [v] MOL'ER: i.e. "MOLIERE"; Pavel P. MIKhAJLOV, Soviet Vice-Consul in NEW YORK.

PHOTO 5.2   Venona Document—March 30, 1945.

MGB

From: WASHINGTON

To: MOSCOW

No: 1822

30 March 1945

Further to our telegram No. 283[a]. As a result of "[D% A.'s]"[i] chat with "ALES"[ii] the following has been ascertained:

1.   ALES has been working with the NEIGHBORS[SOSEDI][iii] continuously since 1935.

2.   For some years past he has been the leader of a small group of the NEIGHBORS' probationers[STAZhERY], for the most part consisting of his relations.

3.   The group and ALES himself work on obtaining military information only. Materials on the "BANK"[iv] allegedly interest the NEIGHBORS very little and he does not produce them regularly.

4.   All the last few years ALES has been working with "POL'"[v] who also meets other members of the group occasionally.

5.   Recently ALES and his whole group were awarded Soviet decorations.

6.   After the YaLTA Conference, when he had gone on to MOSCOW, a Soviet personage in a very responsible position (ALES gave to understand that it was Comrade VYShINSKIJ) allegedly got in touch with ALES and at the behest of the Military NEIGHBORS passed on to him their gratitude and so on.

No. 431   VADIM[vi]

Notes: [a] Not available.
Comments:
   [i] A.: "A." seems the most likely garble here although "A." has not been confirmed elsewhere in the WASHINGTON traffic.
   [ii] ALES: Probably Alger HISS.
   [iii] SOSEDI: Members of another Soviet Intelligence organization, here probably the GRU.
   [iv] BANK: The U.S. State Department.
   [v] POL': i.e. "PAUL," unidentified cover-name.
   [vi] VADIM: Anatolij Borisovich GROMOV, MGB resident in WASHINGTON.

www.nsa.gov/docs/venona

8 August 1969

Navasky again attacked Weinstein and defended Hiss in the pages of *The Nation*. Mounting evidence failed to diminish his belief in Hiss's innocence.[6]

In a 1997 article in *The New Criterion,* Hilton Kramer, a noted liberal social commentator and author, expressed concern for this phenomenon. He took fellow liberals such as Navasky to task for their failure to admit the reality of the situation. He cited a charge Chambers had made in his memoir *Witness* that liberal intellectual defenders of Hiss had "snapped their minds shut in a pro-Hiss psychosis." To Kramer, this bias still persisted in 1997.

HILTON KRAMER, "WHITTAKER CHAMBERS: THE JUDGMENT OF HISTORY"

Nearly half a century has passed since the fateful day in January 1950 when a jury in a Federal court in New York City found Alger Hiss guilty on two counts of perjury. That verdict effectively confirmed the charge brought by Whittaker Chambers that Hiss, his former comrade in a Soviet espionage apparatus in the 1930s, had betrayed his country as a Communist spy while serving as a high official in the U.S. State Department. Hiss, who had been with President Roosevelt at Yalta, had participated in the founding of the United Nations in 1945. He was president of the Carnegie Endowment for International Peace when Chambers first publicly identified himself as a Communist before the House Un-American Activities Committee in August 1948. He went to jail as a convicted felon. Yet for the remaining forty-six years of his life—Hiss died in November 1996 at the age of ninety-two—this once highly respected member of the liberal establishment continued to insist upon his innocence. What is more remarkable, a great many intelligent people—those whom Chambers characterized in *Witness* as the "best people"—continued to believe him, or profess to believe him, even in the face of the mounting post-trial evidence that confirmed his guilt. This is how Chambers described the situation at the end of *Witness:*

> No feature of the Hiss Case is more obvious, or more troubling as history, than the jagged fissure, which it did not so much open as reveal, between the plain men and women of the nation, and those

Source: Hilton Kramer, *The Twilight of the Intellectuals: Culture and Politics in the Era of the Cold War* (Chicago: Ivan R. Dee, 1999), 23–26. Copyright © 1999 by Hilton Kramer, by permission of Ivan R. Dee, Publisher.

who affected to act, think and speak for them. It was, not invariably, but in general, the "best people" who were for Alger Hiss and who were prepared to go to any length to protect and defend him. It was the enlightened and the powerful, the clamorous proponents of the open mind and the common man, who snapped their minds shut in a pro-Hiss psychosis. . . . It was the great body of the nation, which, not invariably, but in general, kept open its mind in the Hiss Case, waiting for the returns to come in. It was they who suspected what forces disastrous to the nation were at work in the Hiss Case, and had suspected that they were at work long before there was a Hiss Case, while most of the forces of enlightenment were poohpoohing the Communist danger and calling every allusion to it a witch hunt.

It was, moreover, an inevitable corollary of this ardently held belief in Hiss's innocence that his accuser had to be stigmatized as a disreputable liar and fraud, if not indeed a malevolent madman. In that pernicious endeavor, which has persisted in some of the "best" circles down to the present day—hence the continued neglect of *Witness*, an autobiography of great literary and historical distinction—Hiss's liberal champions enjoyed an immense advantage. For upon the archetypal figure of the informer there has always been associated something odious and unclean. Americans, in their innocence, tend to be particularly unforgiving in this respect—more unforgiving, in this case, than about evidence of espionage. This, too, was a calamity that Chambers had clearly grasped when he put his life and his career at risk by informing on Alger Hiss.

That in his own self-interest Chambers need not have incurred that terrible risk is not something much appreciated even among people familiar with this celebrated case. It was, after all, within Chambers's power to have sidestepped the entire catastrophe. He could have refused to testify against a former comrade, and in the "best" circles he would have been lavished with praise for defying an unloved Congressional committee. It is worth recalling that in 1948, as a writer for *Time* and *Life*, Chambers was enjoying an immense success in the only decent—and decently paid—job he ever had in his life. He was a happily married man with two young children and a farm in Maryland. He certainly knew what it was likely to cost him if, in naming Hiss as a Communist, he turned informer—and not only in public opprobrium.

"Some ex-Communists are so stricken by the evil they have freed themselves from," he afterwards wrote in *Witness*, "that they inform exultantly against it. No consideration, however humane, no tie however tender, checks them." His own view of the informer's fate was quite different. "By temperament," he wrote, "I cannot share such exultation and stridency, though I understand both. I cannot ever inform against anyone without feeling something die in me. I inform without pleasure because it is necessary."

Everything we know about the Hiss Case—including Chambers's sometimes misguided attempts to shield Hiss himself from the worst charge of all: espionage—attests to the truth of this assertion. Yet the "best people" were so eager to shield themselves from the awful implications of the Hiss Case that they refused to see in Chambers anything but a caricature of irrational anti-Communist wrath. With that caricature firmly established by liberal demonization, the reality of the man himself was effectively removed from enlightened discussion. So, for that matter, was the real Alger Hiss, who, for the "best people" remained safely concealed behind the mask of a New Deal pinup boy, an exemplary figure of virtue and rectitude.

"I always felt that Whittaker was the most misunderstood person of our time," wrote Arthur Koestler at the time of Whittaker Chambers's death in 1961. "When he testified he knowingly committed moral suicide for the guilt of our generation. . . . The witness is gone, the testimony will stand." And so the testimony still stands a half-century later, with added corroboration turning up with greater and greater frequency from hitherto secret archives in Washington, Moscow, and Prague, with every passing year.

Notes

1. Hiss died on November 15, 1996. After his release from prison, he worked as a salesman for a printing company. In 1959, he and his wife Priscilla separated. Although the Supreme Court refused his many appeals for a hearing, he achieved a partial victory when, in August 1975, he was readmitted to the Massachusetts bar. His accuser, Whittaker Chambers, died on July 9, 1961.
2. Allen Weinstein, *Perjury: The Hiss-Chambers Case* (New York: Alfred A. Knopf, 1978).
3. Allen Weinstein, "The Alger Hiss Case Revisited," *The American Scholar* 41 (Winter, 1971–72): 132; see also, *Perjury*, xvii.
4. For background information on the Venona Project, see John Earl Haynes and Harvey Klehr, *Venona: Decoding Soviet Espionage in America* (New Haven: Yale University Press, 1999), 23–56.

5. John Lowenthal, "Venona and Alger Hiss," *Intelligence and National Security* 15 (Autumn, 2000): 119–20. The complete article can be found on pages 98 to 130.

6. Allen Weinstein, *Perjury: The Hiss-Chambers Case* (New York: Random House, 1997); Victor Navasky, "Allen Weinstein's Docudrama," *The Nation* 265 (November 3, 1997): 11–16.

Appendix

The historiography of the Hiss-Chambers controversy and related topics is extensive and continues to grow. This brief bibliography, therefore, offers only a sampling of potential sources that can serve as a starting point for further research.

THE HISS-CHAMBERS CASE

Accounts of the Alger Hiss case began appearing soon after his conviction for perjury, and a debate quickly ensued between those who believed him guilty and those who defended him as an innocent victim. The earliest works were by the principals in the case themselves and other contemporary observers. Alistair Cooke, *A Generation on Trial: U.S.A. v. Alger Hiss* (New York: Alfred A. Knopf, 1950), was published the same year Hiss was convicted. As a foreign observer of the American scene, he tries to put the trial in the context of American culture and politics. Whittaker Chambers, *Witness* (New York: Random House, 1952), is a personal memoir of his experiences in the Communist Party and during the confrontation with Hiss. After his release from prison in 1954, Alger Hiss pleaded his case, *In the Court of Public Opinion* (New York: Alfred A. Knopf, 1957). The Hiss and the Chambers books both rely heavily on the HUAC minutes and trial testimony. Richard Nixon, whose career received a major boost from his central role in the case, weighed in with a chapter in his autobiography, *Six Crises* (Garden City, New York: Doubleday and Company, 1962). In the first chapter devoted to "The Hiss Case," pp. 1–71, he defends his conduct throughout the affair and treats the case as a symptom of the serious Communist threat that all Americans should be prepared to confront.

By the 1970s, new historical sources were available to help historians reassess the major controversial points of the case. This led to significant new studies. John Chabot Smith, a former reporter for the *New York Herald Tribune* who had covered the perjury trials, in *Alger Hiss: The True Story* (New York: Holt, Rinehart, and Winston, 1976), reexamines the evidence in the case and concludes that Hiss was innocent. In contrast, Allen Weinstein, *Perjury: The Hiss-Chambers Case* (New York: Alfred A. Knopf, 1978), is a masterful piece of investigative history that many reviewers believe to be the definitive word on the affair concludes that Hiss was guilty. In a revised edition of this classic work (New York: Random House, 1997), Weinstein incorporates materials made available with the end of the Cold War to further reinforce his judgment. Not everyone, however, was willing to accept Weinstein as the final word. Victor Navasky, "The Case Not Proved Against Alger Hiss," *The Nation,* April 8, 1978, 393–401, argues that Weinstein misquoted and misrepresented many individuals he interviewed for his book. Finally, Sam Tanenhaus's *Whittaker Chambers, A Biography* (New York: Random House, 1997) is an award-winning examination of Chambers's life that further contributes to the scholarship pointing to Hiss's guilt.

A good source for the most recent developments in the Hiss case is a web site launched in 2001 by New York University Libraries. "The Alger Hiss Story: Search for the Truth" (www.nyu.edu/Hiss) presents the case from the perspective of Hiss supporters. But it contains a bibliography and documentary material of interest to all researchers.

MCCARTHY AND MCCARTHYISM

The Hiss affair unfolded during a decade when Americans were profoundly concerned with the domestic threat of Communist subversion that came to be known as the era of McCarthyism. McCarthyism and the man who lent his name to that era, Senator Joseph McCarthy of Wisconsin, is another fertile field for historical inquiry. Following his February 1950 speech in Wheeling, West Virginia, where he claimed to have the names of 205 Communists and fellow-travelers in the State Department, Senator McCarthy became the icon of the anti-Communist movement. Early liberal detractors, notably journalist Richard Rovere in his biography *Senator Joe McCarthy* (New York: Harcourt, 1959), condemn the senator as an opportunistic demagogue. In contrast, conservative works, like William F. Buckley, Jr., publisher of the *National Review,* and L. Brent Bozell's *McCarthy and His Enemies: The Record and Its Meaning* (Chicago: Regnery, 1954) praise the senator for his determined struggle against the Communist threat.

The historical debate has evolved with the perspective of time and the discovery of new evidence, leading to recent more nuanced and balanced treatments of the senator. Two of the more notable are Thomas C. Reeves, *The Life and Times of Joe McCarthy* (Briarcliff Manor, New York: Stein and Day, 1982), and David M. Oshinsky, *A Conspiracy So Immense: The World of Joe McCarthy* (New York: Free Press, 1983).

Reeves's and Oshinsky's books are as much studies of the era of McCarthyism as they are biographies of the infamous senator. They are joined by a number of other important works that examine the broader context of this anti-Communist phenomenon. Earl Latham's *The Communist Controversy in Washington: From the New Deal to McCarthy* (New York: Atheneum, 1969) is a monumental work that traces the issue of Communist subversion in the federal government from the 1930s to McCarthy's ascendancy. Athan Theoharis, in *Seeds of Repression: Harry S. Truman and the Origins of McCarthyism* (New York: Quadrangle, 1977), is one of the first historians to argue that Truman's policies were in part responsible for the emergence of McCarthyism. David Caute, in *The Great Fear: The Anti-Communist Purge Under Truman and Eisenhower* (New York: Simon and Schuster, 1978), examines the broader and more sweeping political and social impact of McCarthyism. Richard M. Fried's *Nightmare in Red: The McCarthy Era in Perspective* (New York: Oxford University Press, 1990) is a more recent treatment that tries to show McCarthyism's influence on future periods in American history. Fried's work contains a particularly valuable bibliographic essay.

OTHER ESPIONAGE CASES

The Alger Hiss affair was a pivotal espionage case, but it was only one of many such cases that captured the attention of the American public during the post-World War II decade. There is a steadily growing historical literature devoted to these cases. J. L. Granatstein and David Stafford, *Spy Wars: Espionage in Canada from Gouzenko to Glasnost* (Toronto: Key Porter Books, 1990), and John Sawatsky, *Gouzenko: The Untold Story* (Toronto: Macmillan, 1984), treat the 1945 defection of Igor Gouzenko and the espionage ring in the Soviet embassy in Canada. Bruce Craig's "A Matter of Espionage: Alger Hiss, Harry Dexter White, and Igor Gouzenko—The Canadian Connection Reassessed," *Intelligence and National Security* 15 (Summer, 2000): 211–24, examines the link between Soviet agents in Canada and Alger Hiss and others in the State Department. He utilizes many recently released archival materials, particularly the Venona documents.

The earliest postwar U.S. incident, the *Amerasia* affair, where classified State Department materials were discovered in the offices of a left-wing scholarly journal, has been examined in Harvey Klehr and Ronald Radosh's *The Amerasia Spy Case: Prelude to McCarthyism* (Chapel Hill: University of North Carolina Press, 1996). The life of Elizabeth Bentley, a reformed Communist agent like Chambers, who played a major role in exposing Soviet espionage, is ably chronicled in Kathryn S. Olmstead's *The Red Spy Queen: A Biography of Elizabeth Bentley* (Chapel Hill: University of North Carolina Press, 2002). Klaus Fuchs, the British scientist who turned over information on the development of the atomic bomb to Soviet agents has been studied recently in Robert C. Williams, *Klaus Fuchs: Atomic Spy* (Cambridge: Harvard University Press, 1987), and Norman Moss, *Klaus Fuchs: The Man Who Stole the Atomic Bomb* (New York: St. Martins, 1987).

Besides the Alger Hiss case, the arrest of Julius and Ethel Rosenberg for turning nuclear secrets over to the Soviet Union has probably generated the most controversy. Louis Nizer's *The Implosion Conspiracy* (Garden City, New York: Doubleday, 1973) is a valuable treatment of the plight of the Rosenbergs. Walter and Miriam Schneir, *Invitation to an Inquest: A New Look at the Rosenberg-Sobell Case* (Garden City, New York: Doubleday, 1983), condemns the government's evidence against the Rosenbergs. In contrast, Ronald Radosh and Joyce Milton, *The Rosenberg File: A Search for the Truth* (New York: Holt, Rinehart, and Winston, 1983), utilizes a vast amount of material acquired through use of the Freedom of Information Act. They conclude that Julius Rosenberg was certainly guilty as charged, although they are critical of the government's and the judge's handling of the case. The case against Ethel, they argue, is less certain. Sam Roberts uses personal interviews and recent archival materials to examine the role David Greenglass, Ethel's brother and witness for the prosecution, played in the trial. His work is entitled *The Brother: The Untold Story of Atomic Spy David Greenglass and How He Sent His Sister, Ethel Rosenberg, to the Electric Chair* (New York: Random House, 2001).

VENONA AND THE SOVIET ARCHIVES

A final topic that deserves attention is the recent scholarship generated by the release of materials from archival sources in the former Soviet Union and the declassification of the Venona documents in the United States. This new information sheds light on Soviet subversion and the activities of the Communist Party in the United States.

Harvey Klehr and John Earl Haynes collaborated with Fridrikh I. Firsov to write *The Secret World of American Communism* (New Haven: Yale

University Press, 1995), and with Kyrill M. Anderson to produce *The Soviet World of American Communism* (New Haven: Yale University Press, 1998). These works, the first two of a larger project, utilize Comintern records housed in Moscow's Russian Center for the Preservation and Study of Documents of Recent History to trace Soviet control, financing, and exploitation for espionage purposes of the American Communist Party from the immediate post-World War I period. Like the Hiss case, this new evidence about Communist Party participation in espionage generated some strong responses. Ellen Schrecker's, *Many Are the Crimes: McCarthyism in America* (Boston: Little, Brown, 1998), offers an alternative, more sympathetic examination of Communists and their leftist sympathizers.

The Venona files complement the information from Soviet sources. Robert L. Benson and Michael Warner, historians with the National Security Agency and the Central Intelligence Agency respectively, have edited a collection of these Venona materials along with commentary, *Venona: Soviet Espionage and the American Response, 1939–1957* (Washington, D.C.: National Security Agency and Central Intelligence Agency, 1996). All of the Venona documents are reproduced on the National Security Agency web site (www.nsa.gov/docs/Venona).

Historical analyses utilizing and tracing the history of the effort to decode the intercepted communications include Harvey Klehr and John Earl Haynes, *Venona: Decoding Soviet Espionage in America* (New Haven: Yale University Press, 1999), and Nigel West, *Venona: The Greatest Secret of the Cold War* (London: Harper Collins, 1999). Allen Weinstein and Alexander Vassiliev, *The Haunted Wood: Soviet Espionage in America—The Stalin Era* (New York: Random House, 1999), combine materials from Soviet KGB archives with the Venona materials to produce a study of Soviet spy activity in America. Jerrold and Leona Schechter's *Sacred Secrets: How Soviet Intelligence Operations Changed American History* (Washington. D.C.: Brassey's, 2002) also exploits these new sources to shed light on Soviet activities, not just in the 1940s and 1950s, but into more recent times. Greg Herken, in *Brotherhood of the Bomb: The Tangled Lives and Loyalties of Robert Oppenheimer, Ernest Lawrence, and Edward Teller* (New York: Henry Holt and Company, 2002), turns to Venona and other sources to examine the careers of the men instrumental in the development of the atomic bomb. Despite the fact that the material from Soviet sources is fragmentary and that its release has slowed in recent years, what has been released has added significantly to understanding of the activities of the Communist Party in the twentieth century.

Index